Contents

Origin of the Cocktail

The origin of the word 'cocktail' is by no means universally agreed, most dictionaries simply give 'orig. unk'. The first use in print of the word cocktail (the drink) was in Hudson, New York, where on 13 May 1806 the editor of the *Balance and Columbian Repository* defined 'Cock tail' as 'a stimulating liquor, composed of spirits of any kind, sugar, water and bitters'.

Over the last two centuries at least a dozen stories have emerged to explain the term's origin. Most involve cockerels or beautiful young women with a name which sounds like cocktail. The more credible explanations are:

1. *Coquetier* is the French name for an egg-cup, in which a Frenchman in New Orleans is said to have served mixed drinks to his guests. In time they came to ask for his *coquetiers* and the name was corrupted to cocktails.

2. An old French recipe containing mixed wines, called *coquetel*, was perhaps carried to America by General Lafayette in 1777.

3. One Betsy Flanagan of Virginia is believed to have served a handsome soldier a mixed drink containing all the colours of a cock's tail. He named it a 'cock-tail'.

The Classic 1000 Cocktails

Robert Cross

foulsham

LONDON • NEW YORK • TORONTO • SYDNEY

foulsham

The Publishing House, Bennetts Close,
Cippenham, Berkshire, SL1 5AP England

ISBN 0 572 02161-5

Copyright © 1996 **Strathearn Publishing Ltd.**

Printed in Great Britain by St Edmundsbury Press Ltd, Bury St Edmunds, Suffolk.

4. In 1769 the term 'cock-tailed' appeared, a racing term used to describe a non-thoroughbred horse. It was the usual practice to dock the tails of such animals, causing the tail to look like that of a cockerel. According to the journals of the time, a 'cock-tailed' horse was one of mixed blood. It is a short step to accept that cock-tail(ed) would soon become accepted as a term to describe anything containing mixed fluids.

5. The centuries-old expression 'cocked tail' describes a horse or person displaying high spirits. It naturally follows that a beverage seen to raise people's spirits would be called a cocktail.

So let's get down to the nitty-gritty.

Cocktails were a small group of recipes mostly based on the 1806 formula, until the 1880s when cocktail began to develop into a generic term for an ever widening class of mixtures.

The actual root of the term is most likely to have come from a two-word expression. The last two remain the only plausible explanations, but with number 5 favourite because it alone accounts for the use of 'stimulating' in the original definition.

Equipment

EQUIPMENT

Buy from a professional catering equipment shop, and also seek out pub/bar utensil supply firms, who you will find are happy to help.

This is a list of the minimum equipment required if you wish to do the job properly.

Standard shaker

The capped variety with built-in strainer. It is essential that the shaker does not leak from the main seal whilst pouring into a glass. *See* Methods.

Boston shaker

Consists of two flat-bottomed cones.

Mixing glass

Used to stir ingredients together. Its size should match your Hawthorn strainer. *See* Methods.

Corkscrew

Try to obtain a quality corkscrew which has a spiral core, rather than the less reliable type consisting of a central nail-like structure surrounded by a raised helix.

Blender, *see* **Crushed ice (Methods).**

Cocktail sticks

Juice extractor and strainer

Long-handled bar-spoon

Decorative muddlers and ornaments

Fruit knife – short and sharp

Glass cloth / tea towel

Hawthorn strainer

Napkins and coasters

Straws – long, short and bendy

Tongues for ice

MEASURES

One single measure is 25 millilitres (ml)

2.5 centilitres (cl)

Measures of $1/6$th gill (23.6 ml), 1 fl oz Imperial (28.4 ml), or 1 fl oz American (29.6 ml) are acceptably close, though using these without making any allowance will slightly affect the alcohol units shown, and the volume produced may be greater than the glass specified is ideally suited for.

1 teaspoon = $1/6$th measure

1 dash = $1/10$th teaspoon

Conversion Table

ML	MSR	FL OZ
25	1	0.9
50	2	1.8
75	3	2.7
100	4	3.6

Cocktail (C)
14 cl/5 fl oz

Rocks,
Old-Fashioned,
Whisky (R)
23 cl/8 fl oz

Highball (H)
28 cl/10 fl oz

Collins (CO)
34 cl/12 fl oz

Pilsner (Pi)
28 cl/10 fl oz

Fluted
champagne (F)
14 cl/5 fl oz

Goblet (G)
34 cl/12 fl oz

Wine (W)
20 cl/7 fl oz

Snifter or
brandy balloon (B)
31 cl/11 fl oz

Double cocktail (D)
23 cl/8 fl oz

Champagne
saucer (CS)
14 cl/5 fl oz

Poco or
Pina Colada (P)
40 cl/14 fl oz

Cordial or
liqueur (L)
8 cl/3 fl oz

Shot glass (S)
5.7 cl/2 fl oz

GLASSWARE

All glassware must be spotlessly clean! If you do not have a glass washer/drier, polish them completely dry with a clean glass cloth after washing to avoid stains.

Test each type of glass to see how many measures it will hold. This will allow you to adjust your quantities to fit the glass exactly.

The importance of using the correct glassware cannot be over-emphasised, as it will ensure the optimum visual impact. Seek out the glass types pictured. These are classic styles which, like grey flannel suits, will always be in fashion. Don't be tempted to buy something which is roughly similar, since non-classic or poor quality products will soon come to offend your eye.

Glassware bearing a distiller's or brewer's name is most desirable.

METHODS

Clean Ice for Home Bars

By holding a glass of defrosted tap water up to the light you will see thousands of white filaments in suspension. This is unacceptable in a clear drink, especially a classic such as a Martini. This effect is mostly evident in hard water areas, where calcium carbonate is the offending mineral. If this effect is evident in your area, neither household water filters nor boiling will remove enough of the minerals concerned.

For the home bar a good remedy can be obtained from your local chemist/drug store in the form of purified *drinking* water. Specify this to avoid being given any other type, e.g. isotonic water for injection.

Purified drinking water has been distilled and costs about twice as much as the finest bottled waters with which it should not be confused; nevertheless this is a trivial cost given the small quantities you are likely to use.

Coconut Cream

Some brands of canned ready-made coconut cream are meant only for culinary purposes; they are unsweetened and usually taste foul. Brands made for cocktails are usually too sweet, too expensive and full of preservatives.

Many bars therefore make their own. Take a chilled (hard) block of pure creamed coconut (usually 200 g). Grate it to break down the grainy texture (you will require one tablespoon of the grated coconut per Pina Colada). Add an equal volume or slightly less of caster sugar and the minimum amount of hot water to dissolve the sugar/coconut mix. Stir until you have a very sweet coconut cream with the texture of a smooth runny paste. It should taste divine and is ready for use when cool. Use the same day. Do not store as it becomes rancid and grainy.

Crushed Ice and Blending

At home you can make crushed ice with a blender but firstly crack/break down large ice cubes with a cleaned hammer or ice pick to reduce the risk of damaging your machine. Using a commercially available blender would avoid this risk.

The ice will liquefy quickly, so produce it immediately before use and ensure the glass to be used is well chilled.

When blending a cocktail with ice the objective is to produce a milkshake-like consistency. Excessive blending will dilute the drink.

Igniting Drinks

Most alcoholic beverages will ignite, but they usually require a little persuasion. Ensure the top layer of a cocktail is a spirit containing at least 40 per cent alcohol (US 80° proof) and is near the rim of the glass. Above the drink, heat up a barspoon full of the same spirit with a lighter. When hot, ignite the spirit in the spoon and gently float the flaming liquid on to the surface of the cocktail.

Do not allow the cocktail to burn for more than a few moments as the glass may crack in the heat and the drinker may burn their lips on the rim.

Shaking

Drinks containing eggs, fruit juices or cream are shaken. The object is to almost freeze the drink whilst breaking down and combining the ingredients.

To 'shake and strain', half fill shaker with whole ice cubes, add ingredients and shake briskly until the exterior of the vessel is very cold. Pour immediately through the built-in strainer or hawthorn strainer, leaving the ice behind. Remember the volume of liquid emerging will have increased as some of the ice will have melted. This is important so you do not produce more drink than the glass will hold.

Do not shake and strain with crushed ice as this will clog the strainer of a standard shaker. Drinks shaken with crushed ice (e.g. Scotch Mist) are intended to be served unstrained.

Wrap a cloth around the seal of the shaker if it is prone to dripping.

To 'shake and pour unstrained', add a glassful of ice and the recipe to the shaker, cover with the top and shake as above. Pour, with the ice, into the same size glass used to measure the ice. Here it is quicker to use a Boston shaker. This technique ensures that the total volume of the drink does not increase, and so fits the glassware used, no matter how much ice melts.

Stirring – Mixing Glass

Stirring is primarily for drinks made up of clear ingredients. The object is to chill and thoroughly mix whilst retaining clarity.

To 'stir and strain', half fill a mixing glass or the bottom half of a shaker with ice cubes, add ingredients and agitate with a long-handled barspoon. After 15–20 seconds, place a hawthorn strainer on top and pour only the liquid into the serving glass.

To 'stir and pour unstrained', prepare as above but use only one glassful of ice and do not strain. Add the entire contents to the same size glass used to measure the ice.

Sherbet/Sorbet (Orange/Lemon etc.)

Dissolve 2 cups of sugar in 1 cup of water and simmer gently in a small saucepan for 2 minutes. Add 1 cup of orange or lemon juice and cool, then freeze. When ready to use it should have a firm ice-cream texture and taste quite sweet but tangy.

Banana/Strawberry/Raspberry Puree

Wash the fruit thoroughly, mash and rub through a sieve to remove lumps and as many pips as possible.

Sugar Syrup (Syrup de Gomme)

This is a useful colourless liquid ideal for sweetening. Most bars make their own, as follows. Dissolve equal volumes of water and sugar, simmer gently for two minutes and allow to cool. Store in an attractive bottle.

Sweet and Sour

A time-saving mix used in many bars where recipes containing lemon juice and sugar syrup (Collins' etc.) are likely to be required in quantity. Simply use in place of the lemon and syrup shown, using the same total quantity.

Blend together 1 egg white, 1 cup/175 g sugar, $1/2$ litre lemon juice, $1/2$ litre water. Keep refrigerated for up to three days.

Tricks of the Trade

Test each of your glasses to see how many spirit measures of fluid they will hold. Fill them with crushed, broken and then whole ice cubes and count how many units of water they will hold in each case. From this you will determine how many measures of liquors etc. to use to make a single cocktail which will fit a particular glass exactly, whether it be simply frosted or filled with ice.

A teaspoon of egg white shaken together with the other ingredients will give otherwise clear drinks a smooth misty look and pleasant thin white head. You will not taste the egg.

Avoid using high quality malt Scotch whisky unless a recipe specifies it. A blend will usually suffice in a mixed drink.

Always mix the cheaper ingredients first (orange juice etc.) so you do not lose precious spirits in the event of error or spillage.

Never shake fizzy drinks. Lemonade, soda, cola, fruit juices and tonic waters should be stored in the fridge ready for inclusion in the cocktail immediately before serving.

Having shaken a cocktail containing cream, wash out the shaker more thoroughly than usual using detergent and cloth to remove the cream which otherwise sticks to the inside. This is unhygienic and may taint the next non-cream cocktail.

All ingredients should be at their peak of condition, especially fruit (freshly sliced) and fruit juices (just squeezed).

Lemon juice should be strained to remove pips before use. Sometimes fine sieving is desirable, usually if the juice is to be added to an otherwise transparent cocktail.

Use only high quality branded products – don't spoil the ship for a ha'p'orth of tar.

Measure quantities accurately especially when using ingredients with strong flavours such as Green Creme de Menthe and Pernod.

When experimenting, try to achieve a balance in the drink by combining something sweet (e.g. fruit liqueur) with something sharp or bitter (e.g. lemon juice). The result is likely to be more palatable. Most successful cocktails achieve this balance. Consider the visual texture, consistency/density, colour, palatability, aroma, taste and presentation.

PARTIES AT HOME

When giving your first cocktail party, limit the number of guests and the range of cocktails on offer.

Ice will be required in large quantity. As a rough guide, on a hot summer evening, four people will require one 3 kg/6.5 lb bag of ice, which can be bought or made well in advance.

Unless you intend to light a barbecue, guests will normally expect you to provide crudités, dips, canapes and/or savoury pastries – the usual party fare.

Cold beer moves faster than anything else, so put plenty in the fridge.

Many recipes can be made in bulk before guests arrive, but not those containing cream or eggs, which will separate or curdle. Pre-mixed drinks should not have ice added until they are ready to be served.

Morning or midday cocktail parties call for low-alcohol drinks. Champagne and fruit juices are ideal – bring on the Buck's Fizz!

YOUR STOCK

One of the joys of being a cocktail enthusiast is the collection and sampling of unusual liqueurs from all over the world. Look for rare potions which are not available back home to add to your collection.

There is an extremely large range of liquors available so, to avoid unnecessary expense, begin with the essentials such as gin, rum etc., and build up by buying ingredients to complete recipes which have caught your eye.

TERMS USED

Add

Incorporate into the drink or vessel. Where appropriate mix gently with a barspoon or add muddler. The current trade jargon is 'build' when adding ingredients directly to a serving glass in this way.

Blend

Blended and poured unstrained. *See* Methods.

Broken ice/Broken ice cubes

Large (2.5 cm/1 in) cubes coarsely chopped to about one-third original size (also known as bar ice). Thus 4 broken ice cubes = about 12 pieces broken ice = 12 slices bar ice. *See* Methods.

Cocktail

This term has changed in meaning since 1806, *see* Origin of the Cocktail. The cocktail *cognoscente* insist that a cocktail is a short alcoholic drink containing three or more ingredients. If it has only two it is a mixed drink. If any mixer is added, e.g. lemonade, it becomes a long drink.

In practice these distinctions are now rarely observed and, especially in the public eye, the definition has widened to cover all such drinks, though if only two ingredients are used they must both be alcoholic e.g. Martini/Stinger.

Crushed ice
Very finely fragmented ice. Always poured unstrained if shaken with recipe. *See* Methods.

Frosted
Glass sufficiently chilled, in fridge/freezer or by filling with crushed ice, to cause cold mist to form on exterior.

Garnish
Decorate/attach to rim of glass.

Ice/Ice-filled
Whole ice cubes/filled with these, i.e. not broken or crushed ice.

Ignite
Set fire to drink. *See* Methods.

Long
Five measures or more of fluid in total.

Mix
Combine ingredients thoroughly, usually using barspoon.

Pour
Add to glass without straining, unless specified.

Pousse-café (after coffee)
Carefully add ingredients, minimum of three, over barspoon in order of density so as to form distinct layers in the glass. Use a straight-sided glass, preferably a tall narrow pousse-café glass. More a style of presentation than a class of drink as there are no common components. Drinks have been served in this way for centuries.

Rim
Coat the rim of glass by moistening and dipping into specified dry material.

Shake
Shaken in shaker with ice until cold. Pour unstrained if crushed ice is specified. *See* Methods.

Shooter
Usually downed in one.

Short

Less than five measures of fluid in total before shaking.

Smooth

When blending with ice, mixture achieves consistency of thick milk-shake.

Spiral

Long (10–25 cm) coiled (1 cm wide) virtually pith-free length of citrus peel. *See* Garnishes.

Stir

Mixed and chilled in mixing glass. *See* Methods. Home users should use clean ice. *See* Methods.

Strain

Pour out, leaving ice and other solids behind. If you have stirred the drink as above, use a hawthorn strainer.

Straight

Neat/straight up/without ice.

Twist

3–6 cm length of pith-free citrus peel, held over the drink and twisted in the centre to release a little essential oil on to the surface. Add twist to drink unless otherwise stated. *See* Garnishes.

PRESENTATION

A cocktail is usually at its peak of appeal when just poured. The guest should wait for the cocktail, rather than the cocktail for the guest. Presentation is all important. A cocktail is a minor work of art which should be pleasing to the eye as well as to the palate.

Always place the completed cocktail on a napkin for your guest.

GARNISHES

Standard garnishes:

A twist (a hand tool is available for this)

A spiral

A wedge

A slice

Imaginative garnishes:

Citrus peel cut into shapes (special cutters are available for more elaborate shapes)

Melon balls, slice of watermelon etc.

Paper parasols, plastic monkeys etc.

RECIPE RATINGS

The glass rating shown with each recipe is a measure of the drink's appeal. All the recipes have been tested.

Average

Very good

Excellent

NB: Some two-glass recipes have been included, where they are variations on a popular drink, or are important or historical cocktails.

KEY

♉♉♉♉ Recipe rating

R ⬜ Code 'R', 'C', etc. with line drawing.
This indicates the recommended glass to use. *See* Glassware.

Citrus flavour etc. A brief indication of flavour.

Alcohol 1.0 One unit of alcohol. This is a useful measure of how much alcohol there is in each recipe.

Aperitifs

From the Latin *aperire* – to open. In cultured circles the aperitif is an indispensable preprandial appetiser and ice-breaker.

Adonis

Wine flavour

Alcohol 1.5

Created in 1886 to celebrate the success of a Broadway musical.

> 2 msr dry sherry
> 1 msr rosso vermouth
> 1 dash orange bitters
> (substitute: dry orange curacao)

Stir and strain, add twist of orange.

C

Bloody Mary

Tomato / Spice flavour

Alcohol 2.0

In 1921 Fernand 'Pete' Petiot of Harry's Bar, Paris, mixed tomato juice, vodka, salt, pepper and Worcestershire sauce. Although tomato and vodka was already a well known combination he named his spiced version a Bloody Mary, according to some accounts after Mary Pickford, the popular screen actress.

In 1933 US Prohibition ended and the following year Petiot accepted an invitation from John Astor of the St. Regis Hotel, New York, to become head barman at its King Cole Grill.

Astor felt some people would be offended by the name Bloody Mary, so Petiot introduced the drink as a Red Snapper. Prince Serge Obolensky asked him to 'spice it up a bit'. Tabasco sauce was added and the result was suddenly all the rage. Petiot later circulated the recipe under its original name.

> 2 msr vodka
> 5 msr tomato juice
> 1/2 teaspoon lemon juice

2 dashes Worcestershire sauce
4 drops Tabasco sauce
1 pinch celery salt
1 small pinch black pepper

Shake and strain through a hawthorn strainer.
Garnish: short celery stem with leaves.

If 1 msr gold tequila is also added,
this becomes a Deadly Mary.

If tequila is used in place of vodka in a
Bloody Mary, this is a Bloody Maria.

If gin is used in place of vodka in a Bloody Mary,
this is now known as a Red Snapper.

G

 Alcohol 3.0

Camp Grenada

Sour fruit flavour
Alcohol 1.0

1½ msr Campari
½ msr grenadine
2 msr grapefruit juice
1 msr pineapple juice
3 msr cold 7UP

Shake and strain into ice-filled glass, add the 7UP.
Garnish: fruit in season.

CO

Ceasefire

Cherry flavour
Alcohol 1.1

½ msr scotch
½ msr cherry brandy
½ msr dry vermouth
5 msr lemonade

Add to ice-filled glass. Garnish: lemon slice
and a cherry, add straws.

H

Diplomat

Herb flavour
Alcohol 1.4

A 1920s classic, originally served straight up.

2 msr dry vermouth
⅔ msr rosso vermouth
1 teaspoon maraschino

Stir and strain into glass three-quarters filled with
broken ice; add cherry on a stick.

R

Ferandina

Vermouth flavour   *Alcohol 1.5*

> 2 msr bianco vermouth
> 1 msr Pimm's No.1.
> 5 msr lemonade

Add to ice-filled glass, add slice of orange.   CO

Frozen Spirits

Spirit flavour   *Alcohol 1.0*

It is quite common in Eastern Europe and Scandinavian countries to keep a bottle of Aquavit, Schnapps or vodka in the freezer and serve it ice cold in a small chilled glass as an aperitif.

In Russia, when vodka is drunk neat and ice cold as an aperitif, the tradition is to raise a toast and smash the empty glass by throwing it into a glowing fireplace. This is to prevent the glass being used to toast anyone else's health.

> 1 msr vodka or spirit of choice

Freeze until gelatinous in texture.
Serve in frosted glass.   S

Gin & It

Herb flavour   *Alcohol 2.1*

'It' being Italian vermouth.

> 1½ msr gin
> 1½ msr Italian rosso vermouth

Add to glass filled with broken ice.
Add cherry on a stick.   R

Key Punch

Lime flavour   *Alcohol 2.0*

> 2 msr dark rum
> 1 msr sugar syrup
> 1 msr lime juice

Add to glass three-quarters filled with broken ice.
Garnish: slice of lime speared with a cherry.
Short straw optional.   R

MANHATTANS

In the 19th century a Manhattan was a term applied to a drink of water drawn from the Manhattan River; it was bottled and distributed widely.

The recipe appeared in bar-guides of the early 1880s and it now seems clear its inventor simply followed the fashion of the day for adding vermouth to popular recipes, in this case the standard Whiskey Cocktail.

There is an old bartenders' tale that the recipe was created around 1874 at the Manhattan Club, New York, for Lady Randolph Churchill, Winston's mother, on the occasion of her banquet in honour of the lawyer and politician Samuel J. Tilden.

Lady Churchill, like her famous son, was no stranger to the demon drink. In 1880, whilst living in London, she once received a payment demand from R. Paine & Sons (Importers of Wines, Spirits and Liqueurs) for the sum of £246. In 1880 that was enough booze to kill a small army!

Manhattan

Vermouth flavour   *Alcohol 2.5*

Originally this was made with one part whiskey to two parts vermouth. Usually two or three dashes of sugar syrup, curacao and bitters were included and the result served straight up. In Manhattan today they are invariably served with ice, and like the Martini, their vermouth content has greatly reduced over the years.

> 2 msr Canadian whisky
> 1 msr rosso vermouth
> 4 drops Angostura

Shake briefly with a glassful of broken ice and pour unstrained. Add cherry on a stick.

R

If no vermouth is used, this is a
Naked Manhattan.

Alcohol 2.0

If only ½ msr rosso is used and ½ msr dry vermouth added, this is a Perfect Manhattan. Garnish: cherry or twist of lemon.

Alcohol 2.5

Replace the whisky in the standard Manhattan for the following popular recipes:

Brandy Manhattan	2 msr brandy/cognac	
Comfortable Manhattan	2 msr Southern Comfort	
Rum Manhattan	2 msr white rum	

Dry Manhattan

Vermouth flavour   *Alcohol 2.5*

Versions of the Manhattan using dry vermouth have been recorded as early as 1884, but the term Dry Manhattan only appeared around 1920. At that time it consisted of a mixture of vermouths – what we now call a Perfect Manhattan.

> 2 msr Canadian whisky
> 1 msr dry vermouth
> 4 drops Angostura

Shake briefly with a glassful of broken ice and pour unstrained. Garnish: lemon twist.   R

Martinez

Dry/Herb flavour   *Alcohol 2.5*

Barlore has it this recipe was created about 1870 by 'Professor' Jerry Thomas. He combined one part gin and two parts rosso vermouth, added a dash of Angostura and two dashes of maraschino. These were shaken and strained to create what he called a Martinez cocktail – after the township to which his first customer was travelling.

Later recipes have the gin/vermouth ratio at 1:1. The trend towards dryness continued, and by 1930 the *Savoy Cocktail Book* shows that this cocktail was being made with dry vermouth.

> 1½ msr gin
> 1½ msr dry vermouth
> 2 teaspoons maraschino
> 1 teaspoon orange bitters
> (substitute: dry orange curacao)

Shake and strain into frosted glass.
Garnish: cherry and lemon twist.   C

MARTINIS

When dry vermouth was first added to gin, probably about the time Noilly Prat appeared in 1843, the resulting 'Gin and French' became a popular combination. Indeed, these two ingredients form the basis of numerous Martini-style nineteenth and twentieth-century recipes.

The Martini is one of the few still popular today. Its history shows this cocktail to be a fashion item whose contents change with the times.

Martini mania began in the 1880s when they were made with rosso vermouth. One of the earliest recipes appears in Harry Johnson's 1888 edition of the *Bartender's Manual*.

It has often been suggested that 'Martini' is a corruption of 'Martinez' and that it was the original Martini. A close look at the facts however, reveals this is incorrect. The standard Gin Cocktail, around since the early nineteenth century, provides the basis of both these drinks.

Just who created the recipe remains a mystery, though one suspect must surely be the Italian-American immigrant population, who may well have introduced Martini rosso vermouth and even the recipe to America years before the brand was widely promoted.

The view held by most professional bartenders for over a century is that, as Johnson specified, a Martini must be stirred not shaken!

Dry Martini

References to the Dry Martini began to appear in US literature from 1903.

Since Martini and Rossi did not begin exporting their dry vermouth to America until 1920–21, it can be deduced that for at least the first 17 years, the Dry Martini must have been made with the only brand of dry vermouth then available – Noilly Prat.

The dry version quickly overtook the old Martini in popularity. By the 1930s the sweet version had become passé and soon fizzled out as a popular drink.

To Make a Martini

The correct implements must be used: a mixing glass, frosted cocktail glass, barspoon and hawthorn strainer are essential.

Any Martini ordered 'on the rocks' should be served in a Rocks glass three-quarters filled with broken ice cubes. This presentation seems to be becoming more common.

Method:

The Martini can be prepared with olive or twist etc. If a twist is specified, *see* Methods and prepare this first.

Ensure the glass has been thoroughly chilled, or fill it with crushed ice and discard this just before use.

Half fill a mixing glass with ice cubes (*see* Clean Ice in Methods) and add the ingredients. Stir with the long-handled barspoon. The Ritz-Carlton Hotel in Boston stir its Martinis exactly 12 times!

Remove glass from fridge, or crushed ice from glass.

Place the hawthorn strainer over the top of the mixing glass and strain into the glass. Add the specified twist or comestible and serve. After squeezing the twist, some people prefer it to be discarded.

Bacardi Martini

Dry / Plain flavour

Alcohol 2.7

2½ msr White Bacardi rum
½ msr dry vermouth

Stir and strain into frosted glass. Add green olive.

C

If a black olive is used this is a Black Devil.

When served on the rocks with a twist of lemon
and no olive,this is known as Rum Martini.

Black Martini

Subtle blackberry flavour

Alcohol 2.8

2½ msr gin
½ msr blackberry brandy

Stir and strain into frosted glass. Add black olive.

C

Chamtini

Raspberry flavour

Alcohol 1.7

1 msr vodka
⅔ msr Chambord

Stir and strain into glass three-quarters filled
with broken ice; add twist of lemon.

R

Dry Martini Cocktail (4:1)

Dry / Plain flavour

Alcohol 3.4

A drink of very subtle flavour.

President F.D. Roosevelt (1882–1945) made one of these in front of the
television cameras to celebrate the end of Prohibition.

3 msr gin
¾ msr dry vermouth
1 teaspoon orange bitters (Optional – popular in
the 1930s. A dash or two of the similar curacao / triple
sec was used in the earliest Martinis).

Stir and strain into frosted glass.
Add either twist of lemon or green olive.

C

When a green olive and a Jalepino pepper are used, this is a Hot Martini.

When a black olive is used, this is a Buckeye Martini.

For an Extra Dry Martini (8:1), use only half the vermouth
shown in a Dry Martini.

Alcohol 3.1

Gibson Martini

Dry / Plain flavour Alcohol 2.7

Created at The Players' Club, New York, for Mr Charles Gibson, an illustrator. It is believed he asked a barman for a cocktail onion to be used in place of the olive in his Dry Martini. This simple act sparked a craze for this cocktail which spread world-wide.

2½ msr gin
½ msr dry vermouth

Stir and strain into frosted glass, add small pearl onion. C

Martini Cocktail (2:1)

Dry / Herb flavour Alcohol 3.1

The standard Martini. A drink of subtle flavour and something of an acquired taste.

2½ msr gin
1¼ msr dry vermouth
1 teaspoon orange bitters (optional)

Stir and strain into frosted glass. Add twist of
lemon or green olive. C

If an olive stuffed with an almond is used, this is a Boston Bullet.

If 1 teaspoon each of lemon vodka and dry orange *Alcohol 3.4*
curacao are included and a lime twist added, this is a
Fourteen Club Martini.

Montgomery

Dry / Plain flavour Alcohol 3.9

Created by Ernest Hemingway at Harry's Bar, Venice. He claimed Monty dared not engage Nazi troops until his Desert Rats' numerical superiority was 15:1, the ratio of gin to vermouth in this cocktail. A very dry Martini.

3¾ msr gin
¼ msr dry vermouth

Stir and strain into frosted glass, add twist of lemon. C

Perfect (Medium) Martini

Dry / Herb flavour Alcohol 3.0

2½ msr gin
½ msr dry vermouth
½ msr rosso vermouth

Stir and strain into frosted glass, add twist of lemon. C

If 1 msr each of vermouths are used and a sprig of mint is used in place of lemon, this is a Cooperstown Cocktail.   *Alcohol 3.5*

If 1/2 msr Mandarine Napoléon is added to a Perfect Martini, this is a Stormy Weather.   *Alcohol 3.5*

Vodka Martini – James Bond Style

Dry / Plain flavour   *Alcohol 2.7*

'Shaken not stirred' is specified here because stirring with ice leaves the drink absolutely clear, whereas Mr Bond prefers the misty effect and extra coldness gained by shaking.

2 1/2 msr vodka
1/2 msr Noilly Prat

Shake and strain into frosted glass. Add green olive. Squeeze lemon twist above surface to spray with oil, and discard.   C

Merry Widow

Herb flavour   *Alcohol 2.7*

Vermouth takes its name from *wermut*, the German word for wormwood, a herb used in the production of aromatised wines since Roman times. Commercial production began around 1750–90.

2 msr gin
1 msr dry vermouth
1 teaspoon Benedictine
1/2 teaspoon Pernod
1 dash Angostura

Stir and strain. Add lemon twist.   C

Negroni Cocktail

Sour herb flavour   *Alcohol 1.8*

In 1919, at the Casoni Bar in Florence, Count Camillo Negroni decided he would prefer his usual 'Americano' with a little gin. Soon everyone wanted the drink 'as Negroni has it'.

1 msr gin
1 msr rosso vermouth
3/4 msr Campari
1 msr soda water (optional)

Stir and strain into glass three-quarters filled with broken ice, add the soda if required.
Garnish: half slice of orange. Originally served with equal measures of liquors.   R

OLD-FASHIONEDS

A spirit-based short drink shaken or simply added to an ice- filled glass containing a bitters-soaked sugar cube.

First appeared at the Pendennis Club, Louisville, Kentucky around 1900. It was made at the request of Colonel James E. Pepper, himself a distiller of bourbon.

Old-fashioned

Medium sour flavour 　　　　　　　　　　　　*Alcohol 2.0*

In 1939 President F. D. Roosevelt mixed one of these for King George VI and Queen Elizabeth.

    2 msr bourbon
    1 sugar cube
    1 dash Angostura
    1 msr soda water (optional)

Place cube in glass and add Angostura. When bitters have been soaked up by cube, three-quarters fill glass with broken ice and add whisky (and soda). Garnish: half slice of lemon and a cherry. Add twist of orange and a muddler.   R

Replace whisky in the following popular Old-fashioneds:

Brandy Old-fashioned	2 msr brandy/cognac	
Canadian Old-fashioned	2 msr Canadian whisky	
Gin Old-fashioned	2 msr gin	
Rum Old-fashioned	1 msr white rum and 1 msr dark rum	
Scotch Old-fashioned	2 msr scotch	
Tequila Old-fashioned	2 msr gold tequila	
Vodka Old-fashioned	2 msr vodka	

Ritz Old-fashioned

Orange bourbon flavour 　　　　　　　　　　　　*Alcohol 2.8*

    2 msr bourbon
    2/3 msr Grand Marnier
    1 teaspoon maraschino
    1 teaspoon lemon juice
    1 teaspoon egg white
    1 sugar cube
    1 dash Angostura
    1 msr soda water (optional)

Rim glass with lemon/caster sugar. Place cube
in glass and add Angostura as above. Shake and
strain into glass three-quarters filled with broken ice.
Add two cherries on a stick. Garnish: half slices of
orange and lemon.

R

Radio City
Sherry flavour Alcohol 1.5

    1 msr sweet sherry
    1 msr dry sherry
    1/2 msr gin
    1 msr 7UP
Add to glass three-quarters filled with broken ice.

R

Rose Water
Subtle fruit flavour Alcohol 0.2

    1/3 msr Campari
    1 teaspoon grenadine
    6 msr lemonade
Add to ice-filled glass.

H

SOURS – STANDARD

The Sour was established as early as the 1850s, with the arrival of the
Brandy Sour.

They are made with very little sweetener and a relatively large amount of
fresh lemon juice; a twist or spiral of lemon is usually added. There is a
sour glass available, but most establishments use a rocks glass. They
should never taste sweet, but sugar can be varied to taste. A little soda
water is always optional, ever since it began to be included in the 1880s.

Amaretto Sour
Almond flavour Alcohol 1.0

    1 1/2 msr amaretto
    1 msr lemon juice
    1/2 msr sugar syrup
Shake and strain into glass filled with broken ice.
Add spiral of lemon; squirt of soda optional.

R

Replace the amaretto in the following popular Sours:
Apricot Sour   1 1/2 msr apricot brandy   *Alcohol 0.8*

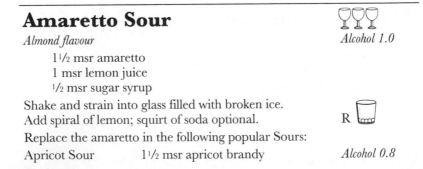

Bourbon Sour	2 msr bourbon	*Alcohol 2.0*
Brandy Sour	2 msr brandy/cognac	*Alcohol 2.0*
Calvados	2 msr calvados	*Alcohol 2.0*
Cherry Sour	1¹/₂ msr cherry brandy	*Alcohol 1.0*
Comfortable Sour	2 msr Southern Comfort	*Alcohol 2.0*
Gin Sour	2 msr gin	*Alcohol 2.0*
Irish Sour	2 msr Irish whiskey	*Alcohol 2.0*
Melon Sour	1¹/₂ msr Midori	*Alcohol 0.9*
Raspberry Sour	1¹/₂ msr Chambord	
	¹/₂ msr white rum	*Alcohol 1.2*
Rum Sour	1¹/₂ msr white rum	*Alcohol 2.0*
	¹/₂ msr golden rum	
Scotch Sour	2 msr scotch	*Alcohol 2.0*
Stone Sour	2 msr Canadian whisky	*Alcohol 2.0*
Tequila Sour	2 msr gold tequila	*Alcohol 2.0*
Vodka Sour	2 msr vodka	*Alcohol 2.0*

Egg Sour

Egg brandy flavour   *Alcohol 1.9*

   1 msr brandy
   1 msr dry orange curacao
   1 msr lemon juice
   ¹/₂ msr sugar syrup
   ¹/₂ an egg

Blend briefly with a glassful of crushed ice,
add spiral of lemon.   R

Fireman's Sour

Lime rum flavour   *Alcohol 2.0*

   2 msr white rum
   1¹/₂ msr lime juice
   1 teaspoon caster sugar
   ¹/₃ msr grenadine
   1 msr soda water

Shake and strain into glass half filled with broken ice,
add the soda. Add twist of lemon. Garnish: orange slice
and a cherry.   R

Pisco Sour

Lime flavour

Alcohol 2.0

2 msr Pisco
juice of ½ a lime
1 teaspoon sugar syrup
½ an egg white
1 dash Angostura

Squeeze lime juice by hand into glass filled with broken ice and add spent shell. Shake remaining ingredients well and strain into glass, add sprig of mint. R

SOURS – WHISK(E)Y FRUIT

A whisk(e)y based fruit-flavoured sour.

Bourbon Triple Sour

Bourbon / Citrus flavour

Alcohol 1.7

1 msr bourbon
1 msr triple sec
1 msr lemon juice
1 teaspoon sugar syrup

Shake and strain into glass filled with broken ice.
Garnish: orange slice and a cherry, add twist of lemon. R

Scotch Melon Sour

Fruit whisky flavour

Alcohol 1.7

1 msr scotch
1 msr Midori
1 msr lemon juice
1 teaspoon sugar syrup

Shake and strain into glass filled with broken ice.
Garnish: orange slice and a cherry, add twist of lemon. R

Simply replace the fruit liqueur in the following recipe to create a Whisk(e)y Fruit Sour:

1 msr bourbon or scotch
1 msr preferred fruit liqueur
1 msr lemon juice
1 teaspoon sugar syrup

Shake and strain into glass filled with broken ice. Garnish: orange slice and a cherry, add twist of lemon.

Southern Tango

Fruity flavour   *Alcohol 1.0*

    1 msr dry vermouth
    1/2 msr Southern Comfort
    2 msr lemonade

Add to glass three-quarters filled with broken ice,
add lemon twist.

H

Ti-Punch

Lime flavour   *Alcohol 2.0*

A traditional French Caribbean aperitif. It is dangerously drinkable.

    2 msr white rum
    1 msr sugar syrup
    1 whole fresh lime

Wash lime, remove top and bottom, and thinly slice
into half rings. Add lime pieces to glass and crush
with flat end of barspoon to release most of the juice.
Add other ingredients and top up with broken ice,
muddle together and add short straw.

R

Champagne Cocktails

Champagne cocktails were traditionally served as an aperitif before a celebratory dinner, but are now popular at any time.

The word champagne is used here as a generic term meaning a high quality sparkling wine. You may prefer to use a Methode Champenoise wine from a region other than Champagne; good quality Italian spumantes and Spanish Cavas are now widely available.

Always store champagne horizontally to keep the wine in contact with the cork.

With all the following recipes, unless otherwise stated:

Always use *dry* champagne which has been thoroughly chilled to between 6.6–8.8° C (44–48° F).

Never shake champagne with the other ingredients.

Always use frosted glassware.

Alfonso

Red wine flavour   *Alcohol 1.8*

When Spanish King Alfonso XIII was deposed in 1931, he spent much of his exile in France. There he sampled this cocktail.

    4 msr champagne
    1 msr Dubonnet
    1 lump sugar
    3 drops Angostura

Add Angostura to sugar lump in frosted glass.
Add large ice cube and the liquors. Squeeze lemon
twist on top and discard.

W

American Glory

Orange flavour   *Alcohol 1.0*

    3 msr champagne
    2 msr orange juice
    2 msr lemonade
Add to ice-filled glass.   **H**

Andalusia

Sweet wine flavour   *Alcohol 1.5*

    3 msr champagne
    1 msr sweet sherry
Add to glass; add a red cherry.   **F**

Aqua Marina

Mint flavour   *Alcohol 2.5*

    4 msr champagne
    1 msr vodka
    ½ msr green creme de menthe
    ½ msr lemon juice
Shake and strain; add champagne.   **F**

Aztec

Subtle fruit flavour   *Alcohol 2.1*
Courtesy of Boero Schnapps.

    3 msr champagne
    ¾ msr Boero watermelon schnapps
    ½ msr gold tequila
Add to glass.   **F**

B2 C2

Herb wine flavour   *Alcohol 4.3*

In Spring 1945, the US 21st Corps crossed the Rhine and liberated a Wehrmacht liquor store. The assortment of liqueurs were soon pressed into service. To make these more palatable in quantity, the following formula was devised.

    1 msr brandy
    1 msr Benedictine
    1 msr Cointreau
    4 msr champagne

Add to glass. Can be made in a large jug with
chopped fruits in season added.

W

Bellini

Peachy flavour — *Alcohol 1.0*

Created in 1943 at Harry's Bar, Venice, by Giuseppi Cipriani on the
occasion of an exhibition of the work of Venetian painter Bellini.

> 3 msr spumante/champagne
> 1½ msr peach juice
> 1 teaspoon sugar syrup

Add to glass. Garnish: slice of peach and a cherry. F

If mango juice is used in place of peach, this is a Mango Bellini.

Black Tie

Wine flavour — *Alcohol 1.5*

Courtesy of Reynac Pineau des Charentes.

> 3 msr cold pineau white
> 1½ msr champagne

Add to glass. Garnish: a black grape.

W

Black Velvet

Also known as Bismarck or Champagne Velvet.

Rich beer flavour — *Alcohol 2.5*

Created in 1861 at Brooks's Club, London. Prince Albert had died and a
steward decided the champagne should also be in mourning, so he mixed
it with Guinness. This became very popular and was the favourite tipple
of Prince Otto Von Bismarck of Germany (1815–98).

Half fill glass with draught or bottled Guinness
and gently top up with champagne. Pi

If lager-beer is used in place of Guinness,
this is a Halsted Street Velvet.

Buck's Fizz

Orange flavour — *Alcohol 1.3*

Created in 1921 by Mr McGarry, a barman at Buck's Club, London. He
specified a ratio of two-thirds champagne to one-third orange.

> 4 msr champagne
> 2 msr orange juice
> 1 teaspoon Grenadine

Add to frosted glass.

W

Champagne Ambon

Banana wine flavour   *Alcohol 1.6*

    4 msr champagne
    1/2 msr Pisang Ambon

Add to glass.   F

Champagne Charlie

Apricot flavour   *Alcohol 1.8*

In 1851 Charles-Camille Heidsieck began producing champagne. His remarkable salesmanship and 'Mr Goodtimes' image earned him the name 'Champagne Charlie'.

    4 msr champagne Charles Heidsieck
    1 msr apricot brandy

Add to glass half filled with broken ice.
Add half slice of orange.   W

Champagne de Mars

Kiwi wine flavour   *Alcohol 1.2*

    2 msr champagne
    1 msr kiwi liqueur
    3 msr cold cola

Add to glass.   W

Champagne Irish Mist

Honey / Wine flavour   *Alcohol 1.8*

    4 msr champagne
    1/2 msr Irish Mist

Add to glass.   F

Champagne Julep

Alcohol 3.5

Mint wine flavour

A Mint Julep topped up with 3 msr champagne.   CO

Champagne Lemon

Lemon wine flavour   *Alcohol 1.0*

    2 msr champagne
    1/2 msr peach schnapps
    2 msr sparkling bitter lemon

Add to glass.   CS

Champagne Napoleon

Orange flavour   *Alcohol 1.8*

In the early hours of 18 March 1814, Napoleon Bonaparte described his battle plans to Mr Jean-Remy Moët, his host, and said 'If I should fail... I want to reward you now for the admirable way you have built up your business, and all you have done for our wines abroad'. He then presented Mr Moet with the Chevalier's Cross of the Legion of Honour, which he took from his own uniform. Beat that for an endorsement.

> ¾ msr Mandarine Napoléon
> 1 msr filtered orange juice
> 3¼ msr champagne

Briefly stir the liqueur and juice with ice and strain into a frosted glass; add the champagne.

F

Champagne Polonaise

Blackberry flavour   *Alcohol 1.9*

> 4 msr champagne
> ½ msr blackberry brandy
> ¼ msr Old Krupnik

Add to glass.

F

Champerno

Aniseed flavour   *Alcohol 1.8*

A favourite of Ernest Hemingway.

> 4 msr champagne
> ½ msr Pernod

Add to glass.

W

When garnished with a wedge of orange, this is a Death in the Afternoon.

Cherry Champagne

Cherry flavour   *Alcohol 1.6*

> 4 msr champagne
> ½ msr cherry brandy

Add to glass.

F

Classic Champagne Cocktail

Cognac / Wine flavour   *Alcohol 1.4*

In 1889 a New York journalist organised a cocktail competition, with a gold medal as first prize. Mr John Dougherty emerged victorious with his Business Brace. He revealed that he had discovered the recipe 25 years earlier in the southern states of the USA. It was exactly the same as that given below, but with the addition of a small quantity of spring water. The precise origin of this recipe remains a mystery.

> 3 msr champagne
> 1/3 msr cognac (substitute: brandy)
> 2 dashes Angostura
> 1 sugar cube

Soak cube in glass with the Angostura.
Add ingredients. Squeeze twist of lemon and discard.
Garnish: half a slice of orange.

F

Lately it has become the fashion to add 1/3 msr Grand Marnier and a dash of sugar syrup.

Cockney Champagne

Lemon wine flavour   *Alcohol 1.8*

> 3 msr champagne
> 3/4 msr gin
> 1/2 msr lemon juice
> 1/2 msr sugar syrup

Add to glass.

F

Di Saronno Mimosa

Fruit wine flavour   *Alcohol 1.1*

Courtesy of Illva Saronno SpA.

> 2 msr champagne
> 3/4 msr Amaretto di Saronno
> 2 msr orange juice

Add to glass. Garnish: half slice of orange.

F

Fiddlers Toast

Citrus wine flavour   *Alcohol 1.6*

    3 msr champagne
    1/2 msr Grand Marnier
    1/2 msr lime juice
    2 msr orange juice
    1 blue curacao-soaked sugar cube

Add all but sugar to glass three-quarters filled with
broken ice. Add slice of orange and float cube on it.
Add short straws.   G

Fireworks

Tangerine flavour   *Alcohol 2.0*

Courtesy of Boero Schnapps.

    4 msr champagne
    1/3 msr gin
    1/2 msr tangerine schnapps

Add to glass with twist of orange.   F

Fraise de Champagne

Strawberry flavour   *Alcohol 1.9*

Courtesy of Marie Brizard Liqueurs, France.

    31/2 msr champagne
    3/4 msr Creme de Fraise Marie Brizard
    1/2 msr cognac

Add to glass.   CS

FRENCHES

Based on the French 75, a French is made in a tall glass like a Collins,
with citrus juice, but half the quantity of base spirit.

French 25

Lemon flavour   *Alcohol 2.7*

    5 msr champagne
    1 msr gold tequila
    1 msr lemon juice
    1/2 msr maple syrup

Add all but champagne to glass, ensure the syrup dissolves.
Fill glass with ice. Add champagne almost to the rim
and mix gently. Garnish: half slice lemon and a
cherry. Add straws.   CO

French 45
Alcohol 2.7

Lemon flavour

A French 75 with Drambuie in place of the Gin
and only half a teaspoon of sugar.   CO

French 65
Alcohol 2.9

Lemon flavour

A French 75 with 2 teaspoons of brandy floated on top.   CO

French 75

Lemon flavour   *Alcohol 2.7*

The original '75 Cocktail' was created by Henry of Henry's Bar, Paris,
during the First World War. He named it after the famous French '75'
light field gun.

In the post-war celebrations, Harry of Harry's Bar, Paris, added
champagne to what was originally a short drink with a gin base and dash
of lemon, and named it a French 75. By 1930 it was world famous and
has recently become a class of drink in its own right.

    5 msr champagne
    1 msr gin
    1 msr lemon juice
    1 heaped teaspoon caster sugar

Add all but champagne to glass, ensure the sugar
dissolves. Fill glass with ice and add the champagne.
Garnish: half slice lemon and a cherry, add straws.   CO

Replace the gin in the following popular Frenches:

French 95   1 msr bourbon

French 125   1 msr cognac

Gagarin

Cherry wine flavour

Alcohol 2.5

Fritz Schaller, Austria. Courtesy of Bols International B.V.

2½ msr Dry Babycham (substitute: champagne)
1 msr vodka
½ msr Bols cherry brandy
½ msr creme de cassis
1 teaspoon lime juice

Stir and strain, add the Babycham.
Garnish: cherry.

C

Gold Velvet

Rich beer flavour

Alcohol 2.3

Half fill glass with lager, add 1 msr pineapple juice
and gently top up with champagne.

Pi

Good Old Days

Herb wine flavour

Alcohol 1.7

4 msr champagne
½ msr Old Krupnik

Add to glass, add a cherry.

F

Great Idea

Fruit wine flavour

Alcohol 0.8

2½ msr champagne
1 msr pineapple juice
1 msr mandarin juice
⅓ msr maple syrup

Dissolve syrup in juices, add champagne.

CS

Green Dragon

Melon wine flavour

Alcohol 1.8

4 msr champagne
1 msr Midori

Add to glass. Garnish: green maraschino cherry.

F

Happy Hollander

Fruit wine flavour   *Alcohol 1.5*

    3 msr champagne
    1/2 msr gin
    1 msr mango juice
    1 teaspoon pineapple syrup
    1 teaspoon lemon juice

Add to glass half filled with broken ice.
Garnish: slice of lemon, add short straws.

W

Henry's Special

Grapefruit wine flavour   *Alcohol 1.3*

    3 msr champagne
    1/3 msr brandy
    1 msr grapefruit juice
    1 teaspoon honey
    1 teaspoon lemon juice

Shake briefly with a glassful of broken ice,
add the champagne.

D

Horn of Plenty

Fruit wine flavour   *Alcohol 1.5*

    3 msr champagne
    1/3 msr Grand Marnier
    1/3 msr Campari
    1/4 msr grenadine

Add to glass. Garnish: half slice orange
and a cherry.

F

Hotel California

Fruity flavour   *Alcohol 2.2*

    4 msr champagne
    1 msr gold tequila
    2 msr mandarin juice
    2 msr pineapple juice

Shake and strain into ice-filled glass,
add the champagne and straws.

P

June Sparkle

Strawberry wine flavour   *Alcohol 1.3*

    3¹/₂ msr champagne
    ¹/₂ msr strawberry liqueur
    1 msr pineapple juice
Add to glass. Garnish: sugar-dipped strawberry.   F

Keep It Up

Orange wine flavour   *Alcohol 1.5*

    3 msr champagne
    ¹/₂ msr cognac
    1 msr orange juice
    1 sugar cube, saturated with 1 dash Angostura
Add to glass with twist of orange,
serve with muddler.   F

Kir Royale

Blackcurrant flavour   *Alcohol 1.6*

    4¹/₂ msr champagne
    ¹/₃ msr creme de cassis
Add to glass.   F

Kiwi Sparkle

Kiwi flavour   *Alcohol 1.3*

    3 msr champagne
    ¹/₂ msr kiwi liqueur
    1 msr kiwi juice
Add to glass.   F

L'Aunisien

Herb wine flavour   *Alcohol 1.5*

M. Pierre-Jean Baillard, France.

    3 msr champagne
    ¹/₂ msr Campari
    ¹/₂ msr white pineau des charentes
Add to glass.   F

La Panthere Rosé

Fruit wine flavour   *Alcohol 3.2*

Created by Marc Boccard-Schuster, Nam Long Le Shaker, London. The
bar of Le Shaker is adorned with first prize medals, mainly golden
shakers, which Marc won in major cocktail competitions all over the
world.

    3 msr champagne
    1½ msr gin
    ½ msr strawberry liqueur
    ½ msr dry orange curacao
    1 msr orange juice

Shake and strain into glass three-quarters filled
with broken ice, add the champagne.
Garnish: small sprig of mint.   G

London Bus

Fruity flavour   *Alcohol 1.0*

    3 msr champagne
    1 msr mandarin juice
    1 msr grapefruit juice
    1 teaspoon passion fruit syrup

Add to glass, add cherry.   F

Mandarine Imperiale

Mandarin flavour   *Alcohol 2.2*

Created by Noel O'Connor, Langan's Brasserie, Piccadilly. Courtesy of Ets. Fourcroy s.a.

    3 msr champagne
    1¼ msr Mandarine Napoléon
    1 msr egg white
    ½ msr lemon juice
    ¼ msr sugar syrup

Shake well and strain, add the champagne.   W

Marilyn Monroe

Wine flavour   *Alcohol 2.3*

In 1668 a monk called Dom Pétrus Perignon became cellarer at the Abbey of Hautvilliers, an important position since the Abbey's financial survival depended upon wine sales. He set about improving the quality of production and soon Hautvilliers wines were achieving twice the price of rival brands.

Dom Perignon champagne was Marilyn Monroe's preferred brand.

    4 msr champagne
    1 msr apple brandy
    1 teaspoon grenadine

Add to glass. Garnish: two cherries on a stick.   CS

Maxim's

Fruit wine flavour   *Alcohol 2.1*

    3 msr champagne
    1/2 msr brandy
    1/2 msr Cointreau
    1 teaspoon raspberry liqueur
    1/2 msr orange juice

Stir and strain, add the champagne and twist of orange. CS

Mimosa

Orange wine flavour   *Alcohol 1.0*

Created around 1925 at the Ritz Hotel Bar, Paris. It took its name from the mimosa flowering plant, whose colour it resembles.

    3 msr champagne
    3 msr orange juice

Add to glass with twist of orange.   W

If 1/2 msr Grand Marnier is added, this is a Grand Mimosa. *Alcohol 1.5*

If 1 msr lime juice cordial is used in place of the orange juice in a Mimosa, this is a Limosa.

If 1 msr lemon juice and 1/2 msr sugar syrup are used in place of the orange juice in a Mimosa, this is a Lemon Mimosa.

Mustique Whammy

Fruit wine flavour   Alcohol 2.1

    3½ msr champagne
    1 msr golden rum
    1 msr orange juice
    ½ msr lemon juice
    ¼ msr grenadine

Shake and strain into glass, add the champagne.   W

Night and Day

Bitter orange flavour   Alcohol 2.4

    3 msr champagne
    ¾ msr cognac
    ½ msr Grand Marnier
    ¼ msr Campari

Add to glass half filled with crushed ice.   W

Palais Royal

Fruit wine flavour   Alcohol 2.2

    3 msr champagne
    1 msr cognac
    ⅓ msr cherry brandy
    1 teaspoon lemon juice

Add to glass half filled with crushed ice.
Garnish: half slice of lemon and a cherry.   W

Passat

Passion fruit flavour   Alcohol 1.5

    2½ msr champagne
    ½ msr triple sec
    ½ msr apricot liqueur
    1 msr passion fruit juice
    1 teaspoon orange juice

Add to glass. Garnish: cherry and lemon slice.   CS

Pernod Fizz

Aniseed flavour   *Alcohol 2.0*

    3 msr champagne
    3/4 msr Pernod
    1 msr mandarin juice

Add to glass three-quarters filled with broken ice.
Garnish: cherry and orange slice.   **W**

Pink Planet

Strawberry flavour   *Alcohol 1.5*

    3 msr champagne
    3/4 msr strawberry liqueur
    2 msr strawberry puree
    1/2 msr lemon juice
    1 teaspoon caster sugar

Rim glass with strawberry liqueur/caster sugar. Blend all
but champagne briefly with three-quarters of a glassful of
crushed ice. Add blended mix and champagne to the glass.
Garnish: half a strawberry, add short straws.   **G**

Pompey Royale

Red wine flavour   *Alcohol 1.0*

    3 msr champagne
    1 msr pomegranate juice
    1/2 msr passion fruit juice
    1/3 msr raspberry syrup
    1 teaspoon caster sugar

Dissolve sugar in juices, add to glass.   **CS**

Pyrenees Greeting

Fruit wine flavour   *Alcohol 1.6*

    3 1/2 msr champagne
    1/2 msr sweet sherry
    1/2 msr melon liqueur
    1 teaspoon lemon juice

Add to glass with twist of lemon.   **F**

Regatta

Herb flavour   *Alcohol 1.9*

    3 msr champagne
    1/2 msr Galliano
    1/2 msr triple sec
    1 teaspoon vodka
    1/2 msr lemon juice

Add to glass.   F

Ritz Fizz

Complex wine flavour   *Alcohol 1.4*

'The law-courts of England are open to all men, like the doors of the Ritz Hotel'. Baron Charles Darling (1849–1936).

    3 1/2 msr champagne
    1 teaspoon amaretto
    1 teaspoon blue curacao
    1 teaspoon filtered lemon juice

Add to glass, float a small rose petal on top.   F

Ritz Bar Fizz

Fruit wine flavour   *Alcohol 1.0*

The recently renovated Ritz Bar of the Ritz-Carlton Hotel in Boston, USA, has been the centre of Boston society since it opened in 1933.

    3 msr champagne
    1 msr pineapple juice
    1 msr grapefruit juice
    1 teaspoon grenadine

Add to glass. Garnish: mint sprig and cherry.   CS

Rose of the Ritz

Raspberry flavour   *Alcohol 2.5*

Courtesy of Hotel Ritz, Paris.

    3 msr champagne
    1 msr cognac
    1 msr raspberry liqueur
    1 teaspoon lemon juice
    15 raspberries

Blend well and pour, add the champagne.   W

Royal Silver

Grapefruit flavour

Alcohol 2.0

    4 msr champagne
    1/2 msr poire williams
    1/2 msr Cointreau
    1 1/2 msr grapefruit juice

Rim glass with grenadine/caster sugar.
Shake and strain, add the champagne.

W

Royal Wild Strawberry

Strawberry flavour

Alcohol 1.6

Courtesy of Marie Brizard Liqueurs, France.

    4 msr champagne
    3/4 msr Fraise des Bois Marie Brizard
    (wild strawberry liqueur)

Add to glass.

CS

Rue Royale

Strawberry flavour

Alcohol 2.1

Courtesy of Marie Brizard Liqueurs, France.

    3 1/2 msr champagne
    1 msr Creme de Fraise Marie Brizard (strawberry liqueur)
    1/2 msr cognac

Add to glass.

CS

Saiki

Fruit wine flavour

Alcohol 1.4

    2 1/2 msr champagne
    1/2 msr creme de banane
    1/2 msr Frangelico
    1 msr orange juice
    1/2 msr lemon juice

Add to glass. Garnish: cherry.

CS

San Remo

Fruity flavour *Alcohol 1.6*

> 3 msr champagne
> 1/2 msr triple sec
> 1/2 msr mandarin liqueur
> 1 msr grapefruit juice

Add to glass. Garnish: slices of grapefruit
and mandarin.

W

Saronno Kir Imperial

Almond flavour *Alcohol 1.7*

M. Zivacco, Municipal Casino, Cannes, France. Courtesy of Illva Saronno SpA.

> 4 msr champagne
> 3/4 msr Amaretto di Saronno

Add to glass with twist of lemon. F

Savoy Affair

Fruity flavour *Alcohol 1.7*

> 4 msr champagne
> 2 teaspoons each: peach brandy,
> strawberry liqueur, passion fruit juice and lime juice

Add to lime/caster sugar-rimmed glass.
Garnish: sugar-dipped strawberry. D

Strawberry Champagne

Strawberry flavour *Alcohol 2.1*

> 3 msr champagne
> 3/4 msr vodka
> 3/4 msr strawberry brandy

Add to glass half filled with broken ice.
Garnish: two halves of a strawberry. W

Strawberry Bandit

Strawberry flavour   Alcohol 1.8

    3 msr champagne
    1/2 msr gold tequila
    1/2 msr creme de fraise
    1 teaspoon grenadine
    1 msr strawberry puree

Blend briefly with a glassful of crushed ice,
add the champagne. Garnish: sugar-dipped
strawberry.

D

Texas Fizz

Fruit wine flavour   Alcohol 2.3

Originally made with soda water, the Texas Fizz recently went up-
market.

    4 msr champagne
    1 msr gin
    1 msr orange juice
    1/4 msr grenadine

Shake and strain into glass three-quarters filled
with broken ice, add the champagne.
Garnish: slice of orange.

H

This is the Night

Fruit wine   Alcohol 1.0

    3 msr champagne
    1 msr passion fruit juice
    2 msr mandarin juice

Add to glass half filled with broken ice.

D

Tomorrow We Sail

Red wine flavour   Alcohol 1.9

    31/2 msr champagne
    1/2 msr LBV port
    1/2 msr dark rum
    1 teaspoon triple sec

Add to glass with twist of orange.

F

Turk's Blood

Red champagne flavour   *Alcohol 1.5*

An old German recipe originally made with strong beer and Burgundy. This version achieved stardom opposite Liza Minelli in the film *Cabaret*.

    3 msr champagne
    2 msr burgundy

Add to glass.   CS

If claret is used in place of burgundy, served with ice and garnished with fruit, this is a Turk's Neck Cup.

Valencia

Fruity flavour

    4 msr champagne
    1 msr apricot brandy
    1 teaspoon dry orange curacao
    1 msr orange juice

Stir and strain, add the champagne.   F
Garnish: half slice of orange.

When Grand Marnier is used in place of curacao, this is a Palm Beach Fizz.

Alcohol 1.8

Hot Drinks

The following recipes all require heatproof glassware. The three essential types are:

Heatproof cups	5–7 fl oz / 14–20 cl	(HPC)
Heatproof goblets	7–10 fl oz / 20–28 cl	(HPG)
Heatproof Irish coffee	8 fl oz / 23 cl	(HPIC)

Glasses should be warm before use.

Apple Comfort

Apple flavour

Alcohol 1.0

    1 msr Southern Comfort
    6 msr hot apple juice

Add to glass.

HPC

Black Stripe

Dark rum flavour

Alcohol 1.5

    1½ msr dark rum
    1 teaspoon molasses (treacle)
    3 msr boiling water

Dissolve molasses in boiling water, add to glass with rum. Add lemon twist.

HPC

Blue Blazer

Honey scotch flavour *Alcohol 2.0*

Created in 1849 by 'Professor' Jerry Thomas at the El Dorado Saloon, San Francisco.

Thomas began his career as a bartender in 1845 at the age of 20 at a saloon in his home town of New Haven, Connecticut. He suffered from wanderlust, and worked in San Francisco, the Yuba River goldfields, Central America, New York, South Carolina, Chicago, St. Louis (Planter's House), and New Orleans, and toured Liverpool, London and Paris.

His genius for inventing highly successful mixed drinks led to him being dubbed 'Professor', and ultimately becoming the most famous and highly regarded bartender of his generation.

Thomas made this drink famous by perfecting the technique of igniting the whisky and tossing the flaming liquid between two silver tankards, thus mixing the ingredients whilst illuminating the bar with liquid fire. President Grant was so impressed he gave Thomas a cigar!

This recipe is delicious on a cold winter evening and is reputed to make even the worst cold or flu a little more bearable. Thomas refused to serve it until the thermometer fell below 10 degrees.

2½ msr scotch
1 msr clear honey (originally sugar)
2½ msr water
¾ msr lemon juice (originally peel only)

Heat in a small saucepan until the honey dissolves.
When hot ignite briefly and pour.
Add twist of lemon. HPC

B.M.A. (Brandy Mocha Almond)

Chocolate / Coffee flavour *Alcohol 0.8*

½ msr brandy
½ msr amaretto
2½ msr hot coffee
2½ msr hot cocoa

Add to glass, sweeten to taste. HPC

Bumpo

Lime rum flavour *Alcohol 2.0*

    2 msr golden rum
    1 msr lime juice
    1 teaspoon caster sugar
    2 msr hot water

Add to glass, dissolve the sugar. Dust with nutmeg.   **HPC**

Canadian Cocoa

Maple milk flavour *Alcohol 1.8*

    ³/₄ msr Canadian whisky
    ³/₄ msr dark rum
    ¹/₂ msr dark creme de cacao
    5 msr milk
    ²/₃ msr maple syrup

Heat milk in small saucepan; when simmering, add
remaining ingredients and pour when syrup is dissolved.   **HPG**

Caribbean Milk

Spiced milk flavour *Alcohol 1.7*

    1 msr dark rum
    1 msr Kahlua
    4 msr milk
    ¹/₂ msr double cream
    1 cinnamon stick
    ¹/₂ slice of lemon

Heat in small saucepan and simmer briefly,
strain into glass.   **HPG**

CHOCOLATE DRINKS

Drinks with a strong flavour of chocolate.

Alhambra

Chocolate flavour *Alcohol 1.0*

    1 msr cognac
    5 msr hot cocoa/chocolate drink – sweetened to taste

Add to glass.   **HPIC**

Hot Rum Chocolate

Chocolate flavour   *Alcohol 1.0*

    1 msr dark rum
    5 msr hot cocoa/chocolate drink – sweetened to taste
    1 tablespoon whipped cream

Combine in glass, top with the cream and sprinkle
with grated chocolate.   HPIC
Replace the rum in the following popular chocolate drinks:

Chocaholic	1 msr brandy	*Alcohol 1.0*
Kahlua Hot Chocolate	1 msr Kahlua	*Alcohol 0.7*
Hot Chocolate Mint (also known as Snuggler)	³/₄ msr peppermint schnapps	*Alcohol 0.6*
Seville Chocolate	³/₄ msr Mandarine Napoléon	*Alcohol 0.8*

Ciderific

Cider flavour   *Alcohol 2.5*

    6 msr dry cider
    1 msr golden rum
    1 stick cinnamon

Heat in a small saucepan and strain into glass
when hot. Add half slice of lemon.   HPG

If 1 msr Apple Schnapps is used in place of
the rum, this is a Hot Spiced Apple Cider.   *Alcohol 2.2*

COFFEES – TOPPED WITH CREAM

Coffee Chaser

Orange coffee flavour   *Alcohol 0.8*

    ¹/₂ msr Kahlua
    ¹/₂ msr Grand Marnier
    5 msr hot black coffee
    1¹/₂ msr whipped cream
    sugar

Add coffee and liquors to glass and sweeten to taste.
Gently float the cream on top, use lightly whipped
whipping cream or, in an emergency, spray-on
sweet cream. Sprinkle with grated chocolate.   HPIC

If $^1/_2$ msr cognac is added to a Coffee Chaser, this is a Parisian Coffee.   *Alcohol 1.3*

Replace Kahlua, Grand Marnier and grated chocolate in the following popular coffees:

Balearic Coffee	$^1/_2$ msr Frigola	
	Sprinkle with nutmeg	*Alcohol 0.3*
Bavarian Coffee	$^1/_2$ msr peppermint schnapps	
	$^1/_2$ msr Kahlua	
	Sprinkle with chocolate	*Alcohol 0.7*
Belgian Coffee	$^3/_4$ msr Elixir d'Anvers	
	Sprinkle with chocolate	*Alcohol 0.7*
Café Don Juan	$^3/_4$ msr dark rum	
	1 msr Kahlua	
	Rim with lemon/sugar	
	Sprinkle with chocolate	*Alcohol 1.5*
Café Grande	$^1/_3$ msr Tia Maria	
	$^1/_3$ msr dark creme de cacao	
	$^1/_3$ msr Grand Marnier	
	Top with cherry	*Alcohol 1.5*
Café Imperial	$^3/_4$ msr Mandarine	
	Napoléon	*Alcohol 0.8*
Café Nelson	$^3/_4$ msr Baileys	
	$^3/_4$ msr Frangelico	
	Sprinkle with chopped hazelnuts	*Alcohol 1.5*
Calypso Coffee	1 msr Tia Maria	
	Sprinkle with chocolate	*Alcohol 0.7*
Calypso Coffee USA	$^1/_2$ msr white rum	
	$^1/_2$ msr dark creme de cacao	
	Top with 1 teaspoon amaretto	*Alcohol 0.8*
Caribbean Coffee	1 msr dark rum	
	Sprinkle with chocolate	*Alcohol 1.0*
Casino Coffee	$^1/_2$ msr brandy	
	$^1/_2$ msr dark creme de cacao	
	$^1/_2$ msr amaretto	
	Sprinkle with chocolate	*Alcohol 1.1*
Chambord Coffee	1 msr Chambord	
	Top with one fresh raspberry	*Alcohol 0.4*
Coffee Break	$^1/_2$ msr brandy	
	$^1/_2$ msr Kahlua	
	Top with cherry	*Alcohol 0.8*

Dutch Coffee	1 msr Oude Genever	
	Sprinkle with nutmeg	*Alcohol 1.0*
Dutch Coffee	1/2 msr Vandermint	
USA	1/3 msr Kahlua	
	Top with 1 teaspoon amaretto	*Alcohol 0.5*
English Coffee	1/2 msr London Dry Gin	
	1/3 msr triple sec	
	1/3 msr Kahlua	
	Top with 1 teaspoon triple sec	*Alcohol 1.0*
French Coffee	1 msr Cointreau	
	1/2 msr Kahlua	
	Top with 1 teaspoon Cointreau	*Alcohol 0.5*
Gaelic Coffee	3/4 msr scotch	
	Sprinkle with chocolate	*Alcohol 0.8*
German Coffee	1/2 msr kirsch	
	Top with black cherry	*Alcohol 0.5*
Irish Mist Coffee	1/2 msr Irish whiskey	
	1/2 msr Irish Mist	
	Top with cherry	*Alcohol 0.9*
Italian Coffee	1/2 msr Strega	
	Sprinkle with nutmeg	*Alcohol 0.5*
Italian Coffee	1/2 msr amaretto	
USA	1/2 msr Kahlua	
	Top with 1 teaspoon amaretto	*Alcohol 0.5*
Jamaican Coffee	3/4 msr white rum	
	1/2 msr Tia Maria	
	Top with 1 teaspoon Tia Maria	*Alcohol 1.0*
Keoke Coffee	1/2 msr brandy	
	1/2 msr Kahlua	
	1/2 msr dark creme de cacao	
	Top with cherry	*Alcohol 1.1*
Lagos Coffee	3/4 msr apricot brandy	
	1/2 msr Kahlua	
	Top with 1 teaspoon amaretto	*Alcohol 0.8*
Mexican Coffee	1 msr Kahlua	
	Sprinkle with chocolate	*Alcohol 0.7*
Mexican Coffee	3/4 msr Gold Tequila	
USA	1/2 msr Kahlua	
	Top with 1 teaspoon Kahlua	*Alcohol 1.0*
Prince Charles Coffee	3/4 msr Drambuie	
	Sprinkle with chocolate	*Alcohol 0.8*

Puerto Rican Coffee	³/₄ msr Captain Morgan spiced rum	
	Top with 1 teaspoon Kahlua	*Alcohol 1.0*
Royale Coffee	1 msr cognac	
	Sprinkle with chocolate	*Alcohol 1.0*
Russian Coffee	1 msr vodka	
	¹/₂ msr Kahlua	
	Top with 1 teaspoon amaretto and a cherry	*Alcohol 1.3*
Scandinavian Coffee	1 msr aquavit	
	Sprinkle with nutmeg	*Alcohol 1.0*
Shamrock Coffee	1 msr Irish Mist	
	Sprinkle with chocolate	*Alcohol 1.0*
Tropical Coffee	1 msr golden rum	
	Sprinkle with cinnamon	*Alcohol 1.0*

Café Disaronno

Almond flavour *Alcohol 0.5*

Courtesy of Illva Saronno SpA.

> ³/₄ msr Amaretto di Saronna
> 5 msr hot black coffee
> sugar
> 1 msr whipped cream

Add to glass and sweeten to taste, float the cream.
Place three coffee beans on top. HPIC

Café Henry the Third

Herb / Orange flavour *Alcohol 1.3*

> ¹/₃ msr Galliano
> ¹/₃ msr Kahlua
> ¹/₃ msr Grand Marnier
> ¹/₃ msr brandy
> 5 msr hot black coffee
> 3 msr whipped cream
> sugar

Rim glass with sugar syrup/cinnamon sugar.
Add to glass and sweeten to taste. Float the
cream on top. HPIC

Irish Coffee

Whiskey / Coffee flavour   *Alcohol 1.3*

The original recipe is said to have been created shortly after the Second World War by Joe Sheridan, head barman at Shannon Airport on the west coast of Ireland. His recipe was rather strong, using about 2 msr whiskey.

The drink only really took off when the San Francisco restaurant Buena Vista became the first to adapt and popularise it. The addition of Kahlua is a recent innovation. Sometimes a teaspoon of Green Creme de Menthe is mixed with the cream before being floated.

> 1 msr Irish whiskey
> 1/2 msr Kahlua
> 5 msr hot black coffee
> 1 1/2 msr whipped cream
> sugar

Add coffee and liquors to glass and sweeten to taste.
Gently float the cream on top.   HPIC

COFFEES – MADE WITH CREAM

Café Toledo

Cream coffee flavour   *Alcohol 1.1*

> 3/4 msr Baileys
> 3/4 msr Kahlua
> 1 teaspoon chocolate syrup
> 5 msr hot black coffee
> 1/2 msr whipping cream
> sugar

Add to glass and sweeten to taste.   HPC

Irish '49

Cream coffee flavour   *Alcohol 1.0*

> 3/4 msr Baileys
> 1/2 msr Irish Mist
> 5 msr hot black coffee
> 1/2 msr whipping cream
> sugar

Add to glass and sweeten to taste.   HPC

Rumba

Rum flavour   *Alcohol 1.3*

    ³/₄ msr Baileys
    ³/₄ msr dark rum
    5 msr hot black coffee
    ¹/₂ msr whipping cream
    sugar

Add to glass and sweeten to taste.   HPC

Tijuana Coffee

Creamy coffee flavour   *Alcohol 0.7*

    1 msr Kahlua
    5 msr hot black coffee
    2 msr lightly whipped cream
    sugar

Add to glass and sweeten to taste. Mix briskly,
allowing froth to form and sprinkle with ground
cinnamon.   HPG

COFFEES – NO CREAM

Black Maria

Coffee rum flavour   *Alcohol 1.3*

    ³/₄ msr Tia Maria
    ³/₄ msr dark rum
    5 msr hot black coffee – sweetened to taste

Add to cup.   HPC
Can also be served cold – shaken and poured into ice-filled goblet.

Café d'Amour

Brandy flavour   *Alcohol 1.3*

    1¹/₄ msr cognac
    5 msr hot black coffee
    zest of ¹/₂ a lemon
    1 stick cinnamon
    sugar to taste

Rim cup with lemon/sugar. Briefly simmer all but cognac in small saucepan. Heat and ignite cognac in soup ladle, add to coffee and extinguish. Strain into cup. If one clove and the zest of half an orange are added to the saucepan before heating, this is a Café Brulot. The cup should not have a sugar rim.   HPC

Grandfather's Coffee

Sweet brandy flavour   *Alcohol 1.4*
    1 msr brandy
    1/2 msr amaretto
    5 msr hot espresso coffee – sweetened to taste
Warm in a small saucepan, pour when hot.   HPC

Dot's Hot Spot

Fruity flavour   *Alcohol 0.6*
    3 msr white grape juice
    3 msr dry cider
    1 teaspoon honey
    1 stick cinnamon
    1 slice of lemon
Heat gently in small saucepan, strain
into glass when hot.   HPC

Glühwein

Spiced wine flavour   *Alcohol 1.5*
    4 msr medium red wine
    1/2 msr brandy
    1 teaspoon caster sugar
    1 slice orange
    1 slice lemon
    1 cinnamon stick
    2 cloves
Simmer gently for 30 seconds and strain into glass.
Often made in quantity as a punch.   HPG

Grog

Spiced rum flavour　　　　　　　　　　　　　　*Alcohol 2.0*

In 1740 Admiral Sir Edward Vernon, nicknamed 'Old Grog' because his cloak was made of a coarse material called grogram, was returning from the Caribbean. To improve efficiency he decided to dilute the crew's rum ration with water, and they named the result Grog. Grog was found to be more palatable when hot. Around 1795 lemon juice was added to combat scurvy, but by 1850 lime was the most common flavouring. Other ingredients were included, but the original recipe was one part strong rum to three parts water.

　　　2 msr dark rum (preferably Purser's)
　　　2 msr water
　　　2/3 msr lime juice
　　　1 teaspoon brown sugar or honey
　　　2 cloves
　　　1 small cinnamon stick

Combine in small saucepan. Heat gently to
dissolve sugar, when hot strain into glass.　　　　　HPC

Hot Buttered Rum

Rum flavour　　　　　　　　　　　　　　*Alcohol 2.0*

　　　2 msr dark rum
　　　2¹/₂ msr water
　　　1 teaspoon brown sugar or honey
　　　1 teaspoon butter
　　　1 small pinch ground nutmeg
　　　4 drops vanilla essence
　　　1 small cinnamon stick

Heat rum, water and sugar in saucepan until
almost boiling. Add to glass with remaining
ingredients and serve when butter melts.　　　　　HPC

Hot Egg Nogg

Milk sour flavour　　　　　　　　　　　　*Alcohol 1.0*

　　　¹/₂ msr brandy
　　　¹/₂ msr dark rum
　　　¹/₂ msr sugar syrup
　　　1 egg
　　　3 msr boiling milk

Blend all but milk until smooth, pour into glass and
add boiling milk. Sprinkle with grated nutmeg.　　　HPG

Hot Gin

Lemon flavour

⚀⚀⚀
Alcohol 2.0

2 msr gin
3/4 msr lemon juice
2 msr boiling water
1 teaspoon sugar
1 cinnamon stick

Add to glass, dissolve sugar.

HPG

Replace the gin in the following:

Hot Orange Brandy	2 msr Grand Marnier	*Alcohol 2.0*
Hot Brandy	2 msr brandy	*Alcohol 2.0*
Hot Sherry	2 msr sweet sherry	*Alcohol 1.0*

Hot Irish

Whisky flavour

Alcohol 1.5

As served in Dublin pubs.

1½ msr Irish whiskey
4 msr boiling water
½ slice lemon studded with cloves
small pinch ground cinnamon

Add to glass and sweeten with brown sugar to taste.

HPG

Hot Jamaican

Spiced rum flavour

Alcohol 2.0

2 msr dark rum (preferably Jamaican)
3 msr water
1 msr lime
½ msr sugar syrup
2 cloves
1 cinnamon stick
½ slice of lime

Heat gently in saucepan, pour unstrained when hot.

HPG

Hot Lemon

Lemon flavour

Alcohol 0.0

A popular cold and flu remedy. A little spirit is optional.

   2 msr lemon juice
   2 teaspoons sugar
   2 msr boiling water

Add to glass, dissolve sugar.

HPC

Hot Scotch Nightcap

Scotch flavour

Alcohol 1.8

   1 msr scotch
   ½ msr Drambuie
   ½ msr dark creme de cacao
   4 msr boiling milk

Add to cup.

HPC

Hot Toddy – *See* Toddies

Irish Cappuccino

Coffee flavour

Alcohol 0.3

   ½ msr Baileys
   1 cup hot cappuccino coffee

Make cappuccino in normal way, adding the Baileys.

HPC

Irish Milk Punch

Milk / Whisky flavour

Alcohol 1.9

   2 msr Baileys
   ¾ msr Irish whiskey
   6 msr hot milk

Add to glass and sprinkle with grated chocolate.
Delicious on a winter evening.

HPC

Kerry Cappuccino

Coffee flavour

Alcohol 0.2

To each cup of cappuccino add one teaspoon
each of Baileys and dark creme de cacao.

HPC

Lamb's Wool (5 people)

Apple beer flavour   *Alcohol 0.8*

This recipe goes back to the seventeenth century, when it was drunk on November 1st – at 'La Mas-ubal' – an occasion dedicated to the angel presiding over fruit and seeds.

    1 quart (40 fl oz / 114 cl) hot ale
    6 roasted apples – cored, peeled and mashed
    1/2 teaspoon nutmeg
    1/2 teaspoon ginger
    sugar

Mix in warm jug and sweeten to taste.   HPG

Mulled Red Wine

Wine flavour   *Alcohol 1.6*

    4 msr full-bodied red wine
    1 msr LBV port
    1 msr water
    1 level teaspoon sugar
    1 teaspoon lemon juice
    1 pinch nutmeg
    1 pinch cinnamon
    1 clove

Heat in small saucepan and strain into glass, do not boil.   HPC

Negus

Spiced wine flavour   *Alcohol 1.4*

Invented by Colonel Francis Negus in the early 1700s and sometimes made in bulk. 'A most refreshing and elegant beverage, particularly for those who do not take punch or grog after supper.' Jerry Thomas, *How to Mix Drinks*, 1862.

    2 msr LBV port
    1 msr claret
    1 msr burgundy
    1 teaspoon brandy
    2 msr water
    1/2 a lemon thinly sliced into rings
    1 small pinch nutmeg
    1 heaped teaspoon sugar

Heat gently, strain into glass when hot.   HPG

Sweet Dreams

Coffee flavour   *Alcohol 1.3*

   2 msr Tia Maria
   6 msr milk
   1 pinch nutmeg

Heat milk and nutmeg until boiling, add to
glass with Tia Maria.   HPG

TEAS

Colonial Boy

Whiskey flavour   *Alcohol 0.8*

   3/4 msr Irish whiskey
   1 dash Angostura
   5 msr hot black tea sweetened to taste

Add to glass.   HPC

Replace the whiskey in the following popular teas:

High Tea	1/3 msr amaretto and 1/3 msr Grand Marnier	*Alcohol 0.7*
Irish Tea	1/2 msr Irish Mist	*Alcohol 0.5*
Tea Thyme	1/3 msr Frigola	*Alcohol 0.2*

Fireside Tea

Tea / Herb flavour   *Alcohol 1.0*

   1 msr dark rum
   5 msr hot black tea sweetened to taste
   1 wedge-shaped slice of lemon
   1 stick cinnamon

Combine in glass, enjoy by the fireside.   HPG

Hot-T

Tea / Orange flavour   *Alcohol 1.0*

   1 msr Cointreau
   5 msr hot black tea

Add tea and spirit to glass, sweeten to taste.
Add slice of orange.   HPC

Indian Tea

Tea / Fruit flavour
Alcohol 1.4

    1 msr gold rum
    3/4 msr amaretto
    5 msr hot black tea sweetened to taste
    spiral peel of half a lemon

Gently simmer tea and peel in small saucepan
for 1–2 minutes. Add liquors and pour, with peel,
into glass.   HPC

TODDIES

The name toddy may have come from 'tarrie', an early seventeenth-
century word for a drink made in the East Indies from fermented palm
tree sap, a form of arrack.

Another possibility is the explanation given in 1721 by Scottish poet
Allan Ramsay. He claimed the name was derived from Tod's Well, once
an important source of water to Edinburgh.

By Ramsay's day the Toddy was well on the way to becoming a popular
traditional antidote to the harsh highland winters, and would soon
appear throughout northern Europe and the Americas.

Whilst most recipes use Scotch whisky, it can be made with any spirit. It
should have one or more spices, a little sweetener and a slice of citrus
fruit – or its juice. Traditionalists prefer to use only malt whisky, spring
water and sugar – served hot.

Danish Toddy

Cherry flavour
Alcohol 2.0

    1 1/2 msr aquavit
    1/2 msr cherry vodka
    1/2 msr lemon juice
    2 msr boiling water
    slice of lemon studded with cloves

Add to glass.   HPC

Galliano Toddy

Scotch / Herb flavour   *Alcohol 1.7*

    1 msr scotch
    ³/₄ msr Galliano
    ¹/₄ msr grenadine
    slice of lemon studded with cloves
    2 msr boiling water
Add to hot glass. Sprinkle with grated nutmeg.   **HPC**

Toddy (Hot Scotch Toddy)

Scotch flavour   *Alcohol 2.0*

    2 msr scotch
    3 msr boiling water
    ¹/₂ msr lemon juice
    1 teaspoon brown sugar or honey
    3 drops Angostura
    slice of lemon studded with cloves

Add to hot glass, stir to dissolve sugar.
Sprinkle with grated nutmeg.   **HPC**
Replace the scotch with Drambuie for
a Drambuie Toddy.

Tea Toddy

Orange tea flavour   *Alcohol 1.0*

    1 msr Cointreau
    5 msr hot tea

Add to glass. Garnish: slice of orange studded
with cloves.   **HPC**

Tom and Jerry (10 people)

Spiced milk flavour   *Alcohol 1.2*

Created by Jerry Thomas around 1852 at the Planters' House Bar, St.
Louis, USA. He refused to serve it until winter's first snowfall.

Stage 1
    2 msr dark rum
    6 eggs
    6 tablespoons sugar (originally twice this quantity)
    ¹/₂ teaspoon ground cinnamon
    ¹/₈ teaspoon ground cloves
    ¹/₈ teaspoon ground allspice

¼ teaspoon baking soda

Whisk thoroughly to produce a batter.

Stage 2

To each glass add:

    1 msr batter

    1 msr brandy

    4 msr boiling milk (originally water)

Sprinkle with grated nutmeg.   HPG

Vruića Rakia

Sour fruit flavour   *Alcohol 2.0*

An East European speciality often made in bulk.

    2 msr plum brandy (Slivovitz)

    1 teaspoon demerara sugar

    2 msr boiling water

Add to small saucepan, dissolve sugar and
serve when hot.   HPC

Long Drinks

Drinks made with five or more fluid measures before shaking.

Ambience

Mandarin flavour
Courtesy of Hennessy Cognac.

Alcohol 2.3

    1 msr VSOP cognac
    1 msr vodka
    1/4 msr Mandarine Napoléon
    4 msr orange juice
    1 msr lime juice
    1/4 msr sugar syrup

Rim glass with lime/caster sugar. Shake and strain into glass three-quarters filled with broken ice. Garnish: slice of lime and a cherry, add straws.

CO

American Dream

Wine flavour

Alcohol 1.5

    3 msr medium red California wine
    1/3 msr bourbon
    1/3 msr rosso vermouth
    3 msr cold cola

Add to ice-filled glass. Garnish: slice of orange and a cherry.

H

Arctic Summer

Lemon / Apricot flavour   Alcohol 1.9

   1½ msr gin
   ¾ msr apricot brandy
   1 teaspoon grenadine
   4 msr sparkling bitter lemon

Add to ice-filled glass. Garnish: cherry and a lemon slice. H

Arthur's Day Dream

Strawberry flavour   Alcohol 2.0

Created at Arthur's Bar, Sydney, Australia.

   2 msr gold tequila
   1 msr lemon juice
   ½ msr strawberry syrup
   3 msr strawberry puree
   2 msr soda water

Blend briefly with three-quarters glassful of
crushed ice, add the soda. Garnish: slice of
lemon and a sugar-dipped strawberry,
add straws.   CO

Australian Virgin

Pineapple flavour   Alcohol 1.5

   1 msr Bundaberg (dark rum)
   2 msr Australian medium white wine
   3 msr pineapple juice
   ½ msr maraschino cherry syrup/juice

Shake and strain into ice-filled glass.
Garnish: cherry.   H

Aztec Surfboard

Tropical fruit flavour   Alcohol 2.0

   1½ msr gold tequila
   ½ msr pisco
   1 teaspoon blue curacao
   3 msr grapefruit juice
   2 msr mango juice
   1 msr passion fruit juice
   1 teaspoon orgeat

Shake and strain into ice-filled glass.   CO

Azzuro

Tropical fruit flavour — *Alcohol 2.0*

Sergio Pezzoli, Belgium. Courtesy of Bols International B.V.

    1 msr Safari
    1 msr Bols blue curacao
    1 msr Pisang Ambon
    2 msr passion fruit juice
    2 msr pineapple juice
    1 teaspoon egg white

Shake and strain into ice-filled glass.
Garnish: fruit in season.

CO

Bacardi Orange

Orange flavour — *Alcohol 2.5*

In 1862 Don Facundo Bacardi bought a small rum distillery in Santiago, Cuba, for $3,500. When a colony of fruit bats settled under the roof of the distillery they inspired the famous bat symbol which still appears on every bottle.

    1³/₄ msr gold Bacardi rum
    ³/₄ msr Grand Marnier
    2¹/₂ msr orange juice
    1 msr soda water
    2 msr lemonade

Add to ice-filled glass, add slice of orange
and straws.

CO

Bacchanalian Cocktail

Fruity flavour — *Alcohol 2.0*

Inspired by Bacchus, the Roman god of wine.

    1 msr white rum
    ¹/₂ msr brandy
    ¹/₂ msr Yellow Chartreuse
    2 msr red grape juice
    1 msr orange juice
    ¹/₂ msr lime juice
    3 msr lemonade

Shake and strain into ice-filled glass, add the
lemonade. Garnish: fruit in season including
seedless grapes.

CO

Bali Punch

Fruity flavour

Alcohol 1.8

1½ msr white rum
½ msr coconut rum
1 msr lime juice
2 msr passion fruit juice
2 msr orangeade
½ msr pineapple syrup

Shake and strain into ice-filled glass, add the
orangeade. Garnish: fruit in season, add straws.

CO

Bar Bandit

Cherry flavour

Alcohol 1.8

1 msr gold tequila
½ msr rosso vermouth
½ msr dry vermouth
½ msr raspberry liqueur
1 teaspoon lime juice
4 msr cherryade

Add to ice-filled glass. Garnish: cherry and
slice of lime.

H

Barcelona

Lemon wine flavour

Alcohol 2.3

2 msr sweet sherry
1 msr Spanish brandy
½ msr Licor 43
⅓ msr lemon juice
2½ msr lemonade

Add to ice-filled glass. Garnish: slice of Seville
orange speared with cherry, and paper parasol.

H

Beef Salad

Lemon flavour

Alcohol 1.9

1½ msr Beefeater gin
½ msr melon liqueur
1 teaspoon Green Chartreuse
4½ msr sparkling bitter lemon

Add to ice-filled glass. Garnish: fruit in season,
add straws.

If ½ msr rye/Canadian whisky is added,
this is a Beef Salad on Rye.

H

Alcohol 2.4

Black Orchid

Fruit/Aniseed flavour   *Alcohol 1.8*

In 1790 Frenchman Dr. Pierre Ordinaire fled the French Revolution and settled in Switzerland. By 1792 he perfected the recipe for an alcoholic elixir flavoured with 15 herbs and other plants. Before his death, he gave the recipe to his housekeeper Madame Henriot, who dispensed it as an aid to digestion. One of her customers, Major Henry Dubied, purchased the recipe in 1797 and began manufacturing it in quantity with his son-in-law and partner, Henri-Louis Pernod. The Pernod brand became so popular that at one time it was part of the French Army's daily rations.

     1 msr Pernod
     1/2 msr Cointreau
     1/2 msr blackberry brandy
     3 msr tonic water
     2 msr lemonade

Add to ice-filled glass, serve with straws.   CO

If the Cointreau is replaced with 1 msr vodka, this is a Jelly Bean.   *Alcohol 2.3*

Black Russian

Coffee flavour   *Alcohol 2.1*

Originally served as a short drink in the 1950s, this became much more popular when cola was added.

     1 1/2 msr vodka
     1 msr Kahlua
     4 msr cold cola

Add to ice-filled glass, serve with straws.   H

Blackberry Cola

Blackberry flavour   *Alcohol 1.5*

     1 1/2 msr blackberry brandy
     1/2 msr dry sherry
     1/2 msr sweet sherry
     4 msr cold cola

Add to ice-filled glass.   H

Blue Hawaiian

Pineapple / Coconut flavour   *Alcohol 2.3*

    1 ½ msr white rum
    ½ msr dark rum
    ½ msr blue curacao
    3 msr pineapple juice
    1 msr coconut cream

Blend briefly with a glassful of crushed ice. Garnish:
cherry and slice of pineapple, add short straws.   G

Blue Lagoon

Orange / Lemon flavour   *Alcohol 1.7*

Created around 1960 when Blue Curacao had just appeared, at Harry's
Bar, Paris, by Harry's son, Andy MacElhone. Andy served this as a short
drink with 1 msr lemon juice in place of the lemonade which is more
common today.

    1 msr vodka
    1 msr blue curacao
    4 msr lemonade

Add to ice-filled glass. Garnish: cherry and
slice of lemon.   H

Blueberry Rumba

Fruity flavour   *Alcohol 1.9*

    1 msr white rum
    ½ msr dark rum
    ¼ msr triple sec
    ¼ msr blue curacao
    ¾ msr blueberry syrup
    2 msr pineapple juice
    2 msr lemonade

Shake and strain into ice-filled glass,
add the lemonade.   H

Boilermaker

Whisky / Beer flavour   *Alcohol 2.0*

In 1953 Welsh poet Dylan Thomas' last drink was at the White Horse
Tavern, New York's fourth oldest bar. He drank boilermakers of beer and
bourbon; some accounts say as many as 20! He stepped outside and
expired. The White Horse has named a bar after him.

    1 msr whisky
    1 glass/ 10 fl oz/ 28 cl cold beer   R Pi

Two separate drinks consisting of any whisky and any beer as a chaser.
Glen Morangie Scotch and draught Guinness are highly recommended.

Bossa Nova

Fruity aniseed flavour   *Alcohol 2.3*

Galliano is named after Major Giuseppe Galliano, to mark his troops'
outstanding courage. In 1895 they were slaughtered by 80,000
Abyssinian warriors.

    1 msr Galliano
    1 msr golden rum
    1/2 msr apricot brandy
    31/2 msr pineapple juice
    1/2 msr lemon juice
    1 teaspoon egg white

Shake and strain into glass filled with broken ice.
Garnish: orange slice and cherry, add straw.   CO

Brain Blender

Fruity flavour   *Alcohol 2.1*

    1 msr Southern Comfort
    1/2 msr white rum
    1/2 msr peach brandy
    1/2 msr creme de banane
    1 teaspoon Benedictine
    1 msr orange juice
    1 msr guava juice
    1 msr mango juice
    1/2 msr lime juice
    1 teaspoon grenadine

Shake briefly with a glassful of crushed ice.
Garnish: fruit in season, add straws.   G

Brandy Punch Cocktail

Brandy flavour Alcohol 2.4

    2 msr brandy
    1/2 msr triple sec
    2 1/2 msr dry ginger ale

Add to glass filled with crushed ice.
Garnish: sprig of mint and fruit in season.

G

BUCKS

Bucks have been around since the 1890s, but are rarely if ever seen
commercially. A Buck is a tall drink made by adding the components directly
to an ice-filled glass. It consists of one base spirit, ginger ale and lemon or
lime juice – but no sugar. It is basically a Rickey made with ginger ale.

Traditionally half a lime or quarter of a lemon is used. This should be
squeezed directly into the glass and its spent shell then added. The
exception is the white rum-based Buck. This can have small quantities of
other flavouring ingredients added, such as fruit juice, syrups or a liqueur.

Apple Buck

Subtle fruit flavour Alcohol 2.5

    2 1/2 msr apple brandy
    juice of 1/4 lemon
    3 1/2 msr ginger ale

Add to ice-filled glass with the spent shell. H

Replace the brandy to make the following popular Bucks:

Brandy Buck	2 1/2 msr brandy
Fast Buck	2 1/2 msr sloe gin
Greek Buck	2 1/2 msr Greek brandy
London Buck	2 1/2 msr gin

Bacardi Buck

Subtle fruit flavour Alcohol 2.3

    1 3/4 msr white rum
    1/2 msr Cointreau
    juice of 1/4 lemon
    4 msr ginger ale

Add to ice-filled glass with the spent shell. H

Bury Me Deep

Fruity flavour   *Alcohol 2.0*

  1½ msr gin
  ½ msr scotch
  ½ msr lime juice
  ½ msr raspberry syrup
  ½ msr passion fruit juice
  3 msr lemonade

Shake and strain into ice-filled glass, add the lemonade. H

Buttock Clencher

Pineapple flavour   *Alcohol 2.2*

  1 msr silver tequila
  1 msr gin
  ¼ msr melon liqueur
  2 msr pineapple juice
  2 msr lemonade

Shake and strain into ice-filled glass, add the lemonade.
Garnish: cherry and a cube of pineapple on a stick. H

C60

Herb flavour   *Alcohol 1.5*

  1½ msr Licor 43
  ½ msr 10-year-old scotch
  5 msr 7UP

Add to ice-filled glass. H

Cablegram

Lemon flavour   *Alcohol 1.8*

The name gives away this drink's 1920s origin. Somehow a Fax Cocktail
doesn't sound as romantic.

  1¾ msr Canadian whisky
  ¾ msr lemon juice
  1 level teaspoon caster sugar
  4 msr ginger ale

Add to ice-filled glass. Garnish: slice of lemon. H

California Rootbeer

Herb cola flavour   *Alcohol 1.6*

    1 msr Galliano
    1 msr Kahlua
    5 msr cold cola

Add to glass filled with broken ice, serve with straws. P

Camp Lawless

Mandarin flavour   *Alcohol 1.8*

Zaleucus, 'lawgiver' to the Locrians in about 650 BC, ordered that wine could only be consumed if mixed with water. Failure to comply was punishable by death.

    1 msr white rum
    1/2 msr Campari
    1/2 msr Galliano
    5 msr mandarin juice

Add rum and juice to glass filled with broken ice, sprinkle Campari and Galliano on top – do not stir. Garnish: cherry and orange slice, add straws. H

Campola

Sour cola flavour   *Alcohol 0.8*

    1 msr Campari
    1/2 msr sweet sherry
    5 msr cold cola

Add to ice-filled glass. Garnish: lime slice and cherry, add straws. H

Caribbean Breeze

Pineapple flavour   *Alcohol 1.8*

    1 1/2 msr dark rum
    1/2 msr creme de banane
    3 msr pineapple juice
    1 teaspoon Rose's Lime Cordial
    2 msr cranberry juice

Shake briefly with a glassful of crushed ice. Garnish: fruit in season, add short straws. G

Carla

Fruity flavour

Alcohol 1.5

    1 1/2 msr young genever
    2 msr orange juice
    1 msr passion fruit juice
    2 msr lemonade

Shake briefly with a glassful of crushed ice and pour, add the lemonade. Garnish: slice of orange and a cherry, add straws.

G

Casablanca

Coconut flavour

Alcohol 2.3

    2 msr white rum
    1/2 msr coconut rum
    4 msr pineapple juice
    1 msr coconut cream
    1/3 msr grenadine

Blend briefly with a glassful of crushed ice, add the Grenadine but do not mix. Garnish: cherry and slice of pineapple.

CO

Cherry Tuesday

Cherry cola flavour

Alcohol 2.0

    1 msr cherry vodka
    1/2 msr dry sherry
    1/2 msr gold tequila
    1/4 msr Amadeus Liqueur
    4 msr cold cola

Add to ice-filled glass.

CO

Chocolate Sailor

Chocolate flavour

Alcohol 2.3

    1 msr gin
    2 msr dark creme de cacao
    3 1/2 msr cold cola

Shake and strain into ice-filled glass, add the cola. Garnish: orange slice and cherry.

G

Cloudy Sky

Sloe flavour

Alcohol 1.3

Created in Philadelphia around 1920.
>   2 msr sloe gin
>   1 msr lime juice
>   2 msr ginger ale

Add to glass filled with broken ice.
Garnish: slice of lime.

H

COBBLERS

There has been much debate as to the origin of the Cobbler. Whilst the modern recipe is undoubtedly American, first mentioned in US literature dated 1809, dictionaries and bar-guides alike have long speculated as to the etymology of its name. This is most likely to derive from 'cobler', an old word for a brewer/innkeeper.

Today a Cobbler is a medium-sized drink augmented with ample ice, usually broken or crushed. A wine, liqueur or spirit base can be used, but it should include only a small quantity of lemon or lime juice if any at all – the exception being the Cherry Cobbler. It should be served with straws, and is characterised by its abundant garnish, usually fruit in season, and often also a sprig of mint.

The liquors are added directly to the ice in the glass. If the recipe specifies powdered sugar, not sugar syrup, this must be dissolved in the glass with water/soda water before the ice is added – and then the liquor(s). In either case the strongest liquors are traditionally added last. The mix should be stirred with a barspoon to encourage a frost to develop on the glass before serving.

Cherry Cobbler

Cherry gin flavour

Alcohol 3.2

>   2 msr London Dry Gin
>   1½ msr cherry brandy
>   ¾ msr sugar syrup
>   ¾ msr lemon juice
>   1 teaspoon creme de cassis

Add to glass filled with crushed ice.
Garnish: slice of lemon, sprig of mint and a cherry, add short straw. Sometimes made shorter in a champagne saucer.

D

Sherry Cobbler

Sherry flavour   Alcohol 1.8

Charles Dickens mentions 'this wonderful invention' in *Martin Chuzzlewit*.

> 3 msr medium sherry
> 1/3 msr triple sec
> 2 msr soda water
> 1/4 msr sugar syrup

Add to glass filled with broken or crushed ice and mix
with barspoon. Garnish: fruit in season, add straws.   G

Replace the sherry in the following popular Cobblers. Where only two
measures are shown use a little extra soda water.

Bourbon Cobbler	2 msr bourbon		Alcohol 2.0
Brandy Cobbler	2 msr brandy		Alcohol 2.0
Claret Cobbler	3 msr claret		Alcohol 0.9
Gin Cobbler	2 msr gin		Alcohol 2.0
Port Cobbler	2½ msr LBV port		Alcohol 1.3
Rum Cobbler	1 msr dark rum 1 msr white rum		Alcohol 2.0
Scotch Cobbler	2 msr scotch		Alcohol 2.0

Generally, with a lower alcohol base such as claret, the quantity should be
increased.

Coconut Grove

Fruity flavour   Alcohol 2.4

> 1½ msr coconut rum
> 1 msr creme de banane
> 1 msr white rum
> 4 msr pineapple juice
> 1 teaspoon lemon juice

Shake and strain into ice-filled glass. Garnish: cherry
and slices of pineapple and lemon.   CO

Codswallop

Fruity flavour   Alcohol 1.9

In the 1850s an inventor called Mr Hiram Codd patented a soda
water/lemonade bottle which was sealed by a glass ball in the neck. The
ball was supported by the pressure of the fizzy drink. To release the drink
one had to strike (wallop) the top of the bottle to break the seal.

1½ msr gin
⅓ msr Campari
⅓ msr raspberry liqueur
⅓ msr lime juice
4 msr lemonade
Add to ice-filled glass.

H

COLADAS

Probably the most popular cocktail in the world, the original Pina Colada is of disputed origin. It certainly comes from Puerto Rico, but was either created by Ramón Marrero Pérez of the Caribe Hilton in 1954, or by Don Ramón Portas Mingot of La Barrachina Restaurant Bar in 1963.

Coladas are variations of the Piña Colada, and always contain white rum, pineapple juice and coconut cream. The big trick is to ensure the freshness of the juice.

Piña Colada

Coconut rum flavour   *Alcohol 2.0*

The name means 'strained pineapple'. To do justice to this world-wide favourite, *see* coconut cream in Methods. In parts of the Caribbean this cocktail may be served in a hollowed-out pineapple and be made from freshly blended pineapple and coconut meat; no cream is used. However, that can be a little grainy in texture, so barkeepers across the world prefer to make a Pina Colada as follows:

Ratios:
3 parts:	2 msr white rum
2 parts:	1⅓ msr coconut cream
4 parts:	2⅔ msr pineapple juice
	1 teaspoon whipping cream
	½ msr caster sugar

Add ingredients to shaker and swirl until sugar is dissolved. Test for sweetness. Shake briefly with a glassful of crushed ice. Garnish: slice of pineapple and a cherry, add straws.

P

If vodka is used instead of rum, this is a Chi Chi or Vodka Piña Colada.

Amaretto Colada

Almond / Coconut flavour

Alcohol 1.9

    1¼ msr white rum
1 msr amaretto
1⅓ msr coconut cream
3 msr pineapple juice
1 teaspoon whipping cream

Blend briefly with a glassful of crushed ice.
Garnish: slice of pineapple and a cherry,
add straws.

P

Substitute the amaretto in the following popular Coladas:

Apple Colada	1¼ msr apple schnapps

Alcohol 2.1

Banana Colada	1¼ msr creme de banane
	2 msr banana purée

Alcohol 1.9

Coffee Colada	1¼ msr Kahlua/Tia Maria

Alcohol 2.1

Flamingo	1 msr sloe gin

Alcohol 1.9

Melon Colada	1¼ msr Midori

Alcohol 2.1

Raspberry Colada	1¼ msr Chambord

Alcohol 1.8

Strawberry Colada	1 msr strawberry liqueur
	1 msr strawberry puree

Alcohol 1.9

Tropicolada	½ msr creme de banane
	½ msr melon liqueur

Alcohol 1.9

Cold Comfort Coffee

Coffee flavour

Alcohol 1.7

    ¾ msr dark rum
¾ msr Southern Comfort
¼ msr dark creme de cacao
4 msr cold coffee – sweetened to taste

Shake and strain into glass filled with crushed ice.

G

COLLINS

Cousin of the Cooler and offspring of the Sling, a Collins is a hot weather drink, not shaken, but made in a tall glass with spirit, lemon or lime juice, sugar, ice, and topped up, usually with soda water.

The name probably came from one John Collins, who was a renowned head waiter at 'Limmer's' in Conduit Street, London, a hotel and coffee house in existence from 1790–1817.

The earliest recipes for a John Collins use Holland's style gin, Genever. When the Collins appeared in America in the 1880s, it was regarded as a glorified Gin Sling; it used soda in place of the Sling's plain water, and lemon juice in place of its lemon peel.

Genever, and consequently the John Collins, never really caught on in the US, until someone used Old Tom Gin, and the ever popular Tom Collins was born.

In the 1880s the Collins was made with a whole tablespoon of sugar, but today they are made slightly dry – invariably with syrup. Where 1 msr lemon juice is specified below, the juice of half a freshly squeezed lemon would be more in keeping with tradition. The soda water should be refrigerated to allow for the minimum use of ice needed to keep the drink cool. Where soda is specified below, bars now often substitute sparkling citrus drinks, to make the result more appealing.

B & B Collins

Lemon brandy flavour

Alcohol 2.0

    1 1/2 msr brandy
    1/2 msr Benedictine
    1 msr lemon juice
    1 msr sugar syrup
    5 msr soda water

Add to frosted glass two-thirds filled with ice, sprinkle the Benedictine on top. Garnish: cherry and slices of orange and lemon, serve with straws.

CO

John Collins

Lemon bourbon flavour

Alcohol 2.0

    2 msr bourbon (originally genever)
    1 msr lemon juice
    3/4 msr sugar syrup
    5 msr soda water

Add to frosted glass two-thirds filled with ice.
Garnish: cherry and slices of orange and lemon,
serve with straws.

CO

Also known as Bourbon Collins or, USA only, a Whiskey Collins.

Mint Collins

Mint flavour   *Alcohol 2.2*

    2 msr vodka
    1/3 msr green creme de menthe
    1 msr lemon juice
    3/4 msr sugar syrup
    5 msr soda water

Add to frosted glass two-thirds filled
with ice. Garnish: sprig of mint.

CO

Rum Collins

Lemon rum flavour   *Alcohol 2.0*

    2 msr dark rum
    1 msr lemon juice
    1 msr sugar syrup
    4–5 msr soda water

Add to frosted glass two-thirds filled with ice.
Garnish: slice of orange and a cherry, serve
with straws. (USA only – use white rum.)

CO

Replace the rum in the following popular Collins':

Brandy Collins	2 msr brandy/cognac
Piscollins	2 msr pisco
Tequila Collins	2 msr gold tequila
Vodka Collins	2 msr vodka

Tom Collins

Lemon gin flavour   *Alcohol 2.0*

Made originally with 'Old Tom' Gin. The name of this gin is
credited to Captain Dudley Bradstreet of London in 1738. To exploit a
legal loophole in the prohibitionist 1736 Gin Act, he hung up a sign in
the shape of a tom cat. Customers would place a sum of money into its
mouth, and from its paw – via a tube – he would dispense an appropriate
measure of the gin.

2 msr gin
1 msr lemon juice
3/4 msr sugar syrup
5 msr soda water

Add to frosted glass two-thirds filled with ice.
Add slice of lemon, serve with straws.

CO

Also known as a Collins and a Gin Collins.

Whisk(e)y Collins

Lemon whisky flavour

Alcohol 2.0

2 msr whisk(e)y
1 msr lemon juice
3/4 msr sugar syrup
5 msr soda water

Add to frosted glass two-thirds filled with ice,
serve with straws. Garnish: slice of orange
and a cherry.

CO

The spirit used in this drink varies around the world so it is easier to ask
for a Scotch Collins or a Bourbon Collins etc.

Cooch Behar

Created by the Maharaja of Cooch Behar.

Tomato flavour

Alcohol 2.0

2 msr pepper vodka
4 msr cold tomato juice
Add to glass three-quarters filled with broken ice.

R

COOLERS

A long drink prepared in the same manner as a Collins, but which usually
contains a spiral of citrus peel, a little trailing over the edge of a tall glass.
Any base liquor can be used, but the recipe should not be shaken unless it
contains egg white.

In the 1880s Coolers were very sweet and sometimes topped with ice
cream. They have become much less sweet, so liqueurs and syrups should
be used in moderation. Lemon juice is not necessarily included. It is
advisable to use refrigerated soda water.

Apricot Cooler

Sour apricot flavour

Alcohol 1.0

    2 msr apricot brandy
    1 msr lemon juice
    1 teaspoon grenadine
    1 dash Angostura
    2 msr soda water
    2 msr lemonade

Add to glass filled with ice and spiral of lemon.

CO

Bridesmaid Cooler

Lemon gin flavour

Alcohol 2.0

    2 msr gin
    1 msr lemon juice
    3/4 msr sugar syrup
    1 dash Angostura
    4 msr ginger ale

Add to glass filled with ice and spiral of lemon.

CO

If half as much sugar syrup is used and the Angostura omitted, this is a Shady Grove Cooler.

Castro Cooler

Citrus flavour

Alcohol 2.3

    1 1/2 msr golden rum
    3/4 msr apple brandy
    2 msr orange juice
    3/4 msr Rose's Lime Cordial
    1/2 msr lemon juice

Add to glass filled with crushed ice and spiral of lime. Garnish: slice of orange and a cherry, add straws.

CO

Chartreuse Cooler

Fruity flavour

Alcohol 1.0

    1 msr Yellow Chartreuse
    2 msr orange juice
    1/2 msr lemon juice
    3 1/2 msr sparkling bitter lemon

Add to glass filled with ice and spiral of orange.

CO

Curacao Cooler

Lemon / Orange flavour

Alcohol 1.6

1 msr triple sec
1/2 msr vodka
1/2 msr blue curacao
1/2 msr lime juice
1/2 msr lemon juice
1/2 msr orange juice
1/2 msr sugar syrup
4 msr lemonade

Add to glass filled with ice and spiral of lime.   CO

Normandy Cooler

Sour lemon flavour

Alcohol 2.0

2 msr calvados
1 msr lemon juice
1 teaspoon grenadine
1/2 msr sugar syrup
4 msr soda water

Add to glass filled with ice and spiral of lemon.   CO

If applejack brandy is used in place of the calvados and the Grenadine is omitted, this is a Harvard Cooler.

Polar Bear Cooler

Fruity rum flavour

Alcohol 2.5

2 msr dark rum
1 msr Punt e Mes
1 msr lemon juice
1/2 msr orange juice
3 1/2 msr cold 7UP

Add to glass filled with crushed or broken ice and spiral of lemon. Garnish: wedge of orange and a cherry, serve with straws.   CO

If grenadine is substituted for the orange juice, this is a Limbo Cooler.

Remmsen Cooler

Gin flavour   *Alcohol 2.0*

Dating from around 1880, this is believed to have been the first spirit-based cooler to appear. Originally it was served without sugar/syrup.

> 2 msr gin
> ³/₄ msr sugar syrup
> 5 msr soda water

Add to glass filled with ice and spiral of lemon.   CO

If scotch is used in place of gin, this is a Remsen Cooler.

Sporran Cooler

Lemon honey flavour   *Alcohol 2.0*

> 2 msr Drambuie
> 1 msr lemon juice
> 1 teaspoon grenadine
> 1 dash Angostura
> 4 msr soda water

Add to glass filled with ice and spiral of lemon.   CO

If dark rum is substituted for the Drambuie
and the Angostura omitted, this is a Rum Cooler.

Tod's Cooler

Subtle fruit flavour   *Alcohol 2.3*

Created in 1910, at the Palace Hotel, Brussels, by Tod Sloan, a famous jockey.

> 2 msr gin
> ²/₃ msr creme de cassis
> ²/₃ msr lemon juice
> 4 msr soda water

Add to glass filled with ice and spiral of lemon.   CO

Corsican

Mandarin flavour   *Alcohol 1.5*

A suitable accompaniment to crêpes suzettes, which can also be made with Mandarine Napoléon.

> 1¹/₂ msr Mandarine Napoléon
> ¹/₂ msr lime juice
> 5 msr 7UP (to top up)

Add to glass three-quarters filled with broken ice.
Garnish: slice of lime speared with cherry, add straw.   H

Corvette

Peach / Sloe flavour

Alcohol 2.3

1½ msr Southern Comfort
1 msr sloe gin
1 teaspoon Campari
4 msr cold lemonade

Add to ice-filled glass.

 H

Costa del Sol

Lemon / Herb flavour

Alcohol 2.5

2 msr white rum
1 msr rosso vermouth
1 msr sugar syrup
½ msr lemon juice
2½ msr soda water

Add to ice-filled glass. Garnish: slice of orange,
paper parasol and cherry.

 H

Count Blythe

Pineapple flavour

Alcohol 2.3

1 msr Pisang Ambon
1 msr dry vermouth
¾ msr gin
½ msr peach brandy
4 msr pineapple juice

Shake and strain into ice-filled glass, add straws.

 CO

Cuba Libre

Lime cola flavour

Alcohol 2.0

In 1893, an army lieutenant in Cuba mixed Bacardi rum with a new soft
drink called Coca Cola and called it 'Cuba Libre'.

2 msr Bacardi white rum
5 msr cold Coca Cola
juice of ½ a lime

Squeeze lime juice directly into glass and add
spent lime shell. Fill with ice and add remaining
ingredients, serve with straws.

 CO

If Southern Comfort is used in place of rum,
this is a Cuba Libre Supreme.

If 1½ msr kirsch is used in place of rum, this is a Kirsch Cuba Libre.

Alcohol 1.5

Cuba Libre Espana

Wine / Lime flavour

Alcohol 1.5

> 1 msr sweet sherry
> ½ msr white rum
> ½ msr dark rum
> juice of ½ a lime
> 5 msr cold Coca Cola

Squeeze lime juice directly into glass and add spent lime shell. Fill with ice and add remaining ingredients, serve with straws.

CO

Cute Fat Bastard in the Sack

Wine flavour

Alcohol 1.1

In the seventeenth century cute was a grape juice syrup sometimes mixed with wine to produce imitation malmsey. Sack was a pale or dry sherry, and fat bastard was a heavy or full-bodied wine made from bastardo grapes, as distinct from a 'tawny' or 'weak bastard'.

> 2 msr red bastardo wine – Doa and Barriada are widely available (substitute: full-bodied red wine)
> 1 msr dry sherry
> 2 msr white grape juice
> ¼ msr sugar syrup
> 2 msr lemonade

Shake and strain into ice-filled glass, add the lemonade. Garnish: half slice of lemon and a cherry.

CO

DAIQUIRIS, FROZEN FRUIT

(*See* also Daiquiris – Short Drinks)

With any fruit Daiquiri ensure you use the same fruit liqueur as the fruit of your choice, and always remove any bitter pith or skin from the fruit before blending. After blending, they should have the consistency of sherbet/sorbet. These are all technically 'frozen' Daiquiris.

Banana Daiquiri

Banana flavour   Alcohol 2.5

2 msr white rum
1 measure creme de banane
1 msr orange juice
1/2 msr lime juice
1/4 of a fresh mashed banana
1 teaspoon whipping cream
1 teaspoon caster sugar

Blend thoroughly, add a glassful of crushed ice,
blend again briefly and pour. Garnish: slices of
pineapple and banana speared with a cherry.
Serve with a thick straw.   G

Cherry Daiquiri

Cherry flavour   Alcohol 2.6

2 msr cherry brandy
1 msr white rum
1/3 msr kirsch
3/4 msr lemon juice
3/4 msr sugar syrup
1/2 msr grenadine
5 maraschino (cocktail) cherries

Blend thoroughly, add a glassful of crushed ice and
blend again briefly. Garnish: slice of lemon and cherry.
The quantities can be halved and served in a
champagne saucer.   G

Coconut Daiquiri

Coconut / Rum flavour   Alcohol 2.4

1 3/4 msr white rum
1 msr coconut rum
1/2 msr lime juice
3/4 msr sugar syrup
3/4 msr coconut cream
1 teaspoon whipping cream
2 teaspoons overproof dark rum

Rim glass with lime/sweet grated coconut. Shake all except
ODR and strain into glass filled with crushed ice.
Garnish: cherry and slice of lime, add short straws.
Sprinkle ODR on top, using barspoon.   G

Peach Daiquiri

Peach flavour   *Alcohol 2.1*

    1½ msr white rum
    1 msr peach schnapps
    ⅓ of a skinned chopped peach
    ½ msr sugar syrup
    ¾ msr lime juice
    ½ msr pineapple juice

Blend until smooth, add a glassful of crushed
ice and blend again briefly. Garnish: wedge
of peach, add thick straws.   G

Strawberry Daiquiri

Strawberry flavour   *Alcohol 2.0*

    1½ msr white rum
    ¾ msr strawberry brandy
    ½ msr orange juice
    2 msr strawberry puree
    ¾ msr lime juice
    ¼ msr grenadine
    1 teaspoon caster sugar

Blend briefly with a glassful of crushed ice.
Garnish: slices of pineapple, lemon, orange and two
halves of a strawberry, serve with thick straws.   G

Davenport

Fruity flavour   *Alcohol 2.5*

    1½ msr Southern Comfort
    1 msr LBV port
    ½ msr dark rum
    ⅓ msr lemon juice
    1 teaspoon grenadine
    3 msr cold cola

Shake and strain into ice-filled glass and add the cola.
Garnish: slice of lemon and a cherry, add straws. H

Dickel Tickle

Fruit / Lemon flavour   *Alcohol 2.0*

    1 msr Geo. A. Dickel whiskey
    ¾ msr Southern Comfort

½ msr Pimm's No.1
¼ msr lime juice
4 msr lemonade
Add to ice-filled glass.

H

Diplomatic Answer

Herb / Orange flavour

Alcohol 2.2

2 msr Ambassadeur (substitute: rosso vermouth)
1 msr brandy
⅓ msr triple sec
4 msr lemonade
Add to glass filled with broken ice.
Garnish: slice of orange, add straws.

P

Disaronno Driver

Orange / Almond flavour

Alcohol 2.0

1½ msr vodka
¾ msr amaretto
4½ msr orange juice
Shake with a glassful of ice and pour unstrained.
Garnish: orange slice.

H

Dizzy Blonde

Aniseed Advocaat flavour

Alcohol 1.5

1¾ msr advocaat
¾ msr Pernod
1 msr orange juice
2 msr lemonade
Add to glass three-quarters filled with broken ice.
Garnish: slice of lemon and green cherry.

G

Dundee Dream

Orange whisky flavour

Alcohol 1.8

1½ msr single grain scotch
½ msr sweet sherry
1 msr mandarin juice
½ msr lime juice
3 msr dry ginger ale
Shake with a glassful of broken ice and pour unstrained,
add the ginger. Garnish: cherry and orange slice.

H

Easy Money

Mango rum flavour

Alcohol 1.8

    1 msr white rum
    1/2 msr dark rum
    1/2 msr coconut rum
    1 msr orange juice
    1/4 msr lime juice
    2 tablespoons mango sherbet/sorbet
    1 teaspoon grenadine

Blend briefly with half a glassful of crushed ice.
Sprinkle the grenadine on top. Garnish: fruit in season.   G

Escape Route

Strawberry flavour

Alcohol 1.7

In 1786 Antonio Carpano established the Carpano Bar, Turin. Situated
behind the Turin Stock Exchange, it offered customers the choice of any
variation of the basic 'Carpano Vermouth', with more sweetness,
bitterness etc. The stockbrokers began referring to the gradations of
bitterness as 'points'.

In 1876 Carpano's Punt e Mes (point and a half) was launched, and has
remained one of the world's most popular vermouths ever since.

    1 msr golden rum
    1 msr Punt e Mes
    1/2 msr strawberry liqueur
    4 msr lemonade

Add to ice-filled glass. Garnish: mint sprig.   H

Even Pair

Pear gin flavour

Alcohol 1.7

    1 msr gin
    1 msr dry vermouth
    1/3 msr pear liqueur
    4 msr tonic water

Shake and strain into ice-filled glass, add the tonic.   H

Eye of the Tiger

Fruity flavour

Alcohol 2.2

    1 msr golden rum
    1 msr coconut rum
    1 msr cranberry juice

1 msr lemon juice
1 msr sugar syrup
1 msr orange juice
½ msr dark rum

Shake and strain into ice-filled glass, sprinkle
the dark rum on top. Garnish: orange slice,
add straws.

H

Fallen Angel

Mint / Lime flavour   *Alcohol 1.6*

1½ msr gin
1 msr lime juice
1 teaspoon white creme de menthe
1 dash Angostura
4 msr lemonade

Add to glass three-quarters filled with broken ice.
Garnish: slice of lime, add short straws.
Sometimes made as a short drink by omitting
lemonade and adding ½ msr sugar syrup.

G

Five Hundred Proof

Fruity flavour   *Alcohol 3.2*

The five spirits' proof rating should total over 500.

½ msr overproof white rum
½ msr 100 proof bourbon
½ msr Green Chartreuse
½ msr 100 proof vodka
½ msr Southern Comfort
1 msr lemon juice
1 msr orange juice
½ msr sugar syrup
½ msr grenadine

Shake and strain into glass filled with
broken ice. Garnish: cherry on a stick.

Pi

FIZZES

First mentioned in articles published in the 1870s, a Fizz is similar to a Collins but is always shaken before adding soda or other sparkling drink. It usually contains no more than half a glassful of ice to ensure it does not inhibit the effervescence of the soda.

They are traditionally served in the morning or at midday, with straws and usually a swizzle stick/muddler. Use chilled soda water and frosted glassware. Any base liquors can be used, but the Fizz should be served immediately after preparation.

Gin Fizz

Lemon gin flavour

Alcohol 2.0

    2 msr gin
    1 teaspoon caster sugar
    1 msr lemon juice
    5 msr soda water

Dissolve sugar, shake and strain into glass half filled with ice, add straws and muddler.

H

If sprigs of mint are added, this is an Alabama Fizz.

Substitute the gin in a Gin Fizz for the following popular Fizzes:

Amaretto Fizz	1½ msr amaretto	*Alcohol 1.2*
Apricot Fizz	1½ msr apricot brandy	*Alcohol 1.2*
Brandy Fizz	2 msr brandy/cognac	*Alcohol 2.0*
Cherry Fizz	1½ msr cherry brandy	*Alcohol 1.2*
Comfortable Fizz	2 msr Southern Comfort	*Alcohol 2.0*
Melon Fizz	2 msr Midori	*Alcohol 1.3*
Rum Fizz	2 msr white rum	*Alcohol 2.0*
Slow Fizz	2 msr sloe gin	*Alcohol 1.3*
Tequila Fizz	2 msr gold tequila	*Alcohol 2.0*
Whisky Fizz	2 msr scotch	*Alcohol 2.0*
Whiskey Fizz	2 msr bourbon	*Alcohol 2.0*
Raspberry Fizz	1½ msr Chambord	*Alcohol 0.7*

Barcelona Fizz

Sherry flavour

Alcohol 1.8

    1 1/2 msr sweet sherry
    1 msr gin
    1/2 msr lemon juice
    1/4 msr sugar syrup
    4 msr soda water

Shake and strain into glass half filled with ice,
add the soda. Garnish: slice of lemon and a
cherry, add straws and a muddler.

H

Bird of Paradise Fizz

Subtle fruit flavour

Alcohol 1.8

    1 1/2 msr gin
    1/2 msr blackberry brandy
    1/2 msr lemon juice
    1/2 msr sugar syrup
    1/2 msr egg white
    4 msr soda water

Shake well and strain into glass half filled with ice,
add the soda. Garnish: slice of lemon and a cherry,
add straws and a muddler.

H

Blackberry Fizz

Blackberry flavour

Alcohol 1.1

    1 1/2 msr blackberry brandy
    1 1/2 msr orange juice
    1 msr lemon juice
    1/4 teaspoon caster sugar
    4 msr lemonade

Dissolve sugar, shake and strain into glass
half filled with ice, add the lemonade.
Garnish: cherry and slice of orange,
add straws and a muddler.

Replace the blackberry brandy with 1 msr gin
and 1/2 msr triple sec for an Orange Fizz.

H
Alcohol 1.4

Hong Kong Fizz

Herb flavour   Alcohol 2.8

Created in the nineteenth century by one Maude Jones, Madame of a Hong Kong brothel. She is said to have consumed several of these every day before lunch.

    ½ msr vodka
    ½ msr gin
    ½ msr Benedictine
    ½ msr Yellow Chartreuse
    ½ msr Green Chartreuse
    ½ msr lemon juice
    4 msr soda water
    ½ teaspoon caster sugar

Dissolve sugar, shake and strain into glass half filled with ice, add the soda, straws and a muddler.

H

Morning Glory Fizz

Sour scotch flavour   Alcohol 2.0

    2 msr scotch
    1⅓ msr lemon juice
    1 teaspoon caster sugar
    ¼ msr egg white
    1 dash Angostura
    4 msr soda water

Dissolve sugar, shake and strain into glass half filled with ice, add the soda. Garnish: slice of orange, add a muddler.

CO

Ramos Fizz – *See* Long and Creamy

Shanghai Gin Fizz

Herb flavour   Alcohol 2.0

    ⅔ msr gin
    ⅔ msr Benedictine
    ⅔ msr Yellow Chartreuse
    ⅔ msr lemon juice
    ½ msr sugar syrup
    4 msr soda water

Shake and strain into glass half filled with ice, add the soda. Garnish: slice of lemon and a cherry, add straws and a muddler.

CO

Texas Fizz – *See* Champagne Cocktails

Vodka Fizz

Fruity flavour   *Alcohol 2.0*

    2 msr vodka
    2 msr orange juice
    1 msr lemon juice
    1 teaspoon caster sugar
    3 msr lemonade

Dissolve sugar, shake and strain into glass half filled
with ice, add the lemonade. Add straws and a muddler.   CO
When half an egg white is included this becomes a
Silver Vodka Fizz.

Fly-swatter

Fruity flavour   *Alcohol 2.2*

    1 msr cognac
    1 msr single grain scotch (substitute: Canadian)
    1 teaspoon Raki (substitute: Pernod)
    3 msr mandarin juice
    2 msr pineapple juice

Add to glass filled with broken ice. Add sprig of
mint and straws.   P

Formula 1

Fruity flavour   *Alcohol 2.6*

Created by Marc Boccard-Schuster. *See* La Panthere Rose, in Champagne
Cocktails.

    2 msr vodka
    ²/₃ msr peach brandy
    ²/₃ wild strawberry liqueur (Fraises de Bois)
    2 msr grapefruit juice
    2 msr tonic water

Add to glass filled with broken ice. Garnish: slice
of lime and small sprig of mint.   CO

Friar Tuck

Mandarin flavour   *Alcohol 2.0*

    1 msr Yellow Chartreuse
    1 msr gin
    3 msr mandarin juice
    3 msr ginger ale

Shake and strain into ice-filled glass, add the
ginger and serve with straws.   CO

Frosty Amour

Subtle fruit flavour   *Alcohol 2.6*

    1 msr apricot brandy
    1 msr vodka
    1 msr Southern Comfort
    1 teaspoon parfait amour
    1 teaspoon creme de banane
    4 msr 7UP

Rim glass with lemon/caster sugar and fill with
ice. Shake and strain into glass, add the 7UP.
Garnish: slice of orange and a green maraschino cherry.   CO

Fuzzy Navel

Orange/Peach flavour   *Alcohol 1.2*

    2 msr peach schnapps
    4 msr orange juice

Shake and strain into ice-filled glass.
Garnish: wedge of orange.   H

If 1 msr vodka is added, this is a Hairy Navel.   *Alcohol 2.2*

Gang UP

Strawberry flavour   *Alcohol 1.6*

    1/2 msr cherry vodka
    1/2 msr gin
    1/2 msr strawberry brandy
    1/2 msr triple sec
    41/2 msr cold 7UP

Add to ice-filled glass.
Garnish: fruit in season, add straws.   H

Gin and Tonic

Gin flavour   *Alcohol 2.0*

Tonic water is a product of the fight against malaria. It contains quinine, an extract of the cinchona nitida tree bark from Java, which was found to arrest the reproduction of malaria parasites, and is effective in alleviating fever and pain. Today, in its highly dilute form, it is appreciated for its 'tonic' effect.

    2 msr gin
    5 msr tonic water
    1/2 teaspoon lemon juice

Add to ice-filled glass. Add half slice of lemon.   H

Gin Lollipop

Orange flavour   *Alcohol 2.0*

S. L. Collins, The Capital Hotel. Courtesy of Gordon's London Dry Gin.

Alexander Gordon, a landowner of Scottish decent, was distilling gin in London as early as 1769. After perfecting the balance of botanicals in Gordon's London Dry Gin, he placed his ancestral family emblem on the label as his seal of approval. This ferocious boar's head still appears on every bottle.

    1 msr gin
    1 msr Southern Comfort
    5 msr orange juice
    1 msr sparkling mineral water

Shake and strain into ice-filled glass, add the water.
Garnish: slice of orange and a cherry.   CO

Goldilocks

Fruity flavour   *Alcohol 1.7*

    1 msr dark rum
    1 msr coconut rum
    3 msr pineapple juice
    2 msr orange juice

Shake and strain into glass filled with broken ice.
Garnish: slice of pineapple.   P

Graffiti

Grape flavour   *Alcohol 1.5*

    1 1/2 msr vodka
    2 msr white grape juice

2 msr cherryade
Add to glass filled with broken ice.
Garnish: seedless grape.

G

Gremlin Fixer

Pineapple flavour

Alcohol 1.6

2/3 msr vodka
2/3 msr Pisang Ambon
2/3 msr dry vermouth
1/3 msr apricot brandy
3 msr pineapple juice

Shake and strain into glass filled with crushed ice.
Garnish: mint sprig.

H

Grocery Boy

Lemon / Fruit flavour

Alcohol 2.0

1 msr white rum
3/4 msr Southern Comfort
1/3 msr triple sec
4 msr sparkling bitter lemon

Add to ice-filled glass.
Garnish: fruit in season, add straws.

H

Haitian Gold

Fruity flavour

Alcohol 2.3

1 msr white rum
1/2 msr Mandarine Napoléon
1/2 msr gold tequila
1/2 msr creme de banane
2 msr guava nectar
1 msr orange juice
1 msr pineapple juice
1 teaspoon strawberry syrup

Blend briefly with a glassful of crushed ice.
Garnish: fruit in season, add straws.

G

Half Man Half Wit

Fruity flavour

Alcohol 2.0

1 1/2 msr white rum
1/2 msr peach schnapps
1/4 msr scotch

2 msr passion fruit juice
2 msr orange juice
1/4 msr grenadine

Shake and strain into glass filled with broken ice,
add the grenadine – do not stir. Garnish: fruit in
season, add straws.

CO

Harvey Wallbanger

Orange flavour   Alcohol 2.6

In the 1970s the following tale was widely circulated. A Californian surfer
called 'Harvey' (surname unknown) decided he would prefer his usual
Screwdriver with a little Galliano. After several of these, he was seen to
bump into furniture and a wall. 'The Wallbanger' became his nickname,
and passed to his favourite drink.

2 msr vodka
3/4 msr Galliano
5 msr orange juice

Add to ice-filled glass, sprinkle the Galliano on top.
Garnish: slice of orange.   H

If the vodka is replaced with gold tequila,
this is a Freddy Fudpucker or Cactus Banger.

If the vodka is replaced with white rum, this is
a Cuban Banger.

Hell Bender

Fruity flavour   Alcohol 2.1

1 msr gin
3/4 msr cherry vodka
1/2 msr sloe gin
2/3 msr passion fruit juice
1 teaspoon caster sugar
31/2 msr lemonade

Shake and strain into ice-filled glass, add the lemonade.   H

Hell Hole

Fruity flavour   Alcohol 2.0

11/2 msr scotch
1/2 msr peach schnapps
1/2 msr dry vermouth
2 msr pineapple juice
3 msr sparkling bitter lemon

Add to ice-filled glass.   CO

109

Henry's Last Hurrah

Sherry flavour *Alcohol 1.8*

    1 1/2 msr sweet sherry
    1/2 msr scotch
    1/2 msr dry sherry
    1/2 msr dry vermouth
    1 teaspoon Drambuie
    1/4 msr lemon juice
    3 1/2 msr lemonade

Add to ice-filled glass. Add half slice of lemon.   G

HIGHBALLS

When this drink rose to prominence in the 1920s many people claimed authorship. It took a special investigation by the *New York Times* – a fact which underlines the social importance of the drink at the time – to establish beyond reasonable doubt that it was created around 1895 by New York barman Mr Patrick Duffy.

Duffy apparently took the name from the nineteenth-century American railroad practice of raising a ball on a pole to urge a passing train driver to speed up. Highball was his term for a drink speedily produced by simply adding the ingredients to a tall glass over ice.

He used one liquor, one mixer (soda or ginger ale) and no more than one garnish – usually a twist of lemon – or none at all. By the 1930s it was, and still is, acceptable to include a dash of bitters, grenadine or triple sec, and to use any sparkling soft drink as a mixer. By the 1950s fruit juices began to be included.

Whilst it is now accepted that up to two mixers can be used, one of which should be sparkling, the inclusion of more than one base liquor is to be avoided. Some long established Highballs use orange juice as a mixer.

Brandy Highball

Sour brandy flavour *Alcohol 2.5*

    2 1/2 msr brandy
    5 msr ginger ale or soda water

Add to a glass three-quarters filled with broken ice.
Add twist of lemon and muddler.   H

Substitute the brandy in the following popular Highballs:

Apple Brandy Highball	2 1/2 msr apple brandy
Bourbon Highball	2 1/2 msr bourbon
Gin Highball	2 1/2 msr gin
Scotch Highball	2 1/2 msr scotch

Carpano Highball
Sweet herb flavour

Alcohol 0.8

    2 msr Punt e Mes
    5 msr lemonade
Add to ice-filled glass. Add twist of orange.

H

Mile Highball
Lemon flavour

Alcohol 1.5

    2 msr Midori
    1 teaspoon kirsch
    5 msr sparkling bitter lemon
Add to glass three-quarters filled with ice.
Add lemon twist.

H

Sky Highball
Pineapple flavour

Alcohol 2.1

    2 msr scotch
    1 teaspoon blue curacao
    5 msr pineapple juice
Add to glass three-quarters filled with ice, sprinkle
the curacao on top, add lemon twist.

H

Seville Highball
Orange/Lemon flavour

Alcohol 1.9

    1³/₄ msr Mandarine Napoléon
    1 teaspoon Pernod
    5 msr sparkling bitter lemon
Add to ice-filled glass. Add orange twist.

H

Highlander
Scotch/Herb flavour

Alcohol 1.5

    ¹/₂ msr Drambuie
    ¹/₂ msr scotch
    ¹/₂ msr dry vermouth
    ¹/₂ msr rosso vermouth
    1 teaspoon lemon juice
    4¹/₂ msr dandelion and burdock (substitute: cola)
Add to ice-filled glass.
Garnish: mint sprig, add straws.

H

High Moon

Fruity flavour   *Alcohol 1.8*

1½ msr raspberry liqueur
1 msr apricot brandy
½ msr cognac
1 teaspoon grenadine
4½ msr sparkling bitter lemon

Add to ice-filled glass. Garnish: cherry and
half slice of lemon.

CO

Hobart

Fruity flavour   *Alcohol 2.1*

All the way from Tasmania.

1 msr mango liqueur
1 msr white rum
½ msr dark rum
2 msr mandarin juice
1 msr pineapple juice
1 msr white grape juice

Shake and strain into ice-filled glass, add straws.   H

Horse's Neck

Brandy flavour   *Alcohol 2.0*

The original 1890s Horse's Neck was a non-alcoholic mix of lemon peel,
ice and ginger ale. By around 1910 bourbon or sometimes brandy was
added, and the result known as a Horse's Neck With a Kick or Horse's
Neck – Stiff.

2 msr brandy or bourbon
1 dash Angostura
4 msr dry ginger ale

Add the spiral rind of a whole lemon to glass with one end
hanging over side. Half fill with ice and add the ingredients. H

Hurricane

Fruity flavour   *Alcohol 2.5*

1½ msr dark rum
1 msr white rum
1 msr lime juice
2 msr passion fruit juice
1 msr pineapple juice
1 msr orange juice

½ msr blackcurrant syrup
Shake and strain into glass filled with broken ice.
Garnish: slice of pineapple and a cherry, add straws. P

Hyatt Club

Fruity flavour   Alcohol 2.4

Altissimo Dario, Hyatt Regency, Brussels. Courtesy of Ets. Fourcroy s.a.

    1⅓ msr white rum
    ⅔ msr Mandarine Napoléon
    ⅔ msr cherry brandy
    4 msr sparkling bitter lemon
Add to ice-filled glass. Garnish: slice of lemon and a cherry. H

Indycar

Subtle fruit flavour   Alcohol 1.4

    1 msr apricot brandy
    1 msr dry vermouth
    ½ msr triple sec
    1 msr passion fruit juice
    3 msr 7UP
Add to ice-filled glass.   H

Jagger's Satisfaction

Subtle fruit flavour   Alcohol 1.8

    1 msr bourbon
    ½ msr Campari
    ½ msr sweet sherry
    ½ msr Rum Tree
    4 msr lemonade
Add to ice-filled glass.   H

Jug Wobbler

Lemon / Herb flavour   Alcohol 2.2

    1 msr gin
    1 msr apple schnapps
    ½ msr dry vermouth
    ¼ msr Pernod
    4 msr 7UP
Add to ice-filled glass.   H

JULEPS

Julep is believed to be derived from an ancient Arabic word translated as 'julab', meaning rose water. By the fourteenth century an 'Iulep' was a syrup of sugar and water, mainly used as a vehicle for medicine.

Samuel Pepys mentioned the Julep in glowing terms, as did poet John Milton.

In 1787 the Julep was first mentioned in US literature, and by about 1800 it had become fully Americanised, complete with mint garnish. It was re-exported to Europe in 1836 by English author Captain Frederick Marryat.

In the US, Juleps were often made with brandy, until bourbon became more widely available after the civil war, and this has remained the most popular base spirit.

There is a silver Julep cup – a tankard – but a Collins glass is currently more popular. The glass should be ice cold before use, and preferably have a white frost coating when served. Melted ice-water contributes a significant volume to a Julep and qualifies it as a long drink.

Juleps are made by dissolving some sugar with a little water in the glass (or using sugar syrup). Sprigs of mint are added and usually crushed, the liquor(s) of choice are added until the glass is more than a quarter but less than one-third full. Fill with crushed ice.

Mint Julep

Bourbon mint flavour   *Alcohol 3.0*

Traditionally served on Kentucky Derby day, the first Saturday in May.

    3 msr bourbon (preferably Kentucky)
    1 msr sugar syrup
    4 fresh sprigs of mint

Add the syrup and mint to glass. Gently crush the mint with the flat end of a barspoon; how much juice you extract depends upon your liking for mint. In some states the tradition is not to crush it at all.

Add the bourbon and stir gently whilst filling the glass with crushed ice. Arrange the sprigs with the stalks down and some leaves on top. Serve with straws and a napkin.   CO

If brandy is used in place of the bourbon, this is a Brandy Julep.

If Southern Comfort is used in place of the bourbon and the sugar syrup halved, this is a Southern Comfort Julep.

Marryat's Mint Julep

Peach brandy flavour

Alcohol 2.5

Also known as Georgia Mint Julep.

1½ msr brandy or cognac
1½ msr peach brandy
12 small sprigs of mint
¾ msr sugar syrup (originally sugar)

Add to glass and fill with crushed ice. Mix gently
so as not to crush mint. Rub rim with piece of
fresh pineapple and serve.

CO

Southern Mint Julep

Peach bourbon flavour

Alcohol 3.0

1½ msr bourbon
1½ msr Southern Comfort
4–5 fresh sprigs of mint
½ msr sugar syrup

Add to glass and fill with crushed ice. Mix gently
so as not to crush mint.

CO

Jungle Juice

Fruity flavour

Alcohol 2.5

Quick and easy to make, delicious on a warm summer's evening.

1¾ msr Pisang Ambon
¾ msr Mandarine Napoléon
¾ msr gin
4 msr orange juice
¾ msr lemon juice

Shake and strain into ice-filled glass. Garnish: slice
of pineapple and a cherry, add straws.

CO

Jungle Wild

Fruity flavour

Alcohol 2.2

1 msr white rum
1 msr Wild Turkey bourbon
⅓ msr Pisang Ambon
2 msr papaya juice
1 msr mandarin juice
⅓ msr lime juice
2 msr lcmonade

Shake and strain into glass filled with broken ice,
add the lemonade. Garnish: fruit in season,
add straws. **P**

Kismet Hardy

Pineapple flavour   *Alcohol 2.1*

    1 msr Cointreau
    3/4 msr dark rum
    1/2 msr amaretto
    3 msr pineapple juice
    1 msr grapefruit juice
    1/2 msr grenadine

Blend briefly with a glassful of crushed ice.
Garnish: cherry and slice of orange. **G**

Kitten Cuddler

Fruity flavour   *Alcohol 1.6*

    1 msr vodka
    1 msr creme de banane
    1 teaspoon Lakka Cloudberry Liqueur
    1 msr pineapple juice
    1/2 msr lemon juice
    1/2 teaspoon grenadine
    3 msr cold Sprite or lemonade

Shake and strain into ice-filled glass, add
the Sprite. Garnish: cherry and slices of
orange and lemon. **CO**

Klondike

Fruity flavour   *Alcohol 2.5*

This is tricky but tasty. It should have two distinct layers of colour – red
on blue/green.

    1 1/2 msr silver tequila
    3/4 msr cognac
    1 msr lime juice
    1 msr mandarin juice
    1/3 msr almond syrup
    1/3 msr blue curacao

Add all but the blue curacao to glass. Fill with just sufficient crushed ice
to make into a sherbet/sorbet. The blue curacao should now be added a
little at a time with a barspoon until the drink turns light blue/green. It
should not be bright blue. The glass should now be about two-thirds full.

To a mixing glass or shaker add:
  3/4 msr dark rum
  1/2 msr grenadine
Make into a sherbet as before. If not bright red add
a little more grenadine. Now add the red sherbet on
top of the blue. Garnish: fruit in season, add straws.   P

Krook's Quencher

Cherry gin flavour   *Alcohol 1.9*

In Dickens' *Bleak House*, Mr Krook's excessive gin drinking and eventual
saturation in spirit leads to his spontaneous combustion.

  1 msr gin
  1 msr cherry brandy
  1/2 msr rosso vermouth
  4 msr cherryade

Add to ice-filled glass. Garnish: mint sprig
and a cherry.   H

Lady in Green

Orange flavour   *Alcohol 2.7*

Courtesy of Marie Brizard Liqueurs, France.

  1 1/3 msr vodka
  1 1/3 msr Anisette Marie Brizard
  1/2 msr blue curacao
  3 1/2 msr orange juice

Shake and strain into ice-filled glass.   H

Lady Killer

Passion fruit flavour   *Alcohol 2.1*

These are all the rage at the Wantagh Arms, Wantagh, a short ride west
of Massapequa, USA.

  1 msr gin
  3/4 msr apricot brandy
  3/4 msr Cointreau
  2 msr passion fruit juice
  2 msr pineapple juice

Shake and strain into ice-filled glass.
Garnish: slices of orange and pineapple.   H

Lark

Orange flavour

Alcohol 2.0

1 msr scotch
1 msr Grand Marnier
¼ msr grenadine
¼ msr lemon juice
4 msr orangeade

Add to ice-filled glass. Garnish: cherry and
slices of orange and lemon.

G

Larney

Vermouth flavour

Alcohol 2.1

1 msr rosso vermouth
¾ msr Irish whiskey
¾ msr Punt e Mes
½ msr Safari
⅓ msr Campari
1 teaspoon grenadine
4 msr lemonade

Shake and strain into ice-filled glass, add the
lemonade. Garnish: orange slice and cherry.

CO

Lemon Tree

Lemon flavour

Alcohol 1.8

1 msr white rum
¾ msr Rum Tree
½ msr coconut rum
½ msr coconut cream
3 tablespoons lemon sherbet/sorbet

Blend briefly with a tablespoon of crushed ice, add straws. H

If orange sherbet is used, this is an Orange Tree.
If mango sherbet is used, this is a Mango Tree.

Lesbian Joy

Sweet wine flavour

Alcohol 1.0

The favoured dessert wines of the ancient Roman banquet were
Falernian, Alban, Caecuban, Chian and Lesbian (from Lesbos).

3 msr medium red wine (preferably Lesbian)
1 teaspoon amaretto
1 teaspoon kirsch
1 teaspoon scotch
3 msr lemonade

Add to ice-filled glass. Garnish: cherry surrounded
by slice of orange, add short straws.

G

Long Beach Iced Tea

Cranberry flavour   *Alcohol 2.4*

> ½ msr gold tequila
> ½ msr white rum
> ½ msr gin
> ½ msr vodka
> ½ msr triple sec
> 3 msr cranberry juice
> 1 msr lemon juice
> ½ msr sugar syrup

Shake and strain into glass three-quarters filled
with broken ice, sprinkle the cranberry on top.
Garnish: wedge of lemon.

CO

If lemonade is used in place of cranberry,
this is a Long Island Lemonade.

Long Island Iced Tea

Lemon cola flavour   *Alcohol 2.4*

In early versions either the triple sec or the tequila were omitted.

> ½ msr white rum
> ½ msr vodka
> ½ msr gold tequila
> ½ msr gin
> ½ msr triple sec
> 1 msr lemon juice
> ½ msr sugar syrup
> 1 teaspoon egg white
> 4 msr cold cola

Shake and strain into ice-filled glass, add
the cola. Garnish: slice of lemon.

CO

If the triple sec is omitted, this is a Texas Tea.

Alcohol 1.9

If blue curacao is used in place of triple sec,
this is a Miami Iced Tea.

Lutteur

Orange / Lemon flavour

Alcohol 2.0

    1 msr VSOP cognac
    ¹/₂ msr vodka
    ¹/₂ msr Mandarine Napoléon
    4 msr sparkling bitter lemon

Add to glass three-quarters filled with broken ice.
Garnish: slice of orange and a cherry, add straws. CO

Mach 6

Pineapple flavour

Alcohol 1.8

    1 msr white creme de cacao
    1 msr sweet sherry
    ¹/₂ msr white rum
    2 msr pineapple juice
    1 tablespoon pineapple chunks
    1 teaspoon grenadine

Blend until smooth, add three-quarters of a
glassful of crushed ice and blend again briefly.
Garnish: pineapple chunk and a cherry,
add straws. CO

MAI TAIS

The history of this drink – it means 'the best' in Tahitian – has been
debated ever since it became popular in the 1950s. The opposing views
are that it was invented either by Trader Vic around 1944, or by Donn
Beach (*see* Zombie) around 1932.

Until tangible evidence for the Beach story is found, it seems likely that
Trader Vic will continue to be credited with full authorship.

Mai Tai (Commercial Mix)

Fruit rum flavour

Alcohol 2.5

*Victor 'Trader Vic' Bergeron (1902–91). Courtesy of Lynn Bergeron, Trader Vic's,
San Francisco.*

Trader Vic was one of the most outstanding restaurateurs of his
generation. His combination of tropical drinks and exotic food soon had
people literally queuing in the street. Today there are a number of his
restaurants around the world, but the jewel in the crown is the Beverly
Hills Trader Vic's, where the world's glitterati are thick on the ground
each evening.

About 1944 he decided to make a cocktail from the finest ingredients he could find. With some input from his head bartender, he came up with a mixture of 2 msr 17-year-old J.Wray & Nephew rum, ½ msr triple sec, ¼ msr orgeat, ¼ msr rock candy syrup and the juice of a lime. This was shaken with a glassful of crushed ice and poured, half the spent lime shell was added, and the result garnished with a sprig of mint.

When he introduced the Mai Tai to Hawaii in 1953 it was too successful. Within a year the entire world supply of 17-year-old rum was exhausted, and he had to reinvent the cocktail using a blend of rums.

    1¼ msr St. James rum
    1¼ msr Appleton gold rum
    (or 2½ msr Mai Tai rum)
    2 msr Mai Tai mix
    juice of 1 large lime

Shake with a glassful of crushed ice. Add half the spent lime shell. Garnish: sprig of mint and fruit stick.   CO

If the above rums or commercial mix are not available, the following is a standard bar recipe.

Mai Tai (Bar Mix)

Fruit rum flavour   *Alcohol 3.0*

    1 msr white rum
    1 msr dark rum
    ⅔ msr triple sec
    ⅓ msr almond syrup
    ⅓ msr sugar syrup
    ¼ msr grenadine
    juice of 1 lime

Shake briefly with a glassful of crushed ice.
Add half the spent lime shell and straws.   CO

There are many other species of the drink which commonly include various fruit juices. The following is a popular version.

Mai Tai (Fruity)

Fruit rum flavour   *Alcohol 2.6*

    1 msr dark rum
    ½ msr white rum
    ½ msr gold tequila
    ½ msr triple sec
    ½ msr amaretto
    1 msr pineapple juice

1 msr orange juice
1/2 msr grenadine
1/4 msr almond syrup
1 dash Angostura
juice of 1/2 a fresh lime
3 msr lemonade

Shake briefly with a glassful of crushed ice.
Add half a spent lime shell and the lemonade.
Garnish: slices of orange, pineapple and a
cherry, serve with straws.

P

Manager's Daughter, The

Lemon / Wine flavour

Alcohol 2.0

1 1/2 msr Dubonnet
1 msr apple brandy
4 msr sparkling bitter lemon

Add to ice-filled glass.

H

Marrakech Express

Grapefruit flavour

Alcohol 2.0

1 msr white rum
1 msr dry vermouth
1 msr white creme de cacao
2 msr grapefruit juice
1 msr mandarin juice
1/2 msr lime juice
1 level teaspoon caster sugar

Shake with a glassful of broken ice
and pour unstrained.

CO

Mean Machine

Blackberry flavour

Alcohol 1.8

1 msr bourbon
1/2 msr gin
1/2 msr blackberry brandy
4 msr lemonade

Add to ice-filled glass.

H

Melanie Pimm

Whisky punch flavour   *Alcohol 2.0*

James Pimm created his No.1 Cup around 1840. Soon Pimm's had to be bottled to fill the demand at home and abroad. His secret recipe has remained unchanged to this day, and is known to only six people.

Pimm's is not usually regarded as an aperitif, more of a summer afternoon mixer base. In a cocktail it gives a more fruity flavour than is offered by vermouth.

1 1/2 msr Pimm's No.1
2/3 msr scotch whisky
1/3 msr lemon juice
5 msr lemonade

Add to ice-filled glass. Garnish: slices of orange, lemon and lime speared with a cherry, serve with straws.

CO

If bourbon is used in place of scotch, this is a Bourbon Pimm's.

Melon Ball

Pineapple flavour   *Alcohol 2.2*

2 msr Midori
1 msr vodka
4 msr pineapple juice

Shake and strain into ice-filled glass. Garnish: melon ball and slice of lime on a stick, add straws.

CO

If garnished with a cherry, this is a Pearl Harbor.

Mexican Chocolate

Chocolate flavour   *Alcohol 2.2*

1 1/2 msr gold tequila
1 msr Kahlua
4 msr chilled chocolate drink/cocoa

Shake and strain into glass filled with crushed ice. Garnish: mint sprig, add short straws.

G

Mississippi Magic

Peach flavour

Alcohol 2.3

1 msr bourbon
1 msr Southern Comfort
1/2 msr dry vermouth
1 msr mandarin juice
1 msr pineapple juice
1/4 msr lime juice
1 msr peach puree

Blend briefly with a glassful of crushed ice, add straws.   G

Mojito

Citrus flavour

Alcohol 2.5

A Cuban Mint Julep with lime. During US Prohibition this old recipe
was revived with great success at the Bodeguita del Medio Bar, Cuba.

2 1/2 msr white rum
juice of half a lime
3–4 sprigs of mint
2/3 msr sugar syrup
1 dash Angostura
2 msr soda water

Gently crush mint in the bottom of the glass, add spent lime
shell, fill up with crushed or broken ice. Shake rum, lime juice,
Angostura and syrup. Strain into glass and add the soda.
Top up with crushed ice if required, and gently
muddle ingredients together; add straws.   CO

Molokai Mike

Fruity flavour

Alcohol 2.0

1 msr white rum
1/2 msr brandy
1 msr orange juice
1 msr lemon juice
1/2 msr almond syrup

Shake and strain into glass two-thirds filled with crushed
ice and mix. In a mixing glass combine: 1/2 msr dark rum,
1/3 msr grenadine and sufficient crushed ice to make a
sorbet/sherbet, and gently add to top of cocktail.
Garnish: fruit in season, add straws.   H

Monkey Wrench

Grapefruit flavour

Alcohol 1.8

    1 3/4 msr white rum
    3 msr grapefruit juice
    3 msr lemonade

Add to ice-filled glass. Garnish: slice of
grapefruit and a cherry, add straws.

CO

Moon River

Apricot / Citrus flavour

Alcohol 2.9

    1 msr apricot brandy
    1 msr gin
    1 msr triple sec
    1/2 msr Galliano
    2/3 msr lime juice
    1/3 msr blue curacao
    1/2 msr sugar syrup

Shake and strain into glass filled with crushed
ice. Add the curacao streaked across the top.

G

Moscow Mule

Ginger / Lime flavour

Alcohol 1.5

In 1947 John Martin, of Heublein & Co., USA, who had acquired the
rights to Smirnoff vodka, was pondering ways of encouraging Americans
to buy it. He was telling his friend Jack Morgan of the Cock 'n' Bull
Saloon in Los Angeles, when Morgan mentioned that he was stuck with a
large quantity of ginger ale. They mixed the two, added a dash of lime
juice, and concluded the resulting 'Moscow Mule' was delicious. Word of
the new cocktail spread rapidly, and soon Smirnoff vodka was in demand
from coast to coast.

    1 1/2 msr Smirnoff vodka
    3/4 msr lime juice
    5 msr dry ginger ale

Add to ice-filled glass.
Garnish: wedge of lime, add straws.

CO

Munchausen

Fruity flavour

Alcohol 1.8

    1 1/2 msr watermelon schnapps
    1 msr lemon vodka
    2 msr pineapple juice

2 msr mandarin juice
1 teaspoon grenadine
2 msr lemonade
Shake and strain into glass half filled with
broken ice, add the lemonade and straws.

CO

Naked Waiter

Lemon flavour   *Alcohol 1.5*

3/4 msr Pernod
3/4 msr Mandarine Napoléon
1 msr pineapple juice
4 msr sparkling bitter lemon
Add to ice-filled glass. Garnish: lemon wedge.   G

Nathalie

Cherry flavour   *Alcohol 2.4*

1 msr cherry vodka
3/4 msr bourbon
1/2 msr Punt e Mes
1/2 msr triple sec
1/2 msr lemon juice
3 msr lemonade
Shake and strain into ice-filled glass, add the lemonade.   G

Navy Grog

Fruity flavour   *Alcohol 2.5*

1 1/2 msr golden rum
1 msr white rum
1 msr orange juice
1 msr lime juice
1 msr pineapple juice
1 msr passion fruit juice
1/2 msr sugar syrup
Blend briefly with a glassful of crushed ice.
Garnish: lime slice and cherry.   G

Nelson's Nightcap

Red wine flavour   Alcohol 1.4

Admiral Lord Nelson enjoyed Marsala wine so much he once purchased 5,000 gallons for the British Navy.

1½ msr LBV port
¾ msr marsala
½ msr dry sherry
1 teaspoon dry orange curacao
1 dash Angostura
3½ msr lemonade

Add to ice-filled glass.   G

Neon Tower

Lemon / Melon flavour   Alcohol 2.4

Barry McDonald. Courtesy of Reunion Tower at Hyatt Regency, Dallas, Texas.

1½ msr Midori
1½ msr Southern Comfort
1 msr lemon juice
½ msr sugar syrup
1 teaspoon egg white
3 msr Slice (substitute: lemonade)

Shake and strain into ice-filled glass, add the Slice.
Garnish: slice of lemon, add straws.   CO

Northside Special

Citrus flavour   Alcohol 2.0

1930s speciality of the Myrtle Bank Hotel, Kingston, Jamaica.

2 msr dark rum (preferably Jamaican)
3 msr orange juice
½ msr lemon juice
2 level teaspoons caster sugar
2 msr soda water

Add all but soda to glass, dissolve sugar and
fill with crushed ice. Add soda and straws.
Garnish: cherry and slices of lemon and orange.   CO

Olaffson's Punch

Citrus flavour   Alcohol 2.1

A Haitian classic.

2 msr dark rum (preferably Haitian)
1 teaspoon maraschino

3 msr orange juice
1¹/₂ msr lime juice
1 teaspoon caster sugar

Dissolve sugar and shake briefly with a glassful of crushed ice. Add short straws and twists of orange and lime.

G

Old Moorhen's Shredded Sporran

Alcohol 2.1

Fruity flavour

1 msr scotch
¹/₂ msr Drambuie
¹/₂ msr Mandarine Napoléon
1 teaspoon parfait amour
2 msr pineapple juice
1 msr guava nectar
¹/₄ msr lemon juice
1 teaspoon almond syrup

Shake briefly with a glassful of crushed ice.
Garnish: slice of lemon and a cherry, add straws.

G

Orchard Orange

Alcohol 2.4

Mandarin flavour

2 msr apple brandy
¹/₂ msr dry vermouth
¹/₄ msr amaretto
3 msr mandarin juice
¹/₂ msr lime juice

Shake and strain into ice-filled glass.
Garnish: fruit in season, add straws.

H

Oyster Bay

Alcohol 1.2

Fruity flavour

1 msr dark rum
1 teaspoon anisette
2 msr mango juice
1 msr grapefruit juice
1 msr pineapple juice
1 msr papaya juice
³/₄ msr lime juice
¹/₂ msr sugar syrup

Shake and strain into ice-filled glass.
Garnish: fruit in season, add straws.

CO

Paris Opera

Aniseed / Orange flavour

Alcohol 2.0

    1 msr Mandarine Napoléon
    1 msr Pernod
    5 msr lemonade

Add to glass three-quarters filled with broken ice.   Pi

Peach UP

Peach / Lemon flavour

Alcohol 1.6

    1 msr peach schnapps
    1/2 msr gin
    1 msr dry vermouth
    4 msr cold 7UP

Add to ice-filled glass.   H

Peek in Pandora's Box

Orange flavour

Alcohol 1.9

    1 3/4 msr scotch
    1/4 msr Campari
    1 teaspoon Strega
    1 1/2 msr mandarin juice
    3 msr ginger ale

Add to ice-filled glass.   H

Peppermint Depth Charge

Beer flavour

Alcohol 2.0

    1 msr peppermint schnapps
    1 glass / 10 fl oz / 28 cl cold beer

Add schnapps to beer.   Pi

Any flavour of Depth Charge can be produced
by adding the appropriate schnapps.

Picker's Peach

Peach rum flavour

Alcohol 2.6

    1 1/2 msr white rum
    1 msr peach schnapps
    1/2 msr dark rum
    1 msr orange juice
    3/4 msr lemon juice
    1/2 teaspoon caster sugar

¹/₃ of a ripe peeled peach
1 teaspoon Pêcher Mignon (optional)
Blend until smooth, add a glassful of crushed
ice and blend again briefly. Garnish: wedge-shaped
slice of peach speared with a cherry, add straws.　CO

Pimm's Turbo
Fruity flavour　　　　　　　　　　　　　*Alcohol 1.7*
　　1 msr Pimm's No. 1
　　1 msr gin
　　4 msr lemonade
Add to ice-filled glass. Garnish: slice of lemon and a cherry.　G

Pina Colada – *see* Coladas

Pina Vina
Pineapple flavour　　　　　　　　　　*Alcohol 0.9*
An ideal accompaniment for a lunchtime salad.
　　3 msr medium white wine
　　¹/₂ msr lemon juice
　　3oz/85g pineapple chunks
Blend with a glassful of crushed ice until
smooth. Garnish: slice of lemon speared
with pineapple chunk and a cherry.　　　G

Pink Pussycat
Fruity flavour　　　　　　　　　　　　*Alcohol 2.0*
　　2 msr gin
　　3 msr pineapple juice
　　2 msr grapefruit juice
　　¹/₃ msr grenadine
Shake and strain into ice-filled glass.
Garnish: slice of grapefruit and a cherry.　　CO

Pisang Garuda
Fruity flavour　　　　　　　　　　　　*Alcohol 2.3*
Garuda, the fabulous mythical part-human bird described in ancient
Hindu Sanskrit, is the national emblem of Indonesia. Pisang Ambon is
based on an old Indonesian recipe.

1½ msr Pisang Ambon
1 msr white rum
½ msr Mandarine Napoléon
4 msr sparkling bitter lemon

Rim glass with grenadine/caster sugar. Shake
and strain into ice-filled glass, add the bitter lemon.
Garnish: colourful fruit in season redolent of
plumage, add straws.

CO

Planter's Punch

In 1879, Fred L. Myers founded the Myers's Rum distillery in Jamaica
and celebrated by creating what he named a Planter's Punch. This
concoction became the house speciality at Kelly's Bar, Sugar Wharf,
Jamaica, and its popularity soon began to spread.

Planter's Punch (Original)

Orange flavour   *Alcohol 1.7*

Fred L. Myers. Courtesy of Myers's Rum, Jamaica.

1⅔ msr Myers's dark rum
4 msr orange juice
juice of ½ a lime
1 teaspoon grenadine
1 teaspoon caster sugar

Shake and strain into glass filled with crushed ice.
Garnish: cherry and slice of orange.

H

Planter's Punch (Americanised)

Fruity flavour   *Alcohol 2.3*

1 msr Myers's dark rum
1 msr white rum
½ msr creme de banane
1 msr lime juice
1 msr pineapple juice
2 msr mandarin juice
½ msr grenadine
1 dash Angostura
2 msr soda water

Shake and strain into ice-filled glass, add
the soda. Garnish: fruits in season, add sprig of
mint and straws. Sprinkle with grated nutmeg.

P

POLAR-COLAS

Made with liquor, lemon juice and one small, very cold bottle of cola (185–200ml), to which the ingredients are added using a funnel. It is usually necessary to pour away a small quantity of cola to do this. A bar towel or rubber bung is placed over the top of the bottle and pressure applied while it is briefly inverted to mix the ingredients. The bottle is placed in a large glass (tankard, stein or British pint), and this is filled with broken ice to keep the bottle cold. A straw is added to the bottle.

Captain Cola

Rum cola flavour   *Alcohol 1.5*

    1 msr Captain Morgan spiced rum
    1/2 msr armagnac
    1 teaspoon lemon juice
    1 bottle cold cola

Make as above.   Bottle

Cola-Rolla

Lemon cola flavour   *Alcohol 1.8*

    1/2 msr dry orange curacao
    1/2 msr cognac or brandy
    1/2 msr vodka
    1/2 msr lemon juice
    1 bottle cold cola

Make as above.   Bottle

Mandeville-Polar

Rum cola flavour   *Alcohol 1.6*

    1 msr dark rum
    1/2 msr white rum
    1 teaspoon Pernod
    1/2 msr lemon juice
    1 teaspoon grenadine
    1 bottle cold cola

Make as above.   Bottle

If made in a rocks glass over ice using less cola, this is a Mandeville.

Poca-Hola

Bitter cola flavour   *Alcohol 1.1*

    3/4 msr Punt e Mes
    3/4 msr Campari
    1/2 msr Noilly Prat
    3/4 msr lemon juice
    1 bottle cold cola

Make as above.   Bottle

Polar-Roller

Orange cola flavour   *Alcohol 1.0*

    1/2 msr Cointreau
    1/2 msr armagnac
    1 teaspoon lemon juice
    1 bottle cold cola

Make as above.   Bottle

Prawn Salad

Fruity flavour   *Alcohol 2.0*

    1 1/2 msr Pimm's No.1
    1/3 msr Glayva
    1/3 msr Mandarine Napoléon
    1/3 msr scotch
    4 msr lemonade

Add to ice-filled glass.
Garnish: fruit in season, add straws.   H

Quick Thrill

Wine flavour   *Alcohol 1.1*

    3 msr medium red wine
    1/3 msr dark rum
    3 msr cold cola

Add to ice-filled glass.   G

Rebel Raider

Mandarin flavour   *Alcohol 1.8*

    1 1/2 msr Rebel Yell bourbon
    1/2 msr sweet sherry
    1 teaspoon Campari

3 msr mandarin juice
3 msr lemonade

Shake and strain into ice-filled glass,
add the lemonade.

CO

RICKEYS

This unsweetened cocktail of spirit, lime juice and soda water was first made around 1893 in Shoemakers Restaurant, Washington, USA, for one Joe Rickey, a Congressional lobbyist who preferred to be known as Colonel Jim.

Rickeys based on other spirits were once popular, but have not stood the test of time as has the original Gin Rickey. The slightest trace of sugar in a Gin Rickey and it would be a Gimlet, though both cocktails evolved independently.

Gin Rickey

Lime gin flavour   *Alcohol 2.0*

2 msr gin
1/2 a fresh lime
4 msr soda water

Squeeze lime juice directly into glass half filled
with ice, add spent shell and gin.
Mix with barspoon and add soda.

H

Replace the gin to make the following Rickeys:

Apple Rum Rickey	1 msr apple brandy 1 msr white rum	*Alcohol 2.0*
Apricot Rickey	2 msr apricot brandy	*Alcohol 1.0*
Aquavit Rickey	2 msr aquavit 1 teaspoon kummel	*Alcohol 2.3*
Bourbon Rickey	2 msr bourbon	*Alcohol 2.0*
Brandy Rickey	2 msr brandy or cognac	*Alcohol 2.0*
Rum Rickey	2 msr white rum	*Alcohol 2.0*
Sloe Gin Rickey	2 msr sloe gin	*Alcohol 1.3*
Vodka Rickey	2 msr vodka	*Alcohol 2.0*

Royal Turkey

Fruity flavour

Alcohol 2.2

1 msr Wild Turkey bourbon
1 msr sloe gin
1 msr apricot brandy
2 msr pineapple juice
3 msr 7UP

Shake and strain into ice-filled glass, add the 7UP.
Garnish: fruit in season, add straws.

 P

Rum Runner

Fruity flavour

Alcohol 2.7

1 msr blackberry brandy
1 msr dark rum
1 msr creme de banane
1/2 msr white rum
1/2 msr pineapple juice
1/2 msr grenadine
1/2 msr lemon juice
1 teaspoon almond syrup

Blend briefly with a glassful of crushed ice.
Garnish: orange slice and cherry, add straws.

G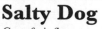

Salty Dog

Grapefruit flavour

Alcohol 2.0

2 msr vodka
4 msr grapefruit juice

Rim glass with grapefruit/salt. Shake and strain into glass
three-quarters filled with broken ice, add spiral of grapefruit. H
If no salt rim is used, this is a Greyhound.

SANGAREES

The Sangaree is a nineteenth-century American mix influenced by the
traditional Spanish red wine based drink Sangria (blood drink). In the
early twentieth century they acquired soda water. They can be made with
fortified wines, ales and spirits. They are sweetened and added to an ice-
filled glass. Traditionally the spirit-based versions are dusted with nutmeg.

Brandy Sangaree

Brandy flavour   *Alcohol 2.8*

    2½ msr brandy
    ½ msr sugar syrup
    2½ msr soda water
    ½ msr LBV port

Add to glass filled with broken ice, sprinkle the
port on top. Dust with nutmeg and add straws.   H

Replace the brandy to make the following Sangarees:

Bourbon Sangaree	2½ msr bourbon	
Gin Sangaree	2½ msr gin	
Scotch Sangaree	2½ msr scotch	
Sherry Sangaree	2½ msr sweet sherry	*Alcohol 1.5*

Fruit Sangarees such as peach, apricot or cherry can also be made by
using a fruit brandy in place of the spirit and omitting the sugar syrup.

Saoco

Coconut flavour   *Alcohol 2.0*

A classic Caribbean cocktail.

    2 msr white rum
    4 msr coconut milk – the fluid centre of a coconut
    (not coconut cream)

Shake briefly with a glassful of crushed ice,
add straw. Often served in a coconut.   G

Screwdriver

Orange flavour   *Alcohol 2.0*

A drink which appeared as recently as the 1950s. Barlore has it this drink
acquired its name when a US oilman in Iran was seen to stir one with his
screwdriver. It is tempting to believe the name is connected with the
account given by N. E. Beveridge in *Cups of Valor*, which describes how
US marines stationed at Tientsin in 1945 attempted to make their own
gin. An 18-inch screwdriver was used to stir the brew, and the result
known as Screwdriver Gin.

    2 msr vodka
    4½ msr orange juice

Add to ice-filled glass.
Garnish: slice of orange and a cherry.   H

If white rum is used in place of vodka,
this is a Rum Screw or Cuban Screw.

If only 1 msr vodka is used but 1 msr sloe gin is added, this is a Slow Screw.   *Alcohol 1.6*

If only 1 msr vodka is used but 1 msr Wild Turkey 101 is added, this is a Wild Screw.   *Alcohol 2.3*

If ½ msr blue curacao is added to a Screwdriver, this is a Green Eyes.   *Alcohol 2.3*

If 3 msr 7UP are added to a Screwdriver, this is a Screw-Up.

CO

Sea Breeze

Fruity flavour   *Alcohol 1.5*

    1½ msr vodka
    2 msr grapefruit juice
    3 msr cranberry juice

Shake briefly with three-quarters glassful of broken ice and pour unstrained. Garnish: wedge of lime.   H

If pineapple is used in place of grapefruit, this is a Bay Breeze.

Seven and Seven, 7 & 7

Subtle citrus flavour   *Alcohol 2.0*

A recipe conceived and successfully publicised by the two manufacturers involved.

    2 msr 7 Crown Canadian whisky
    5 msr cold 7UP

Add to ice-filled glass. Garnish: slice of lime.   H

Shandy

Beer flavour   *Alcohol 1.0*

    beer
    lemonade

Add to glass in equal measure.   Pi

Sixteen and a Half

Herb / Lemon flavour   *Alcohol 1.5*

    1 msr 7 Crown Canadian whisky
    ½ msr Punt e Mes
    ½ msr Pimm's No.1
    ½ msr lime juice
    4 msr 7UP

Add to ice-filled glass.   H

SLINGS

Sling is an Americanism which first appears in literature dated 1759. It appears to be derived from the German word schlingen, meaning 'to swallow quickly'. A Sling, like a Cooler and a Gimlet, was also the name of an implement found in bars, being a device used to handle barrels.

A true Sling should only be diluted with plain cold water. Today, few Slings use this because it is rather boring for modern tastes. Instead most qualify by including ice and excluding any sparkling soft drink.

A Sling should contain lemon or lime juice and sugar/syrup or a sweet liqueur. Any base spirit and any fruit juices can be used. It may be shaken and strained into an ice-filled glass or simply added to ice in the glass.

Gin Sling

Lemon gin flavour   *Alcohol 2.0*

    2 msr gin
    2/3 msr sugar syrup
    1 msr lemon juice
    2 msr cold water

Add to ice-filled glass with twist of lemon.
Sprinkling with nutmeg is optional.

G

Replace the gin in the following Slings:

Bourbon Sling	2 msr bourbon
Brandy Sling	2 msr brandy
Rum Sling	2 msr dark rum
Scotch Sling	2 msr scotch whisky
Vodka Sling	2 msr vodka

Iron Bar Sling

Cherry flavour   *Alcohol 2.1*

    1 msr gin
    1 msr cherry brandy
    1/3 msr Southern Comfort
    2 msr orange juice
    1 msr lime juice
    1 msr pineapple juice
    1/4 msr grenadine

Shake and strain into ice-filled glass.

H

Singapore Sling

Cherry gin flavour   *Alcohol 2.2*

This world-famous cocktail was created in 1915 by Ngiam Tong Boon, a Hainanese-Chinese bartender working at Raffles Hotel, Singapore.

    1 msr gin
    1 msr cherry brandy
    1/2 msr Cointreau
    1 msr lime juice
    1 msr pineapple juice
    1 msr orange juice
    1/4 msr grenadine
    1 teaspoon Benedictine
    1 dash Angostura

Shake and strain into glass filled with broken ice, sprinkle the Benedictine on top.
Garnish: slice of pineapple and a cherry, add straws.

H

Note: use a highly coloured cherry brandy, as the end result should be slightly pink. Raffles Hotel Bar does not use soda water in this recipe.

Sydney Sling

Subtle herb flavour   *Alcohol 2.9*

    1 1/2 msr white rum
    1 msr cherry brandy
    1/2 msr triple sec
    1/3 msr Yellow Chartreuse
    3/4 msr lime juice
    2 msr pineapple juice
    1 1/2 msr orange juice
    1 dash Angostura

Shake and strain into ice-filled glass. Garnish: sprig of mint, slices of lime, lemon, orange and a cherry speared with an umbrella, add straws.

CO

Western Sling

Cherry gin flavour   *Alcohol 2.3*

    2 msr gin
    1/2 msr cherry brandy
    1 msr lemon juice
    2/3 msr sugar syrup
    1 teaspoon grenadine
    3 msr pineapple juice

Shake and strain into ice-filled glass.
Garnish: cherry and slice of
orange. Add a twist of lemon and straws.

CO

Slippery Surprise

Fruity flavour

 Alcohol 1.8

1½ msr scotch
½ msr creme de banane
2 msr peach juice
2 msr grapefruit juice
½ msr passion fruit juice

Shake with three-qurters of a glassful of broken ice
and pour unstrained. Garnish: fruit in season, add straws. G

Slow Gin and Tonic

Lemon gin flavour

 *Alcohol 2.2*

The sloe gin takes the dry edge off the usual 'G & T', whilst providing
colour, fragrance and a pithy fruitiness.

1½ msr gin
1 msr sloe gin
⅓ msr lemon juice
5 msr tonic water

Add to ice-filled glass with half slice of lemon.   CO

Slow Comfortable Screw

Fruity flavour

Alcohol 2.3

1 msr vodka
¾ msr Southern Comfort
¾ msr sloe gin
5 msr orange juice

Shake and strain into glass filled with
broken ice. Garnish: cherry, add straws.   CO

If ½ msr Galliano is sprinkled on top, this is a   *Alcohol 2.8*
Slow Comfortable Screw Against the Wall.

Slow Screw, Mildly Comfortable, Slightly Wild

Orange flavour

Alcohol 2.3

¾ msr sloe gin
¾ msr vodka

½ msr Southern Comfort
½ msr Wild Turkey 101
4 msr orange juice
2 msr lemonade

Shake and strain into glass filled with
broken ice, add the lemonade.
Garnish: cherry, add straws.

P

Snowball

Advocaat flavour   Alcohol 0.9

Still a top-selling mix especially in northern Europe, where it is available
bottled ready-made. Though regarded as a wimp's drink it is, in fact, a
delicious low-alcohol recipe.

2 msr advocaat
¼ msr Rose's Lime Cordial
5 msr lemonade

Add to ice-filled glass.
Garnish: cherry on a stick.

CO

If 1 msr vodka is added, this is a   Alcohol 1.9
Vodka Snowball.

If ¾ msr strawberry brandy is added,   Alcohol 1.3
this is a Strawberry Snowball.

If ¾ msr cherry vodka is added, this is a   Alcohol 1.7
Cherry Snowball.

Soho Twist

Sparkling wine flavour   Alcohol 2.0

1½ msr white rum
½ msr sweet sherry
¼ msr LBV port
1 teaspoon Drambuie
½ msr lime juice
4 msr ginger ale

Add to ice-filled glass. Add spiral of
lemon and short straws.

G

Spritzer

Dry flavour   *Alcohol 0.9*

A popular low-alcohol drink. The name appears to come from the German 'spritz', to squirt, a reference to the soda water.

    3 msr cold dry white wine
    4 msr soda water
Add to ice-filled glass.
Garnish; half slice of lemon.   CO

If red wine is used and 1/2 msr strawberry   *Alcohol 1.2*
liqueur added, this is a Spritzer de Fraise.

Strangeways to Oldham

Mandarin flavour   *Alcohol 2.0*

    1 msr dark rum
    1 msr gin
    1/2 msr Rose's Lime Cordial
    2 msr mandarin juice
    1 msr passion fruit juice
    2 msr lemonade
Shake and strain into ice-filled glass,
add the lemonade and straws.   CO

If white rum is used in place of gin, this is
an Easy Way To Oldham.

Strip and Yell

Lemon flavour   *Alcohol 1.9*

    1 1/4 msr Rebel Yell bourbon
    3/4 msr peach schnapps
    1/4 msr Strega
    4 1/2 msr sparkling bitter lemon
Add to ice-filled glass with spiral of lemon.   H

Submarino

Beer flavour   *Alcohol 2.0*

Courtesy of Sauza Tequila.

    1 msr silver tequila
    1 glass (28 cl) Mexican beer
Add tequila.   Pi

If gin is substituted for tequila and added to
any beer, this is known as a Dog's Nose.

Sunbeam

Fruity flavour

Alcohol 1.9

1 msr Midori
1 msr Jim Beam bourbon
1/2 msr creme de banane
2 msr mandarin juice
2 msr pineapple juice
1/4 msr grenadine

Shake and strain into ice-filled glass,
add the grenadine, but do not mix.

H

Sun City

Fruity flavour

Alcohol 2.2

1 msr white rum
1/2 msr dark rum
1/2 msr Galliano
1/2 msr apricot brandy
2 msr pineapple juice
juice of 1/4 of a lime
4 msr lemonade

Shake and strain into ice-filled glass, add the
spent shell and the lemonade, add straws.

P

Surprise Browst

Fruity flavour

Alcohol 1.5

'Browst' is an old Scottish term for brewing.

1 msr single grain scotch
1 msr creme de banane
4 msr grapefruit juice
1/3 msr grenadine

Shake and strain into ice-filled glass,
sprinkle the grenadine on top but do not mix.
Garnish: cherry, add straws and muddler.

CO

SWIZZLES

Originating in the West Indies and first noted by a traveller in 1813, a Swizzle is made with spirit, lime juice, sugar syrup or a liqueur, crushed ice and sometimes soda water. Originally other ingredients such as fruit juices tended to be added only in small quantity for colour or subtle flavouring, but now it seems anything goes – but the drink must still be swizzled.

Apple Swizzle

Apple flavour   *Alcohol 2.3*

    1½ msr apple brandy
    ¾ msr dark rum
    3 msr sparkling apple juice
    1½ msr lime juice
    ¾ msr sugar syrup

Shake all but the apple juice and strain into frosted glass. Almost fill with crushed ice and swizzle briefly to frost the glass; add the apple juice, a swizzle stick and straws.   CO

Gin Swizzle

Lime gin flavour   *Alcohol 2.5*

    2½ msr gin
    2 msr soda water
    1½ msr lime juice
    ¾ msr sugar syrup
    1 dash Angostura

Shake all but soda and strain into frosted glass filled with crushed ice. Swizzle briefly to frost the glass, add the soda. Add swizzle stick and straws.   CO

Replace the gin in the following swizzles:

Blue Swizzle	2½ msr white rum	*Alcohol 2.7*
	⅓ msr blue curacao	
Bourbon Swizzle	2½ msr bourbon	*Alcohol 2.5*
Brandy Swizzle	2½ msr brandy	*Alcohol 2.5*
Green Swizzle	2½ msr white rum	*Alcohol 2.7*
	⅓ msr green creme de menthe	
Red Swizzle	2½ msr white rum	
	⅓ msr grenadine	
Rum Swizzle	1½ msr dark rum	
	1 msr white rum	

Tartan Swizzle   2½ msr scotch

Whilst the above are the most common versions, any spirit can be used in a Swizzle: gin, tequila, vodka etc.

Mai Tai Swizzle

Citrus rum flavour   *Alcohol 2.8*

Donn Beach, Don the Beachcomber Restaurant, Hollywood.
Courtesy of Phoebe Beach.

1½ msr Myers's dark rum
1 msr white rum
½ msr triple sec
1 msr grapefruit juice
juice of ½ a lime
¼ msr almond syrup/Falernum
1 dash Angostura
1 dash Pernod

Shake and strain into glass filled with crushed ice, add the spent lime shell and swizzle briefly.
Garnish: slice of pineapple and mint sprigs.   H

Queen's Park Swizzle

Lime rum flavour   *Alcohol 2.0*

A one-time speciality of the Queen's Park Hotel, Trinidad.

2 msr dark rum (preferably Trinidad, Demerara)
2 dashes Angostura
½ msr sugar syrup
juice of ½ a lime
4 mint leaves
2 msr soda water

Squeeze lime, add juice and shell to glass. Fill with crushed ice and mint leaves. Add rum, Angostura and syrup then swizzle until glass frosts. Add the soda and straws. Garnish: fresh sprig of mint.   H

Syracuse Special

Sherry flavour   *Alcohol 1.9*

    1¹/₂ msr sweet sherry
    ³/₄ msr bourbon
    ¹/₂ msr dry sherry
    ¹/₂ msr dry vermouth
    ¹/₄ msr lemon juice
    3 msr lemonade

Add to ice-filled glass. Garnish: seedless grape
and sprig of mint.

G

Tequila Sunrise

Orange flavour   *Alcohol 2.0*

The origin of this recipe can be traced back to Mexico in the early 1930s.

    2 msr gold tequila
    ¹/₂ msr grenadine
    4 msr orange juice

Stir and strain orange and tequila into ice-filled glass,
add the grenadine, allowing it to sink to bottom.
Garnish: orange slice and a cherry.

H

If equal measures of pineapple and orange juice
are used, this becomes a Florida Sunrise.

If Geo. A. Dickel whiskey is used in place of
tequila, this is a Dickel Soon Rise.

Texas Sunset

Fruity flavour   *Alcohol 1.7*

Courtesy of Reunion Tower at Hyatt Regency, Dallas, Texas.

    ³/₄ msr white rum
    ¹/₂ msr apricot brandy
    ¹/₂ msr Bacardi 151 rum (substitute: overproof white)
    2 msr orange juice
    1 msr lemon juice
    ¹/₂ msr sugar syrup
    1 teaspoon egg white
    ³/₄ msr grenadine

Shake briefly with three-quarters of a glassful of
broken ice and pour unstrained. Sprinkle the
grenadine on top; do not stir.

CO

Titanic Uplift

Orange / Fruit flavour

Alcohol 2.2

2 msr Midori
1 msr Plymouth gin
4 msr orange juice

Shake and strain into glass three-quarters filled with broken ice. Garnish: three melon balls, green, red and orange (use food colourants). Serve with a straw.

CO

If grapefruit juice is used in place of orange, this is a Grapefruit Glory.

Tree House

Citrus flavour

Alcohol 2.0

1½ msr Rum Tree
1 msr gold tequila
1 msr grapefruit juice
1 msr pineapple juice
4 msr sparkling bitter lemon

Add to ice-filled glass. Garnish: mint sprig and cherry, add straws.

P

Trouser Rouser

Fruity flavour

Alcohol 1.8

1½ msr scotch
½ msr creme de banane
2 msr mango juice
1 msr pineapple juice
½ msr lime juice
1 teaspoon egg white

Shake and strain into glass three-quarters filled with broken ice. Garnish: sprig of mint and a cherry.

CO

Troya

Grapefruit flavour

Alcohol 1.7

1 msr amaretto
½ msr scotch
½ msr Cointreau
4 msr grapefruit juice

Shake with a glassful of broken ice and pour unstrained. Garnish: slice of pineapple, 2 cherries and a sprig of mint.

CO

Viking's Helmet

Lime flavour

Alcohol 2.3

1½ msr aquavit
¾ msr Swedish vodka
¾ msr lime juice
⅓ msr pineapple syrup
3 msr ginger ale

Add to ice-filled glass with lime twist.

H

West Indian Punch

Fruit rum flavour

Alcohol 2.4

2 msr dark rum
¾ msr creme de banane
1 msr orange juice
1 msr pineapple juice
¾ msr lime juice

Shake briefly with a glassful of crushed ice.
Garnish: fruit in season, add straws.
Sprinkle with grated nutmeg.

H

Wild Cherry

Cherry flavour

Alcohol 2.0

1½ msr Wild Turkey
½ msr cherry brandy
¼ msr white creme de cacao
4 msr cherryade

Add to ice-filled glass. Garnish: cherry
and mint sprig.

H

Winning Horse

Fruit cola flavour

Alcohol 1.8

1 msr Southern Comfort
½ msr dark rum
½ msr rosso vermouth
4½ msr cold cola

Add to ice-filled glass.
Garnish: slice of orange and a cherry.

G

Woo-Woo

Cranberry / Peach flavour   *Alcohol 1.8*

Formerly a Teeny-Weeny Woo-Woo, this had its 15 minutes of fame
when Peach Schnapps first became popular in the 1980s.

    1½ msr peach schnapps
    1 msr vodka
    4 msr cranberry juice

Shake and strain into ice-filled glass.   H

Yellow Fingers

Light / Fruity flavour   *Alcohol 2.5*

John-Anthony Albicocco, proprietor of the rather swish Co-Co's Water
Cafe overlooking the bay at Huntington, Suffolk County, USA,
recommends the following cocktail to favoured guests.

    1 msr Southern Comfort
    1 msr vodka
    ½ msr Galliano
    1 msr orange juice
    2 msr lemonade
    ½ msr egg white
    10 drops blue curacao

Shake all but the curacao and lemonade very
well and strain into glass. Add the lemonade.
Garnish: slice of orange and a cherry. Using a
dropper or thin straw, place the blue curacao
drops in neat rows on frothy white surface.
Serve immediately.   D

Zombie

Fruity flavour   *Alcohol 2.9*

Created in 1934 by Donn Beach at Don the Beachcomber Restaurant,
Hollywood. This was America's first South Sea Island themed restaurant,
and Donn's exciting rum creations with exotic food to match were a great
success, resulting in a chain of Beachcomber restaurants.

Donn was the originator of 63 exotic cocktail recipes, still popular to this
day.

Barlore has it that he produced this cocktail for a guest suffering with a
hangover, who reported feeling like a zombie.

    ½ msr white rum
    1 msr golden rum
    ½ msr dark rum

½ msr cherry brandy
½ msr apricot brandy
2 msr pineapple juice
1 msr orange juice
¾ msr lime juice
½ msr papaya juice
¼ msr almond syrup/Falernum
⅓ msr overproof dark rum

Shake briefly with a glassful of crushed ice.
Garnish: sprig of mint and slices of lime and
pineapple, add straws. Sprinkle the ODR on top,
using long-handled barspoon.

CO

Zulu

Fruit cola flavour

Alcohol 1.9

1 msr dark rum
1 msr dark creme de cacao
½ msr creme de banane
1 msr lime juice
1 teaspoon grenadine
1 teaspoon Pernod
4 msr cold cola

Shake and strain into ice-filled glass, add the cola.
Garnish: slice of lime and a cherry.

CO

Long and Creamy

Drinks made with five fluid measures or more before shaking, and containing at least a third of a measure cream, milk or ice-cream.

Alaskan Orange

Orange flavour

Alcohol 2.3

    2 msr Van Der Hum (substitute: Mandarine Napoléon)
    3/4 msr brandy
    4 tablespoons vanilla ice-cream

Blend briefly with half a glassful of crushed ice.
Garnish: grated orange zest, chocolate and nutmeg.

G

Baileys Milk Shake

Baileys / Coffee flavour

Alcohol 2.3

    1 1/3 msr Baileys
    1 msr white rum
    2/3 msr Kahlua
    3 tablespoons vanilla ice-cream
    1 msr whipped cream

Blend briefly with half a glassful of crushed ice,
float the whipped cream on top.
Garnish: cherry on a stick, add straws.

H

Banana and Coffee Cream Soda

Banana / Coffee flavour   *Alcohol 1.9*

    1½ msr Kahlua
    ½ msr dark rum
    ½ msr creme de banane
    1½ msr whipping cream
    ½ msr lime juice
    4 msr cold soda water
    ½ a ripe banana – mashed

Blend all but soda with a half glassful of
crushed ice, add the soda and straws.
Garnish: cherry and slices of banana and lime.   P

Banana Banshee

Banana flavour   *Alcohol 1.3*

    1 msr white creme de cacao
    1 msr creme de banane
    ½ msr dry sherry
    ⅓ of a banana – mashed
    3 tablespoons vanilla ice-cream

Blend briefly with half a glassful of crushed ice.
Garnish: slice of banana and a cherry.   G

If 1 msr vodka is added, this is a   *Alcohol 2.3*
Screaming Banana Banshee.

Banana Bombshell

Banana flavour   *Alcohol 2.0*

    1½ msr white rum
    1 msr creme de banane
    1 msr coconut cream
    1 msr sugar syrup
    1 msr whipping cream
    4 msr pineapple juice
    ⅓ of a banana – mashed

Blend with half a glassful of crushed ice until smooth.
Garnish: cherry, a slice of pineapple and a slice
of lemon, with excess peel hanging over side
of glass like fuse.   G

Banana Split

Strawberry / Banana flavour   *Alcohol 1.9*

    1 msr creme de banane
    1 msr strawberry liqueur
    1/2 msr dry sherry
    1/3 of a banana – mashed
    1 msr strawberry puree
    3 tablespoons vanilla ice-cream
    1 msr dark creme de cacao

Blend briefly and pour, sprinkle the cacao on top.
Garnish: strawberry and slice of banana, add straws.   G

Barnaby's Buffalo Blizzard

Sweet herb flavour   *Alcohol 2.2*

Courtesy of Barnaby's Restaurant, Buffalo.

In 1977 snowbound victims of a memorable blizzard had nothing better to
do for three days but invent new cocktails. They all agreed this was the best.

    1 msr white creme de cacao
    1 msr Galliano
    3/4 msr vodka
    2 msr milk
    1 teaspoon grenadine
    2 tablespoons vanilla ice-cream
    1 1/2 msr whipped cream

Blend briefly with half a glassful of crushed ice.
Top with the whipped cream. Garnish: cherry.   CO

Barrier Reef

Orange flavour   *Alcohol 3.3*

    2 msr gin
    1 msr triple sec
    1/3 msr Grand Marnier
    1/2 msr blue curacao
    4 tablespoons vanilla ice-cream

Blend briefly and pour into ice-filled glass.
Garnish: blue maraschino cherry, slices of
pineapple and orange, add thick straws.   P

Bonaparte Velvet

Mandarin flavour   *Alcohol 2.1*

    1 msr Mandarine Napoléon
    1 msr cognac
    1 teaspoon Frangelico
    3 tablespoons vanilla ice-cream

Blend briefly with half a glassful of crushed ice.
Garnish: orange slice and a cherry, add straws.   H

Brandy Puff

Brandy flavour   *Alcohol 2.0*

Before Prohibition, Puffs were a popular category of drink in the US.
They are no longer seen commercially.

    2 msr brandy
    3 msr milk
    3 msr soda water

Shake and strain, add the soda.   G
Any spirit can be used, but was usually gin, whisky or rum.

Brazilian Monk

Hazel / Coffee flavour   *Alcohol 2.0*

    1 msr Frangelico
    1 msr Kahlua
    1 msr dark creme de cacao
    1/2 msr dry sherry
    4 tablespoons vanilla ice-cream

Blend briefly. Garnish: mint leaf and cherry
on a stick, sprinkle with grated chocolate.   H

Brown Cow

Coffee flavour   *Alcohol 1.0*

    1 1/2 msr coffee liqueur
    6 msr cold milk

Add to ice-filled glass. Sprinkle with nutmeg, add a straw.   CO
If dark rum is used in place of liqueur, this is a Rum Cow.   *Alcohol 1.5*

Brute

Almond flavour

Alcohol 1.2

   1 msr amaretto
   1 msr dark creme de cacao
   3 tablespoons vanilla ice-cream

Blend briefly with half a glassful of crushed ice.
Garnish: cherry, add straws.

CO

Cherry Chocolate Freeze

Cherry / Chocolate flavour

Alcohol 1.3

   1 msr cherry brandy
   1 msr dark creme de cacao
   1/2 msr chocolate syrup
   2 tablespoons vanilla ice-cream

Blend briefly with half a glassful of crushed ice.
Garnish: sprig of mint mint and cherry on a
stick. Sprinkle with grated chocolate, add straws.

G

Chocolate Monkey

Banana / Chocolate flavour

Alcohol 1.0

   1 msr creme de banane
   1/2 msr white rum
   3/4 msr chocolate syrup
   1/3 of a banana – mashed
   3 tablespoons chocolate ice-cream
   1 1/2 msr whipped cream

Blend briefly with half a glassful of crushed ice,
float the whipped cream on top. Garnish: slice of
banana and a cherry, add straws.

P

Chocolate XS

Chocolate flavour

Alcohol 2.3

   1 msr dark rum
   1 msr dark creme de cacao
   1 msr Baileys
   3/4 msr chocolate syrup
   3 msr milk
   1/3 teaspoon sieved cocoa
   1 tablespoon chocolate ice-cream
   1 msr whipped cream

Blend briefly with a tablespoon of crushed ice,
float the whipped cream on top and serve
with straws. You should be ashamed of yourself! H

Cocobanana

Banana flavour Alcohol 2.1

    1 msr white rum
    1 msr creme de banane
    1/2 msr amaretto
    1/2 msr coconut rum
    3 msr pineapple juice
    1 msr coconut cream
    1/3 of a banana – mashed
    3 tablespoons vanilla ice-cream

Blend briefly with half a glassful of crushed ice.
Garnish: fruit in season, add straws. P

Country Cream

Sweet fruit flavour Alcohol 1.8

    1 msr coffee liqueur
    1 msr pear liqueur
    1/2 msr Campari
    1/3 msr raspberry liqueur
    3 tablespoons vanilla ice-cream

Blend briefly with half a glassful of crushed ice, add straws. G

Crime of Passion

Fruit rum flavour Alcohol 1.0

    1 msr dark rum
    1 msr passion fruit juice
    2 tablespoons vanilla ice-cream
    1/3 msr raspberry syrup
    3 msr cream soda

Beat or blend briefly, pour and add the soda.
Garnish: slice of orange and a cherry, add straws. G

Dreamsicle

Orange flavour

Alcohol 1.2

    1 msr triple sec
    1 msr white creme de cacao
    2 tablespoons vanilla ice-cream
    2 tablespoons orange sherbet/sorbet

Blend briefly with half a glassful of crushed ice.
Garnish: slice of orange and a cherry, add straws.

H

EGG NOGGS

In the seventeenth century Nog was a strong beer brewed in East Anglia, in England, and a noggin was a small mug of beer or liquor. It was quite common there and in America to adulterate such drinks with beaten egg (*see* Flips) and this practice appears to be the origin of the Egg Nogg.

Traditionally consumed on Christmas morning, Egg Noggs are often made in bulk. They can be thickened to taste with extra egg yolk or cream, or thinned with milk.

Baltimore Egg Nogg

Milk brandy flavour

Alcohol 2.0

    1 msr brandy
    1 msr madeira
    1/2 msr dark rum
    4 msr milk
    1/2 msr sugar syrup
    1 small beaten egg

Shake and strain into glass, sprinkle with grated nutmeg. G

Egg Nogg

Brandy/Advocaat flavour

Alcohol 2.0

    1 msr dark rum
    1 msr brandy
    11/2 msr milk
    1 msr whipping cream
    1/2 msr sugar syrup
    1 small beaten egg

Shake well and strain, sprinkle with nutmeg. G

Holiday Egg Nogg (Serves 10)

Rum / Advocaat flavour Alcohol 1.2

    6 msr rum
    6 msr bourbon
    6 beaten eggs
    6 oz/175 g sugar
    1/2 teaspoon salt
    15 fl oz/42 cl whipping cream
    15 fl oz/42 cl milk

Mix in punch bowl until sugar dissolves and chill for four hours. Mix and sprinkle with grated nutmeg.

W

Friesian

Hazelnut flavour Alcohol 1.5

    1 msr Amaretto
    1 msr Frangelico
    3 tablespoons vanilla ice-cream
    1 teaspoon chocolate syrup

Blend briefly with half a glassful of crushed ice. Garnish: cherry, add straws.

CO

Frozen Black Irish

Sweet coffee flavour Alcohol 1.5

    1 msr Kahlua
    1 msr Baileys
    1/2 msr vodka
    2 tablespoons vanilla ice-cream

Blend briefly with half a glassful of crushed ice. Garnish: sprig of mint, add straws.

D

Frozen Coconut

Coconut flavour Alcohol 2.0

    1 1/2 msr white rum
    1 msr coconut rum
    3 tablespoons coconut ice-cream

Rim glass with egg white/sweet grated coconut. Blend briefly with half a glassful of crushed ice. Garnish: cherry on a stick, add short straws.

G

Frozen Gael

Sweet coffee flavour

Courtesy of Invergordon Distillers.

Alcohol 1.4

　　1 msr single grain scotch
　　1 msr Baileys
　　2 tablespoons vanilla ice-cream

Blend briefly with a tablespoon of crushed ice.
Garnish: orange slice.

D

Frozen Irish Coffee

Coffee flavour

Alcohol 1.5

　　1½ msr Irish whiskey
　　5 msr cold black coffee – sweetened to taste
　　1 tablespoon vanilla ice-cream

Shake briefly with three-quarters of a glassful
of crushed ice, top with the ice-cream. Sprinkle
with grated chocolate, add straws.

H

Frozen Key Lime

Lime flavour

Alcohol 1.5

　　1 msr white rum
　　½ msr dark rum
　　1½ msr lime juice
　　3 tablespoons vanilla ice-cream

Blend briefly with half a glassful of crushed ice.
Garnish. slice of lime and a cherry, add short straws.

G

Gamble

Fruity flavour

Alcohol 1.5

　　1 msr apricot brandy
　　¾ msr Mandarine Napoléon
　　½ msr sweet sherry
　　1 msr mango juice
　　3 tablespoons vanilla ice-cream

Blend briefly with half a glassful of crushed ice.

G

Hammer Horror

Coffee flavour Alcohol 1.7

    1 msr vodka
    1 msr Kahlua
    4 tablespoons vanilla ice-cream
Blend briefly and sprinkle with
grated chocolate, add straws.

H

Island Affair

Fruity flavour Alcohol 1.5

    1¼ msr melon liqueur
    ½ msr Cointreau
    ⅓ msr blue curacao
    1½ msr orange juice
    2 msr mango juice
    1 msr whipped cream

Shake and strain all but cream and curacao into
glass three-quarters filled with broken ice. Add
curacao, allowing it to sink to bottom, float the cream
on top. Garnish: fruit in season, add straws.

P

Island Delight

Cherry rum flavour Alcohol 2.0

    1 msr cherry vodka
    ½ msr white rum
    ½ msr dark rum
    3 tablespoons vanilla ice-cream
    1 msr whipped cream
    1 teaspoon grenadine
Blend briefly with half a glassful of crushed ice.
Top with the whipped cream and sprinkle the
Grenadine on top.

G

Jamaican Iced Coffee

Rum / Coffee flavour Alcohol 1.6

    1 msr dark rum
    1 msr Tia Maria
    ¾ msr whipping cream
    4 msr cold black coffee
Shake and strain into glass filled with crushed ice.
Add short straws and sprig of mint.

G

Kahlua Cream Soda

Coffee flavour

Alcohol 1.2

    2 msr Kahlua
    1½ msr whipping cream
    4 msr soda water

Shake and strain, add the soda and straws.   H

Kaiser's Jest

Sweet mint flavour

Alcohol 1.3

    1 msr white creme de cacao
    1 msr peppermint schnapps
    2 tablespoons vanilla ice-cream

Blend briefly with half a glassful of crushed ice, add straws. D

Las Vegas

Fruity flavour

Alcohol 1.5

    1½ msr gold tequila
    2 msr coconut cream
    2 msr orange juice
    2 msr pineapple juice
    1 msr whipping cream

Blend briefly with half a glassful of crushed ice.
Garnish: slice of pineapple, add straws.   P

If vodka is used in place of tequila, this is a Vodka Las Vegas.

Lazy Daze

Fruit / Mint flavour

Alcohol 2.5

    1 msr vodka
    1 msr coffee liqueur
    1 msr melon liqueur
    ⅓ msr green creme de menthe
    1¼ msr whipping cream
    2 msr lemonade

Shake and strain into ice-filled glass, and
add the lemonade. Float the cream on top.
Garnish: cherry and sprig of mint.   H

Leprechaun's Coffee

Coffee flavour

Alcohol 1.7

    1½ msr Baileys
    ¾ msr Irish whiskey
    5 msr cold black coffee

Shake and strain into glass three-quarters filled with broken ice.

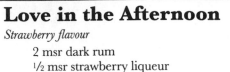

H

Love in the Afternoon

Strawberry flavour

Alcohol 2.3

    2 msr dark rum
    ½ msr strawberry liqueur
    1 msr orange juice
    ¾ msr coconut cream
    ½ msr sugar syrup
    ½ msr whipping cream
    3–4 strawberries

Blend until smooth, add half a glassful of crushed ice and blend again briefly. Garnish: strawberry, add straws.

P

Martian Sex Monster

Melon / Herb flavour

Alcohol 2.1

    1 msr melon liqueur
    ¾ msr Galliano
    ¾ msr cognac
    3 tablespoons vanilla ice-cream

Blend briefly with half a glassful of crushed ice. Sprinkle the melon liqueur on top, add straws.

H

Ménage à Trois

Strawberry / Chocolate flavour

Alcohol 1.0

    1 msr vodka
    1½ msr strawberry puree
    1 msr coconut cream
    2 tablespoons chocolate ice-cream

Blend briefly and sprinkle with grated chocolate. Garnish: strawberry, add short straws.

R

MILK PUNCHES

These are a long, spirit or liqueur-based drink made with cold milk.

Bourbon Milk Punch

Bourbon flavour   *Alcohol 2.0*

    2 msr bourbon
    1/2 msr sugar syrup
    5 msr full cream milk

Shake and strain into ice-filled glass. Garnish: cherry
on a stick, sprinkle with grated nutmeg or cinnamon.   CO

Replace the bourbon in the following popular Milk Punches:

Brandy Milk Punch	2 msr brandy/cognac	*Alcohol 2.0*
Comfortable Milk Punch	2 msr Southern Comfort	*Alcohol 2.0*
Rum Milk Punch	1 msr white rum 1 msr dark rum	*Alcohol 2.0*
Rye Milk Punch	2 msr Canadian whisky	*Alcohol 2.0*
Scotch Milk Punch	2 msr Scotch whisky	*Alcohol 2.0*

Butterscotch Milk Punch

Sweet scotch flavour   *Alcohol 1.6*

    1msr Drambuie
    1/2 msr scotch
    1 teaspoon Cointreau
    4 msr milk
    1/3 msr sugar syrup

Shake and strain into ice-filled glass, sprinkle with nutmeg. H

Milky Way Punch

Apricot flavour   *Alcohol 1.7*

    2/3 msr dark rum
    2/3 msr bourbon
    2/3 msr apricot brandy
    41/2 msr milk

Shake and strain into ice-filled glass,
sprinkle with cinnamon.   H

Mistress

Sweet fruit flavour   *Alcohol 2.1*

    1½ msr gin
    1 msr white creme de cacao
    1 teaspoon Campari
    2 msr pineapple juice
    1 msr passion fruit juice
    1 msr whipping cream

Shake and strain into ice-filled glass, sprinkle
the Campari on top. Add cherry.   H

Mozart Eiskaffee

Chocolate coffee flavour   *Alcohol 1.0*

    2 msr Mozart
    4 msr cold black coffee sweetened – to taste
    1 tablespoon vanilla ice-cream
    1 msr whipped cream

Blend briefly with half a glassful of crushed ice,
top with the whipped cream. Garnish: grated chocolate. CO

Nuts Banane

Sweet banana flavour   *Alcohol 1.6*

    1 msr Frangelico
    1 msr creme de banane
    ½ msr kirsch
    1 msr whipping cream
    ½ a banana – mashed

Blend with half a glassful of crushed ice until smooth.
Garnish: slice of banana and a cherry. CO

One Ball Left

Sweet mint flavour   *Alcohol 1.7*

    1 msr cognac
    1 msr peppermint schnapps
    3 msr cream soda
    1 msr whipping cream

Shake and strain into ice-filled glass, add the soda.
(Some types of soda will cause the cream to congeal.) H

Peanut Coffee Frenzy

Peanut flavour   *Alcohol 1.0*

    1½ msr Kahlua
    3 msr cold milk
    2 tablespoons vanilla ice-cream
    ½ msr smooth peanut butter
    3 msr 7UP

Blend briefly with half a glassful of crushed ice, add the 7UP. P

Pistachio Rumba

Pistachio flavour   *Alcohol 2.0*

    2 msr white rum
    3 tablespoons pistachio ice-cream

Blend briefly with half a glassful of crushed ice. Garnish:
slice of lime and cherry on a stick, add short straws.   G

Plantation Coffee

Coffee flavour   *Alcohol 1.8*

    1 msr golden rum
    ½ msr Grand Marnier
    ½ msr dark creme de cacao
    4 msr cold black coffee
    ¾ msr double cream

Shake and strain into glass filled with crushed ice.
Sprinkle with grated chocolate, add short straws.   G

Ramos Fizz

Lemon flavour   *Alcohol 2.0*

Created around 1888 at Henrico Ramos's Imperial Cabinet Saloon, New
Orleans, USA. The precise formula was a closely guarded secret until the
saloon closed in 1920 due to Prohibition. Only then did Henrico's
brother, Charles Henry, reveal this recipe.

    2 msr Old Tom gin
    (substitute: gin and dash of sugar syrup)
    3 drops orange flower water
    (substitute: dry orange curacao)
    1 msr lemon juice
    ¾ msr lime juice
    1 msr egg white
    1 msr full cream milk or light (whipping) cream

1 teaspoon powdered (caster) sugar
3 msr soda water

Shake with half a glassful of crushed ice and
pour unstrained, add the soda and straws.

H

Root Beer Float

Sweet herb flavour   *Alcohol 1.7*

1 msr Cointreau
1 msr Kahlua
4 msr cold cola
1/2 msr lemon juice
1 tablespoon vanilla ice-cream

Add ice-cream to glass half filled with ice.
Add remaining ingredients gently, add straws.

CO

Rum Sunday

Sweet rum flavour   *Alcohol 1.6*

1 msr dark rum
1/2 msr sweet sherry
1/2 msr grenadine
3 tablespoons vanilla ice-cream
2 teaspoons overproof dark rum

Blend briefly with half a glassful of crushed ice.
Float the overproof rum and sprinkle with
grated chocolate.

CO

Strawberry and Coffee Cream Soda

Banana / Coffee flavour   *Alcohol 1.9*

1 1/2 msr Kahlua
1/2 msr dark rum
1/2 msr strawberry liqueur
1 msr whipping cream
1/2 msr lime juice
3 msr cream soda
2 msr strawberry puree

Blend all but soda briefly with half a
glassful of crushed ice, add the soda.
Garnish: slice of banana between two
halves of a strawberry, add straws.

P

Strawberry Cascade

Strawberry flavour *Alcohol 2.6*

Mr Henryk Mulla, Cascades Cocktail Lounge, courtesy of the Terrace Inter-
Continental Hotel, Adelaide, South Australia.

    1 msr vodka
    1 msr Galliano
    1 msr Kahlua
    5 msr strawberry puree
    2 msr whipping cream

Blend all but Kahlua briefly with half a
glassful of crushed ice, sprinkle the Kahlua
on top. Garnish: sugar-dipped half strawberry,
serve with straws.   P

Strawberry Cream

Strawberry flavour *Alcohol 1.0*

    1 msr gin
    3 msr strawberry puree
    1/2 msr lemon juice
    1 teaspoon caster sugar
    2 tablespoons strawberry ice-cream

Blend briefly with half a glassful of crushed ice.
Garnish: half a sugar-dipped strawberry, add straws.   G

Strawberry Fetish

Strawberry flavour *Alcohol 1.5*

    1 1/2 msr strawberry schnapps (substitute: liqueur)
    1/2 msr Frangelico
    1/4 msr grenadine
    1 msr whipping cream
    2 msr lemonade
    1 msr soda water

Shake and strain into glass filled with broken ice,
add the lemonade and soda. Garnish: strawberry.   CO

Strawberry Knockout

Strawberry flavour   *Alcohol 1.3*

½ msr amaretto
½ msr kirsch
1 msr white creme de cacao
4 msr strawberry puree
1 msr whipping cream
2 msr whipped cream

Blend briefly with half a glassful of crushed ice, top with the
whipped cream. Garnish: strawberry, add straws.   P

Waikiki Beach

Fruity flavour   *Alcohol 1.8*

1½ msr white rum
½ msr amaretto
½ msr coconut cream
2 msr pineapple juice
1 msr whipping cream
1 msr passion fruit juice

Rim glass with egg white/sweet grated coconut.
Shake and strain into ice-filled glass.   G

Will to Live

Mandarin flavour   *Alcohol 2.0*

1 msr Mandarine Napoléon
1 msr amaretto
⅓ msr cognac
3 tablespoons vanilla ice-cream

Blend briefly with half a glassful of crushed ice.
Garnish: orange slice and a cherry, add straws.   H

If Pisang Ambon is used in place of   *Alcohol 1.7*
Mandarine Napoléon, this is a Green Banana.

Non-Alcoholic

Acapulco Gold
Fruity flavour

>   3 msr pineapple juice
>   1 msr coconut cream
>   1 msr whipping cream
>   ½ msr grapefruit juice

Shake and strain into glass half filled with broken ice.   H

Apple of My Eye
Apple flavour

>   2 msr apple juice
>   ⅓ msr blackcurrant syrup
>   1 msr whipping cream

Blend briefly with a glassful of crushed ice.
Sprinkle with cinnamon.   R

Banana Boat
Banana flavour

>   ½ a mashed banana
>   3 msr milk
>   1 msr pineapple juice
>   1 msr coconut cream

Blend briefly with half a glassful of crushed ice.
Garnish: slice of banana and a cherry.   CO

Bingo

Fruity flavour

    1 msr papaya juice
    1 msr orange juice
    1 msr coconut cream
    1 msr pineapple juice
    1/2 msr lime juice
    1 msr strawberry puree
    1/4 msr grenadine

Blend briefly with a glassful of crushed ice, add straws.   G

Bitter Experience

Sparkling citrus flavour

    2 msr orange juice
    1/2 msr lime juice
    2 msr sparkling bitter lemon

Add to glass filled with broken ice, add short straws.   G

Bora-Bora

Pineapple flavour

    3 msr pineapple juice
    3 msr dry ginger ale
    1/2 msr grenadine
    1 teaspoon lime juice

Shake and strain into ice-filled glass, add
the ginger. Garnish: slice of lime and a cherry.   G

Brontosaurus

Citrus flavour

    3 msr grapefruit juice
    1/2 msr lime juice
    1/2 msr grenadine
    3 msr lemonade

Shake and strain into ice-filled glass, add the
lemonade. Garnish: celery stick.   H

Canadian Pride

Grapefruit flavour

Made from the evaporated sap of the *acer saccharum* tree, the unique
flavour of maple syrup gives added dimension to this cocktail, whilst

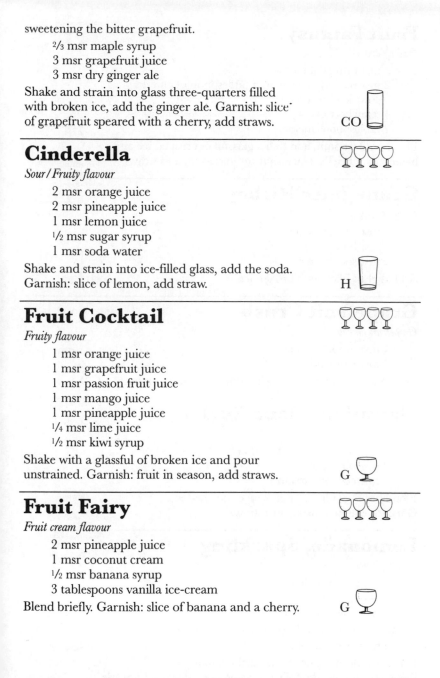

sweetening the bitter grapefruit.

> ²/₃ msr maple syrup
> 3 msr grapefruit juice
> 3 msr dry ginger ale

Shake and strain into glass three-quarters filled with broken ice, add the ginger ale. Garnish: slice of grapefruit speared with a cherry, add straws.   CO

Cinderella

Sour / Fruity flavour

> 2 msr orange juice
> 2 msr pineapple juice
> 1 msr lemon juice
> ¹/₂ msr sugar syrup
> 1 msr soda water

Shake and strain into ice-filled glass, add the soda. Garnish: slice of lemon, add straw.   H

Fruit Cocktail

Fruity flavour

> 1 msr orange juice
> 1 msr grapefruit juice
> 1 msr passion fruit juice
> 1 msr mango juice
> 1 msr pineapple juice
> ¹/₄ msr lime juice
> ¹/₂ msr kiwi syrup

Shake with a glassful of broken ice and pour unstrained. Garnish: fruit in season, add straws.   G

Fruit Fairy

Fruit cream flavour

> 2 msr pineapple juice
> 1 msr coconut cream
> ¹/₂ msr banana syrup
> 3 tablespoons vanilla ice-cream

Blend briefly. Garnish: slice of banana and a cherry.   G

Fruit Fantasy

Fruity flavour

    3 msr orange juice
    2 msr pineapple juice or a tablespoon of chunks
    1/2 msr kiwi syrup
    4 strawberries
    2 tablespoons melon

Blend until smooth, add half a glassful of crushed ice and
blend again briefly. Garnish: fruit in season, add straws.   P

Grape Juice Rickey

Fruity flavour

    2 msr red grape juice
    1 msr lime juice
    2 msr soda water

Add to glass filled with broken ice.   H

Grapefruit Crush

Grapefruit flavour

    4 msr grapefruit juice
    4 msr lemonade

Add to ice-filled glass.Garnish: mint sprig, add a straw.   CO

Hawaiian Island Surfer

Fruity flavour

    4 msr orange sherbet/sorbet
    2 msr pineapple juice
    1 msr coconut cream

Blend briefly with half a glassful of crushed ice.
Garnish: fruit in season, add straws.   G

Lemonade, Sparkling

Lemon flavour

    1 1/2 msr lemon juice
    1 1/2 msr sugar syrup
    4 msr cold soda water

Shake and strain into frosted glass, add the soda.
Garnish: slice of lemon; add straws.   R

If 1 1/2 msr orange juice replaces the lemon juice,
this is an Orangeade. If lime juice is used, this is a Limeade.

Lemonade, Pink

Lemon flavour

    1¹/₂ msr lemon juice
    1¹/₂ msr sugar syrup
    ¹/₃ msr grenadine
    4 msr cold water

Shake and strain into ice-filled glass.
Garnish: cherry and lemon slice, add straws.
If no grenadine is used, this is a Still Lemonade.

H

Lemon Ice-Cream Soda

Lemon / Vanilla flavour

    1¹/₂ msr lemon juice
    1¹/₂ msr sugar syrup
    3 msr soda water
    2 tablespoons vanilla ice-cream

Blend briefly with half a glassful of crushed ice,
add the soda and mix gently. Serve with straws.

P

Magic Island

Fruity flavour

    3 msr pineapple juice
    1 msr grapefruit juice
    1 msr coconut cream
    ¹/₂ msr whipping cream
    1 teaspoon grenadine

Blend briefly with three-quarters of a glassful of crushed ice.
Garnish: fruit in season, add short straws.

G

Mandate

Mandarin / Lemon flavour

    4 msr mandarin juice
    3 msr sparkling bitter lemon
    1 teaspoon raspberry syrup

Add to ice-filled glass.

G

Merlin's Treat

Fruity flavour

    2 msr mango juice
    1 msr pineapple juice

1 msr orange juice
1/2 msr strawberry syrup
2 msr dry ginger ale

Shake and strain into ice-filled glass, add
the ginger. Garnish: fruit in season, add straws.
Sprinkle with grated nutmeg.

G

Mickey Mouse

Cola / Vanilla flavour

> 5 msr cold cola
> 1 tablespoon vanilla ice-cream
> 1 msr whipped cream

Add cola, then ice-cream to ice-filled glass. Top with
the whipped cream. Garnish: two cherries and
grated chocolate. Serve on a napkin with straws.

H

Mock Daisy Crusta

Lime / Fruit flavour

> 1 1/2 msr lime juice
> 1 msr sugar syrup
> 1/2 msr raspberry syrup
> 1/4 msr grenadine
> 3 msr soda water

Rim glass with lime / caster sugar, add spiral of
lime and fill up with crushed ice. Stir lime juice
and both syrups, strain into glass. Add the soda
and sprinkle the grenadine on top.

G

Passion Cooler

Fruity flavour

> 2 msr pineapple juice
> 2 msr mango juice
> 1 msr orange juice
> 1 msr passion fruit juice
> 1/3 of a banana – mashed

Blend briefly with half a glassful of crushed ice.
Add spiral of orange peel. Garnish: slice of
banana and cherry.

G

Peach Magnifico

Fruity flavour

>   2 msr peach juice
>   1 msr mango juice
>   4 msr dry ginger ale

Add to ice-filled glass. Garnish: fruit in season. **G**

Pineapple Island

Pineapple / Coconut flavour

>   2 tablespoons pineapple pieces
>   2 tablespoons coconut ice-cream

Blend with half a glassful of crushed ice until smooth.
Garnish: slice of pineapple and a cherry, add straws. **CO**

Pomola

Fruit cola flavour

>   1 msr lime juice
>   5 msr cold cola
>   1/3 msr grenadine

Add to ice-filled glass. Garnish: cherry and
slice of lime, add straws. **H**

Queen Charlie

Subtle fruit flavour

>   1/2 msr grenadine
>   3 msr soda water
>   3 msr lemonade

Add to ice-filled glass. Garnish: fruit in season, add straws. **H**

Rosemary

Strawberry flavour

>   3 msr strawberry puree
>   1 msr guava juice
>   1 msr pineapple juice
>   1/4 msr lime juice
>   1 teaspoon strawberry syrup
>   2 msr lemonade

Shake and strain into glass three-quarters filled
with crushed ice, add the lemonade.
Garnish: lime slice and strawberry, add straws. **H**

175

Shirley's Sister

Strawberry flavour

> 3 msr lemonade
> 3/4 msr grenadine
> 2 tablespoons strawberry ice-cream
> 1 teaspoon chocolate syrup

Half fill glass with broken ice. Add lemonade and Grenadine.
Fill up with the ice-cream and top with the chocolate.
Garnish: strawberry, add straws.　H

Southern Ginger

Ginger mint flavour

> 5 msr dry ginger ale
> 1 sprig of mint
> 1/2 msr sugar syrup
> 1/2 msr lemon juice

Crush mint gently in glass, fill up with broken ice.
Add remaining ingredients and mix gently,
serve with straws.　H

St. Clement's

Citrus flavour

> 2 msr orange juice
> 2 msr sparkling bitter lemon

Add to glass filled with broken ice.
Garnish: slices of orange and lemon, add straws.　H

Strawberry Kiss

Strawberry flavour

Who could fail to enjoy a cocktail of strawberries and cream?

> 3 msr strawberry puree
> 1 1/2 msr pineapple juice
> 1/2 msr lemon juice
> 1/2 msr whipping cream
> 1/2 teaspoon caster sugar

Blend briefly with half a glassful of crushed ice.
Garnish: half a caster sugar-coated strawberry.　G

Strawberry Salad

Strawberry flavour

  2 msr strawberry puree
  1 msr apple juice
  1 msr papaya juice
  1 msr pineapple juice
  2 msr soda water

Shake and strain into glass filled with broken ice,
add the soda. Garnish: fruit in season, add straws.   P

Strawberry Split

Strawberry flavour

  2 msr strawberry puree
  1 msr apple juice
  1 msr pineapple juice
  ½ msr lime juice
  ⅓ msr strawberry syrup
  2 msr lemonade

Blend briefly with half a glassful of crushed ice,
add the lemonade. Garnish: strawberry, add straws.   P

Summer Rain

Fruity flavour

  1 msr raspberry puree
  1 msr grapefruit juice
  1 msr pineapple juice
  2 msr orange sherbet/sorbet
  1 msr lemonade

Blend briefly with half a glassful of crushed ice,
add the lemonade. Garnish: fruit in season, add straws.   H

Summertime Soda

Citrus/Vanilla flavour

  1 msr orange juice
  1 msr grapefruit juice
  1 msr lemon juice
  1 teaspoon caster sugar
  3 msr soda water
  1 tablespoon vanilla ice-cream

Dissolve sugar in juices, add with soda to glass three-quarters filled with ice. Top with the ice-cream. Garnish: fruits in season, add straws.   H

Tarzan's Juicy Cooler

Fruity flavour

Yoghurt is an unusual ingredient in a cocktail, but works very well here by providing a refreshing complement to the fruit juices.

> 3 msr orange juice
> 3 msr pineapple juice
> 1/4 msr grenadine
> 1/2 msr lemon juice
> 1 tablespoon strawberry yoghurt
> 2 teaspoons clear honey

Blend briefly with half a glassful of crushed ice. Garnish: slice of orange speared with a cherry, add straws.   H

Tenderberry

Strawberry flavour

> 2 msr dry ginger ale
> 1/2 msr grenadine
> 1 msr double cream
> 3 msr strawberry puree
> 1 teaspoon caster sugar

Blend briefly with three-quarters of a glassful of crushed ice, add the ginger ale. Garnish: strawberry.   H

Ugly Virgin

Fruity flavour

> 2 msr tangerine/mandarin juice
> 2 msr grapefruit juice
> 2 msr lemonade

Shake and strain into ice-filled glass, add the lemonade. Garnish: slice of Ugli fruit, add straws.   H

VIRGINS

Non-alcoholic versions of popular cocktails.

Virgin Bellini

Peach flavour

2 msr peach juice
1 teaspoon grenadine
2 msr soda water

Add to glass.

W

Virgin Colada

Pineapple flavour

3 msr pineapple juice
2 msr coconut cream
1/3 msr whipping cream
3/4 msr lime juice

Shake and strain into glass filled with crushed ice.
Garnish: slice of pineapple and a cherry,
add a straw.

G

Virgin Raspberry Daiquiri

Raspberry flavour

3 msr raspberry puree
2 msr pineapple juice
1/2 msr lemon juice
1 teaspoon caster sugar
1/2 msr raspberry syrup

Blend briefly with half a glassful of crushed ice.
Garnish: raspberries.

G

Virgin Mary

Tomato flavour

A Bloody Mary without vodka.

G

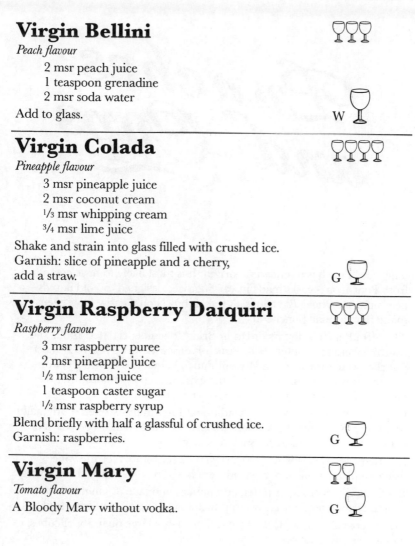

Punches and Cups

The word Punch is of uncertain origin. It is most likely to have come from Puncheon – casks made in varying sizes designed to hold liquids – a beer puncheon held 72 gallons. A punch bowl could easily have been made from a small puncheon.

The term Punch is first recorded in British documents dated 1632, and by 1671 there are references to Punch Houses. However, in 1632 most punches were similar to the Wassail Punch below, made with ale, brandy or wine. It was only in 1655, with the exploration of Jamaica, that the basis of most punches was discovered – rum.

Cups, also made in bulk, are a traditional English drink offered originally to hunting party members before departure. These tend to be based on wine or lower-alcohol spirits such as sloe gin.

In either case, specialised glassware can be substituted for the wine glasses indicated. Alcohol measures are based on an 11 cl/4 fl oz serving.

If a drink is too strong or bitter, add either lemonade or ginger ale to taste. Always offer alternatives to punch, including alcohol-free drinks.

Where possible, use a block of ice rather than a large quantity of cubes, to avoid excessive dilution.

Bacardi Champagne Punch
(30 people)

Fruit / Champagne flavour   *Alcohol 1.5*

    50 cl white Bacardi rum
    10 cl triple sec
    10 cl amaretto
    5 cl grenadine

5 cl sugar syrup
1 pineapple cut into wedges (or large tin of chunks)
2 x 75 cl bottles champagne
1 litre sparkling water

Combine ingredients in bowl, cover and chill
for minimum 2 hours, add champagne, water
and a little ice when ready to serve. Add 5–10
frozen strawberries.

 W

Boatman's Cup (21 people)

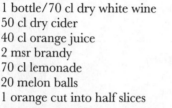

Fruity flavour　　　　　　　　　　　*Alcohol 0.6*

1 bottle/70 cl dry white wine
50 cl dry cider
40 cl orange juice
2 msr brandy
70 cl lemonade
20 melon balls
1 orange cut into half slices

Mix and chill all but fruit and lemonade in a
punch bowl for 2–3 hours. Add remaining
ingredients when ready to serve.

 W

Bombay Punch (40 people)

Champagne / Wine flavour　　　　　　*Alcohol 2.3*

1/2 litre sweet sherry
1/2 litre brandy
3 msr triple sec
3 msr maraschino
2 litres champagne
1 litre sparkling water
6 msr lemon juice
5 msr sugar syrup

Add to punch bowl with sufficient ice to chill.
Add sliced fruits in season and serve.

W

Boston Punch (16 people)

Apple wine flavour

Alcohol 1.3

75 cl champagne
28 cl cider
14 cl brandy
2 msr triple sec
3 msr dark rum
4 msr lemon juice
40 cl sparkling water
1 tablespoon sugar

Dissolve sugar and combine ingredients in punch bowl. Add thin wedges of apple and sufficient ice to chill.

W

Brandy Punch (7 people)

Brandy flavour

Alcohol 2.6

50 cl brandy
12 cl dark rum
3 cl lemon juice
20 cl water
30 cl dry ginger ale
1 sliced orange
1 tablespoon pineapple chunks
1 tablespoon raspberries

Combine in punch bowl. When ready to serve, add ginger ale and sufficient ice to chill.

W

Bride's Bowl (27 people)

Fruit / Champagne flavour

Alcohol 1.9

25 cl brandy or cognac
3 cl cherry brandy
50 cl gold rum
12 cl lemon juice
20 cl orange juice
40 cl pineapple juice
1 pineapple cut into wedges (or large tin of chunks)
1 sliced orange
2 x 75 cl bottles champagne

Combine ingredients in a punch bowl, cover and chill for at least 2 hours. Add champagne and a little ice when ready to serve.

W

Champagne Pineapple Punch
(15 people)

Fruity flavour   *Alcohol 1.0*

   50 cl sauternes
   30 cl pineapple juice
   10 cl lemon juice
   60 g caster sugar
   200 g pineapple chunks
   75 cl champagne

Add all but champagne to large jug and mix until
sugar dissolves. Chill for minimum 2 hours.
To serve, pour into individual glasses until
two-thirds full and top up with the champagne.
Allow a few chunks of pineapple to fall into each glass.   W

Champagne Punch (30 people)

Champagne flavour   *Alcohol 1.2*

   2 litres champagne
   3 msr brandy
   2 msr maraschino
   3 msr triple sec
   1 litre sparkling water
   200 g / 7 oz sugar

Add sugar to bowl and dissolve in the spirits plus a little
water. When ready to serve, add champagne, water, fruits
in season and sufficient ice to chill.   W

Champagne Spray Punch
(28 people)

Fruity flavour   *Alcohol 0.6*

   75 cl champagne
   25 cl creme de cassis
   5 cl lime juice
   4 tablespoons clear honey
   1 litre cranberry juice
   1 litre sparkling water – or less according to taste

Dissolve honey in juice and add with remaining
ingredients to punch bowl and mix. Add sufficient
ice to chill. Garnish: 3 or 4 slices of lime.   W

Confetti Punch (40 people)

Orange / Wine flavour   *Alcohol 1.2*

    70 cl white rum
    1½ litres dry sparkling wine
    1 litre lemonade
    70 cl white grape juice
    50 cl orange juice
    10 halved strawberries

Chill ingredients for minimum 2 hours. When
ready to serve, combine in bowl with a little ice.

W

El Grito (14 people)

Strawberry flavour   *Alcohol 2.0*

Traditionally served at the Mexican *Fiestas Particias*.

    70 cl gold tequila
    70 cl strawberry puree
    10–15 cl sugar syrup (to taste)
    6 washed, sliced strawberries

Add to punch bowl with sufficient crushed
ice to make contents slushy.

W

Fish House Punch (16 people)

Lemon flavour   *Alcohol 1.3*

The various recipes for this punch all stem from that first served in 1732
by Captain Samuel Morris at the 'State in Schuylkill', a social club on the
Schuylkill River, Philadelphia, USA. Members would meet at the Fish
House, fry their fish and drink the punch – they still do.

    14 cl lemon juice
    75 g caster sugar
    30 cl cognac or brandy
    14 cl peach brandy
    14 cl dark rum
    1 litre sparkling water

Combine and chill for minimum 2 hours, add
water when ready to serve. Add slices of lemon.

W

Fruit Juice Cup (24 people)

Fruity flavour

Alcohol 0.5

70 cl red lambrusco sparkling wine
10 cl dark rum
50 cl orange juice
10 cl lemon juice
20 cl pineapple juice
10 cl sugar syrup
1 litre ginger ale

Add slices of orange and lemon. Add to bowl with ample ice
to chill and serve immediately. Exotic fruit juices can be added
in small quantity according to taste. This cup can be fortified
with white rum, but don't forget to count the units!   W

Ginger Punch (17 people)

Citrus / Ginger flavour

Alcohol 0.7

70 cl dry white wine
4 msr/10 cl golden rum
15 cl grapefruit juice
30 cl orange juice
70 cl dry ginger ale

Combine in large jug and chill for 1–2 hours,
add the ginger when ready to serve.   W

Knockout Punch (12 people)

Herb cider flavour

Alcohol 0.8

1 litre cider
1 msr gin
1 msr Benedictine
1 msr brandy
1 msr peach brandy
30 cl lemonade

Combine in large jug and chill for 1–2 hours,
add the lemonade when ready to serve.   W

Parisiana Punch (11 people)

Brandy wine flavour

Alcohol 1.9

> 75 cl champagne
> 30 cl madeira
> 12.5 cl/5 msr cognac
> ½ cup/100 g sugar
> 2 lemons washed

Cut lemons into half slices. Add all ingredients except champagne to a large jug and mix until sugar dissolves. Chill for 2–3 hours and add champagne when ready to serve.

W

Pimm's No.1 Cup (25 people)

Fruity flavour

Alcohol 0.8

> 70 cl Pimm's No.1
> 200 cl lemonade/sparkling citrus drink

Add to bowl with ice block. Add slices of lemon, apple, orange, cucumber and a sprig of mint.

W

Roman Punch (27 people)

Champagne/Orange flavour

Alcohol 1.6

> 1½ litres champagne
> 50 cl dark rum
> 2 msr/5 cl triple sec
> 3 beaten egg whites
> 700 g/24 oz sugar
> 60 cl orange juice
> 20 cl lemon juice
> grated zest of one orange

Mix all but champagne and rum. Combine in bowl with ample ice and orange slices.

W

Sangria (12 people)

Fruity flavour

Alcohol 1.3

There are many versions of Sangria; in Spain they often contain a measure or two of the local liqueur. Here is a basic recipe with which to experiment.

> 75 cl medium red Spanish wine
> 4 msr Spanish brandy
> 20 cl soda water (or lemonade)

juice of 1 orange and 1 lemon
sliced whole orange, lemon and lime
1 tablespoon caster sugar (or to taste)

Combine ingredients in jug half filled with ice,
dissolve sugar and add soda. Serve immediately.

W

Sauternes House Punch

(14 people)

Sweet wine flavour   *Alcohol 1.6*

1½ litres sauternes
1 msr Grand Marnier
1 msr dry orange curacao
1 msr maraschino
125 g/4 oz sugar

Dissolve sugar in wine and combine all
ingredients in large jug with ample ice to cool.
Add fruits in season.

W

Scorpion Punch (11 people)

Fruit/Wine flavour   *Alcohol 2.1*

30 cl white rum
70 cl dry white wine
5 cl brandy
3 cl almond syrup
5 cl lemon juice
5 cl orange juice

Mix together in large ice-filled jug, add
slices of orange and sprig of mint.

W

Somerset Punch (16 people)

Fruity flavour   *Alcohol 0.6*

1 litre dry cider
15 cl dry white wine
2 msr apple brandy
15 cl orange juice
5 cl/2 msr lemon juice
15 cl apple juice
30 cl dry ginger ale

Combine in punch bowl with large block of ice.
Add sliced strawberries.

W

Strawberry Punch (20 people)

Strawberry flavour   *Alcohol 1.2*

    70 cl white sparkling wine
    70 cl medium red wine
    20 cl brandy
    10 cl strawberry liqueur
    1 msr lemon juice
    5 cl strawberry syrup
    50 cl lemonade

Combine in punch bowl with large block of ice, add sliced strawberries.

W

Toledo Punch (90 people)

Wine flavour   *Alcohol 1.1*

Based on the recipe given by Harry Johnson in his *Bartender's Manual*, 1882. Johnson, a straight-talking Californian, opened his first bar in Chicago around 1868.

To a large punch bowl add 1 lb/450 g sugar (start with half this and add more to taste), 1 litre soda water, juice of 2 lemons, 1/2 litre/50 cl cognac, 1 small bunch wintergreen or mint sprigs, 2 washed oranges – thinly sliced into half rings, 1/2 a pineapple – diced, 5–6 washed and halved strawberries and seedless grapes.

Dissolve the sugar in the above, then add: 3 x 75 cl bottles champagne, 1/2 litre/50 cl ordinary brandy, 2 x 75 cl bottles claret, 2 x 75 cl bottles white Rhine wine, 3 litres water. Add a block of ice and serve.

W

Trinidad Rum Punch
(20 people)

Alcohol 1.6

Lemon rum flavour

    1 litre water
    500 g sugar
    75 cl dark (preferably Trinidad) rum
    40 cl lemon or lime juice
    1 teaspoon Angostura

Boil water and dissolve the sugar. Add remaining ingredients. Serve hot and sprinkle with nutmeg. Originally a red hot poker was plunged into punch before serving – mainly for effect.

W

Tropical Punch (30 people)

Fruity flavour   *Alcohol 1.3*

70 cl gold rum
50 cl apricot liqueur
75 cl pineapple juice
75 cl grapefruit juice
30 cl orange juice
20 cl papaya juice
10 cl mango juice
10 cl passion fruit juice
5 cl lemon juice

Combine in bowl, add fruits in season and
sufficient ice to chill.

W

Wassail Bowl/Punch
(7 people)

Alcohol 2.0

Sweet beer flavour

There are numerous old English and Welsh Wassail recipes in circulation,
most are served hot and they commonly use cored, mashed, baked
apples, beaten eggs, various spices, madeira, brandy and cider. The
following is a basic version with which to experiment.

3.5 litres ale or dark beer
125 g/4 oz sugar
20 cl sweet sherry
1 teaspoon ground nutmeg
1 teaspoon ground ginger
7 hot cored baked apples

Heat all but apples gently in large saucepan until
sugar dissolves. Place apples in individual Wassail
bowls and add the hot mix. Serve with dessert spoons.

Winter Wine (4 people)

Spiced wine flavour   *Alcohol 1.4*

35 cl red wine
2 msr cognac or brandy
1 small pinch cinnamon
1 tablespoon honey
2 msr water

Heat in small saucepan and pour just before   HPC (Heat-
boiling. Add slice of lemon to each cup.   proof cup)

Short Drinks

Drinks made with less than five measures of fluid before shaking.

Abracadabra
Citrus flavour   *Alcohol 1.5*

    1½ msr white rum
    1½ msr mandarin juice
    1½ msr grapefruit juice
    ½ teaspoon caster sugar

Shake and strain into glass filled with crushed ice.   D

Absinthe Cocktail
Aniseed flavour   *Alcohol 1.8*

    1½ msr Pernod
    ½ msr anisette
    ¾ msr water
    1 teaspoon sugar syrup

Stir and strain.   L

If a teaspoon of maraschino is added,   *Alcohol 2.0*
this is an Absinthe Italiano.

Acapulcoco
Coconut flavour   *Alcohol 2.4*

    1 msr gold tequila
    1 msr Kahlua
    ⅔ msr dark rum
    ½ msr coconut cream

Shake and strain. Garnish: cherry
and slice of orange.   C

Affinity

Herb / Scotch flavour   *Alcohol 2.0*

Big in the 1920s but now strictly for the enthusiast.

    1 msr scotch
    1 msr rosso vermouth
    1 msr dry vermouth
    1 dash Angostura

Shake and strain, squeeze twist of lemon
above drink and discard.   C

After Nine

Coffee flavour   *Alcohol 1.2*

    ³/₄ msr Kahlua
    ³/₄ msr peach Schnapps
    ³/₄ msr Baileys

Make pousse-café. Shooter.   L

Agent Provocateur

Orange flavour   *Alcohol 2.4*

    1 msr white rum
    ¹/₂ msr Mandarine Napoléon
    ¹/₂ msr dry orange curacao
    ¹/₄ msr coconut rum
    ¹/₄ msr melon liqueur
    ¹/₄ msr lime juice
    1 teaspoon parfait amour

Shake briefly with a glassful of crushed ice.
Garnish: slice of lime and a cherry.   R

Albert 2000

Orange / Herb flavour   *Alcohol 2.7*

Caielli Giovanni, Grand Hotel Villa d'Este, Italy. Courtesy of Ets. Fourcroy s.a.

    1 msr vodka
    1 msr dry vermouth
    ²/₃ msr Mandarine Napoléon
    ²/₃ msr triple sec

Shake and strain into glass filled with
broken ice, add cherry on a stick.   R

Algonquin

Pineapple whisky flavour

Alcohol 2.4

 2 msr rye/Canadian whisky
 1 msr dry vermouth
 1 msr pineapple juice

Shake and strain into glass three-quarters filled with broken ice. Garnish: slice of orange and cherry.

 R

Algonquin Bar Punch

Lemon / Herb flavour

Alcohol 1.5

 1½ msr sloe gin
 ½ msr dark rum
 1 msr lemon juice
 ½ msr sugar syrup
 ½ msr raspberry syrup

Shake and strain into glass filled with crushed ice. Garnish: fruit in season, add short straws.

 R

Amigo

Fruity flavour

Alcohol 1.5

Teo Leinson, Finland. Courtesy of Bols International B.V.

 1 msr white rum
 ¾ msr Bols Creme de Bananes
 ¼ msr Bols Apricot Brandy
 1½ msr pear juice
 1 dash grenadine

Shake and strain.

 C

Amsterdam

Orange flavour

Alcohol 1.8

 1½ msr gin
 ½ msr triple sec
 ¾ msr mandarin juice

Shake with a glassful of broken ice and pour unstrained.

R

Andalusian Smile

Wine flavour

Alcohol 1.8

    1 3/4 msr dry sherry
    1/2 msr white rum
    1/2 msr cognac
    1 dash Angostura

Shake and strain into glass three-quarters
filled with broken ice.

R

Angler's Cocktail

Gin flavour

Alcohol 1.7

    1 1/2 msr gin
    1/4 msr grenadine
    1 teaspoon dry orange curacao
    1 dash Angostura

Add to glass filled with broken ice.

R

Apollo 1

Fruity flavour

Alcohol 2.2

    1 1/3 msr apple brandy
    2/3 msr Cointreau
    1/3 msr Pimm's No.1.

Shake with a glassful of broken ice
and pour unstrained.

R

If a teaspoon of Licor 43 is added,
this is an Apollo 44.

Alcohol 2.3

Après Ski

Sweet mint flavour

Alcohol 1.7

    1 msr vodka
    1/2 msr Pernod
    1/4 msr green creme de menthe
    3 msr lemonade

Add to glass three-quarters filled with broken ice.
Garnish: slice of lime and sprig of mint.

R

Apricot Crush

Apricot flavour Alcohol 1.3

1½ msr apricot brandy
½ msr white rum
1 msr orange juice
½ msr lemon juice

Shake and strain into glass filled with crushed ice.   CS

Apricot Tree

Apricot flavour Alcohol 1.4

1 msr apricot brandy
1 msr Rum Tree
½ msr dry vermouth
1 msr apricot juice
1 msr pineapple juice

Shake and strain.   C

Arrowhead

Fruit rum flavour Alcohol 1.8

1 msr dark rum
½ msr Southern Comfort
½ msr creme de banane
¼ msr lime juice
2½ msr lemonade

Add to glass three-quarters filled with broken ice.   R

Artists' Special

Fruit scotch flavour Alcohol 1.5

Created around 1920 at the Artists' Club, Rue Pigalle, Paris.

1 msr scotch
1 msr sweet sherry
½ msr grenadine
½ msr lemon juice

Shake and strain.   C

AVENUES

A short drink based on sweet sherry and made in the glass – which has been frosted. Any fruit liqueur can be used, but this should constitute only a subtle contribution to the overall flavour.

First Avenue

Orange sherry flavour   *Alcohol 1.4*

In 1835 Manuel Maria Gonzalez became established as a sherry producer. He was joined in 1855 by Englishman Robert Blake Byass, and the name Gonzalez Byass was born. Today the company is the world's largest producer of sherry.

  1½ msr sweet sherry
  ½ msr Cointreau
  ¾ msr soda water
  1 teaspoon Campari

Add to glass filled with broken ice.   R

Simply replace the Cointreau in the following popular Avenues:

Second Avenue   ½ msr peach schnapps   *Alcohol 1.1*
Third Avenue   ½ msr melon liqueur   *Alcohol 1.1*

AWOL

Fruit scotch flavour   *Alcohol 1.7*

  ½ msr amaretto
  1 msr scotch
  ½ msr dry orange curacao
  ¾ msr lime juice

Shake and strain into glass filled with broken ice.
Garnish: orange wedge.   R

B-52

Coffee flavour   *Alcohol 1.3*

  1 msr Kahlua
  1 msr Baileys
  2 teaspoons Grand Marnier

Make pousse-café. Shooter. Sometimes served stirred and strained into ice-filled rocks glass.   L

B and B

Herb / Brandy flavour   *Alcohol 2.0*

  1 msr brandy or cognac
  1 msr Benedictine

Stir and strain.   L

Bacardi Cocktail

Citrus flavour   Alcohol 1.5

In 1936 the New York Supreme Court ruled that this cocktail could only be made using Bacardi rum. Who are we to argue?

    1½ msr Bacardi white rum
    1 msr lemon or lime juice
    ½ msr sugar syrup
    1 teaspoon grenadine

Shake and strain. Garnish: cherry on a stick.   CS

Bacchus

Sharp / Fruity flavour   Alcohol 2.5

    2 msr brandy
    1 msr apricot brandy
    1 msr lime juice

Add to glass filled with broken ice and twist of lime.   R

Bacon and Tomato Sandwich

Fruit rum flavour   Alcohol 1.5

    ¾ msr Pimm's No.1
    ½ msr dark rum
    ½ msr white rum
    2 msr lemonade

Add to glass three-quarters filled with broken ice.   R

Baileys Comet

Baileys flavour   Alcohol 1.5

    1 msr Baileys
    1 msr Vodka

Add to glass half filled with broken ice.   R

Bairn, The

Orange scotch flavour   Alcohol 2.9

    2 msr single grain scotch
    ¾ msr Cointreau
    1 teaspoon Campari

Add to glass three-quarters filled with broken ice.   R

Barbarella

Lemon / Herb flavour   *Alcohol 2.0*

> 1 msr Plymouth gin
> ³/₄ msr dry vermouth
> ¹/₂ msr Galliano
> 1 teaspoon blue curacao
> 2 msr sparkling bitter lemon

Shake and strain into glass half filled with
broken ice, add the lemon. Garnish: blue cherry
and lemon slice.   R

BATIDAS

A fruity Brazilian drink based on aguardente de cana (cachaça), a full-
bodied raw version of white rum popular in South America. The spirit is
mixed with fresh fruit and sugar before blending with ice to produce Batida
Strawberry, Batida Pineapple etc.

Batida Abaci (pineapple)

Pineapple flavour   *Alcohol 1.5*

> 1¹/₂ msr cachaça
> 1 msr pineapple juice
> 1 tablespoon pineapple pieces or chunks
> ¹/₂ teaspoon caster sugar

Blend with a glassful of crushed ice until smooth,
serve with short straws.   G

Replace the pineapple with mango juice for a Batida Mango.

Batida Morango (strawberry)

Strawberry flavour   *Alcohol 2.0*

> 2 msr cachaça
> ¹/₃ msr strawberry syrup
> 2 strawberries
> ¹/₂ teaspoon caster sugar

Blend with a glassful of crushed ice until smooth.
Garnish: sugar-dipped strawberry, add straws.   G

Bayou

Fruit brandy flavour *Alcohol 1.8*

> 1½ msr cognac
> ½ msr peach brandy
> 1 msr mango juice
> ⅓ msr lime juice

Shake with a glassful of broken ice and pour
unstrained. Garnish: peach slice. R

Beach Peach

Peach flavour *Alcohol 1.9*

> 1½ msr white rum
> ¾ msr peach brandy
> 1 msr peach juice
> ½ msr lime juice
> 1 teaspoon pineapple syrup

Shake and strain into glass half filled
with broken ice. R

Beam Me Up Scotty

Coffee flavour *Alcohol 1.2*

> ¾ msr Kahlua
> ¾ msr creme de banane
> ¾ msr Baileys

Make pousse-café. Shooter. L

Beef on Rye

Lemon flavour *Alcohol 2.0*

> 1½ msr Beefeater gin
> ½ msr rye/Canadian whisky
> ½ msr passion fruit syrup
> 2 msr sparkling bitter lemon

Shake and strain into glass half filled with
broken ice, add the lemon. R

If aquavit is used in place of rye, this is a Danish Beef.

Bennet Cocktail

Lime flavour   *Alcohol 2.1*

A 1920s recipe originally served straight up and without the syrup.

    2 msr gin
    ²/₃ msr lime juice
    ¹/₃ msr sugar syrup
    1 dash Angostura

Shake and strain into glass filled with broken ice.   R

Best Year

Pineapple flavour   *Alcohol 1.6*

    1 msr vodka
    ¹/₂ msr blue curacao
    ¹/₂ msr Licor 43
    1¹/₂ msr pineapple juice
    ¹/₂ msr Rose's Lime Cordial

Shake and strain into glass filled with broken ice.   R

Between the Sheets

Sharp flavour   *Alcohol 2.8*

    1¹/₄ msr brandy or cognac
    1 msr white rum
    ¹/₂ msr Cointreau
    ³/₄ msr lemon juice
    ¹/₂ msr sugar syrup

Shake and strain. Garnish: slice of lemon.   C

Big Toe

Sweet coffee flavour   *Alcohol 1.8*

Frangelico was the name given by local farmers to a hermit living around 1650 by the River Po, Italy. The name is a corruption of Fra Angelico, Friar of the Angels, which suggests he may once have been a monk. He created many liqueurs, the best known being predominantly flavoured with hazelnuts, as is the popular liqueur which bears his name today.

    ¹/₂ msr Frangelico
    ¹/₂ msr amaretto
    ¹/₂ msr Kahlua
    ¹/₂ msr Baileys
    ¹/₂ msr white rum
    ¹/₂ msr dark creme de cacao

Stir and strain. Garnish: cherry on a stick. L

Biscay

Fruity flavour   Alcohol 1.8

Rum production began in the West Indies in the seventeenth century. Still a major industry, its social, political and economic importance over the centuries cannot be overstated.

> 1 msr white rum
> 1/2 msr Rum Tree
> 1/2 msr Mandarine Napoléon
> 1 teaspoon lime juice
> 1 msr lemonade

Add to glass half filled with broken ice.
Garnish: cherry, add orange twist.   R

Black Death

Blackberry flavour   Alcohol 1.8

> 1 msr bourbon
> 1 msr dry vermouth
> 1/3 msr blackberry brandy
> 1 teaspoon lemon juice

Shake and strain into glass filled with
broken ice, add lemon twist.   R

Blackjack

Coffee flavour   Alcohol 1.8

> 1 msr cognac
> 1/2 msr kirsch
> 1/2 msr coffee liqueur
> 2 msr cold black coffee

Shake with three-quarters of a glassful of
broken ice and pour unstrained.   R

Black Magic

Coffee flavour   Alcohol 2.0

> 1 1/2 msr vodka
> 3/4 msr Tia Maria
> 1 teaspoon lime juice

Shake with a glassful of broken ice and pour
unstrained, add lime twist.   R

Blackout

Blackberry gin flavour Alcohol 0.8

½ msr gin
½ msr blackberry brandy
¼ msr lime juice
¼ msr sugar syrup

Shake and strain. Shooter. S

Black Widow

Coffee flavour Alcohol 1.7

1 msr white rum
1 msr Kahlua

Add to glass three-quarters filled with broken ice. R

Blarney Stone

Scotch / Herb flavour Alcohol 2.3

2 msr Irish whiskey
1 teaspoon triple sec
½ teaspoon Pernod
½ teaspoon maraschino
1 dash Angostura

Add to glass filled with broken ice.
Add orange twist and mint sprig. R

Blow Job

Orange / Coffee flavour Alcohol 1.2

½ msr Grand Marnier
½ msr coffee liqueur
½ msr creme de banane
1 teaspoon whipping cream

Stir and strain, float the cream. Add two halves
of a cherry on a stick. Shooter. L

Bluebeard

Blueberry flavour Alcohol 2.5

1½ msr vodka
1 msr cognac
½ msr blueberry syrup

Stir and strain. B

Blue Star

Sour orange flavour   *Alcohol 1.6*

> 1 msr gin
> ³/₄ msr Lillet or Noilly Prat
> ¹/₃ msr blue curacao
> 1 msr orange juice

Shake and strain into glass filled with crushed ice.
Garnish: cherry and slice of orange.   CS

Blushing Barmaid

Lemon flavour   *Alcohol 1.0*

> ³/₄ msr amaretto
> ³/₄ msr Campari
> 3 msr sparkling bitter lemon

Add to glass half filled with broken ice.   R

Bobby Burns

Whisky / Herb flavour   *Alcohol 2.3*

Named after Robert Burns (1759–96), the Scottish poet and song writer, best known for 'Auld Lang Syne'.

> 1¹/₂ msr scotch
> 1¹/₂ msr rosso vermouth
> 1 teaspoon Benedictine

Add to glass three-quarters filled with
broken ice, add twist of lemon.   R

If a dash of Angostura and a teaspoon of sugar syrup
are substituted for the Benedictine, this becomes a
Flying Scotsman.

If a teaspoon of sugar syrup is substituted for the
Benedictine, this becomes a Harry Lauder.

Boca Chica

Tropical fruit flavour   *Alcohol 1.8*

N. Homeijer, Holland. Courtesy of Bols International B.V.

> 1 msr vodka
> ²/₃ msr Pisang Ambon
> ²/₃ msr coconut rum
> 2 msr guava nectar
> ¹/₃ msr passion fruit syrup

Shake and strain. Garnish: cherry
and orange slice.

C

Bombay

Herb flavour

Alcohol 2.7

1½ msr brandy
¾ msr dry vermouth
¾ msr rosso vermouth
1 teaspoon Pernod
2 teaspoons triple sec

Shake and strain into glass filled with crushed ice.

CS

Bonaparte

Mandarin flavour

Alcohol 1.8

1 msr cognac
¾ msr Mandarine Napoléon

Stir and strain.

B

Bonny Prince

Scotch flavour

Alcohol 2.0

1½ msr scotch
½ msr dry vermouth
¼ msr Drambuie

Stir and strain into glass three-quarters
filled with broken ice.

R

If lime juice is used in place of dry vermouth,
this is a Bonny Prince Charlie.

Alcohol 1.8

Boomer

Fruity flavour

Alcohol 1.0

⅔ msr gold tequila
½ msr apricot brandy
½ msr orange juice
¼ msr lemon juice
¼ msr sugar syrup

Shake and strain. Shooter.

L

Bordij

Fruit wine flavour

Alcohol 1.9

>   2 msr red Bordeaux wine
>   1 msr cognac
>   3/4 msr creme de cassis

Stir and strain into ice-filled glass.

W

Bosom Caresser

Rich wine flavour

Alcohol 1.7

>   1 msr madeira
>   3/4 msr brandy
>   1/2 msr triple sec
>   1 teaspoon grenadine
>   1 egg yolk

Shake well and strain.

C

Boss, The

Sweet bourbon flavour

Alcohol 1.8

>   1 1/2 msr bourbon
>   1/2 msr amaretto

Add to glass filled with broken ice, add cherry on a stick. R

Brandy Champarelle

Herb flavour

Alcohol 2.0

An old recipe of about 1890, originally made pousse-café and with twice the volume shown here. Also known as Champerelle or Shamparelle.

>   3/4 msr triple sec
>   3/4 msr cognac
>   1/2 msr anisette
>   1/2 msr Green Chartreuse

Stir and strain.

L

Brandy Fino

Brandy flavour

Alcohol 2.0

>   1 1/2 msr cognac
>   1/2 msr dry sherry
>   1/4 msr Glayva

Stir and strain.

B

Brave Bull

Coffee flavour

Alcohol 1.7

    1 msr gold tequila
    1 msr Kahlua

Add to glass filled with broken ice,
add twist of lemon.

R

If 2 msr cold cola are added, this is a Bandit's Coffee.

If served straight up and a flaming teaspoon
of Sambuca is floated on top, this is a Raging Bull.

Alcohol 1.9

Breakfast

Wine flavour

Alcohol 1.7

    2 msr LBV port
    1 msr dark creme de cacao
    1 teaspoon golden rum
    1/2 msr lemon juice
    1 teaspoon egg white

Shake well and strain, sprinkle with
grated nutmeg.

C

Bronx

Herb flavour

Alcohol 2.3

Created around 1906 by top barman Johnny Solon at the old Waldorf
Astoria, New York. The story goes he named it following a trip to the
Bronx Zoo.

    1 1/2 msr gin
    3/4 msr rosso vermouth
    3/4 msr dry vermouth
    3/4 msr orange juice

Shake and strain into glass three-quarters filled
with broken ice – originally straight up in a
cocktail glass. Garnish: slice of orange.

R

Bloody Bronx – replace orange with blood orange juice.

Dry Bronx – replace rosso with dry, 1 1/2 msr vermouth in total.

Golden Bronx – include 1 egg yolk, shake well.

Silver Bronx – replace rosso with 1/2 msr egg
white, increase orange to 1 1/2 msr, shake well.

Alcohol 1.9

205

Brown Derby
Lime rum flavour

Alcohol 1.5

    1½ msr dark rum
    1 msr lime juice
    1 teaspoon maple syrup

Shake and strain into glass three-quarters filled
with broken ice, or serve straight up.   R

Cactus Juice
Lemon flavour

Alcohol 2.0

    2 msr gold tequila
    1 teaspoon Drambuie
    1 msr lemon juice
    1 teaspoon caster sugar

Dissolve sugar, shake with a glassful of
broken ice and pour unstrained.   R

Café Kirsch
Coffee flavour

Alcohol 1.0

    1 msr kirsch
    2 msr cold black coffee
    1 msr sugar syrup
    ½ msr egg white

Shake well and strain.   C

Caipirinha
Lime flavour
Alcohol 2.0

Pronounced 'caipireeni', the name means 'peasants' drink' in Brazil,
where it is served in every bar. It's the cocktail which makes up for the
malaria shot.

    2 msr aguardente de cana – cachaça
    1 small fresh lime
    1½ teaspoons caster sugar

Wash lime and remove top and bottom, cut into
8 segments. Add lime pieces and sugar to glass,
crush until the juice is released. Add cachaça,
and muddle together briefly ensuring the sugar
has dissolved. Add broken ice to fill glass and
muddle together. Garnish: ring of lime.   R

If vodka is used in place of cachaça,
this is a Caipiroska.
If white rum is used, this is a Caipirissima.

Calvarniac

Orange brandy flavour   *Alcohol 2.0*

Calvados is recorded as having first been produced in Normandy by Gilles de Gouberville in 1553, when it was known as 'eau de vie de cidre'.

   1 msr calvados
   2/3 msr Grand Marnier
   1/3 msr cognac
   1 msr lemonade

Add to glass half filled with broken ice,
add lemon twist.   R

Camel's Coffee

Coffee flavour   *Alcohol 2.0*

   3/4 msr Kahlua
   1/2 msr cognac
   1/2 msr Strega
   1/2 msr white rum
   1 msr cold coffee

Shake and strain into ice-filled glass.   R

Camshaft

Passion fruit flavour   *Alcohol 1.3*

   1 msr vodka
   1/2 msr Campari
   1 msr passion fruit juice
   1 msr orange juice
   1 msr lemonade

Add to glass half filled with broken ice.   R

Canada Cocktail

Orange whisky flavour   *Alcohol 2.1*

   1 1/2 msr Canadian whisky
   1/2 msr Cointreau
   3 drops Angostura

Add to glass filled with broken ice and sprig of mint.   R

Canadian Black

Blackberry flavour

Alcohol 1.8

    1 1/2 msr Canadian whisky
    1/2 msr blackberry brandy
    1/4 msr lemon juice

Shake and strain into glass filled with crushed ice. CS

Canario

Mandarin flavour

Alcohol 1.5

    1 1/2 msr pisco
    1 1/2 msr mandarin juice
    1 teaspoon pineapple syrup
    1/4 msr lime juice
    1 teaspoon caster sugar

Dissolve sugar, shake and strain into glass filled
with crushed ice. Garnish: lime twist. D

Canton

Mandarin flavour

Alcohol 0.8

    1 1/2 msr rice wine
    1/4 msr triple sec
    2 msr mandarin juice
    1 teaspoon grenadine

Shake and strain into glass three-quarters filled
with broken ice, add orange twist and a cherry. R

Captain's Cocktail

Lime rum flavour

Alcohol 1.8

    1 msr white rum
    1/2 msr Captain Morgan spiced rum
    1 msr lime juice
    1/2 teaspoon caster sugar
    1/2 msr LBV port

Shake and strain into glass filled with crushed ice.
Sprinkle the port over one half of the surface,
drink from the port side! CS

Caribbean Harvest

Tropical fruit flavour   *Alcohol 2.0*

    1 msr white rum
    1 msr coconut rum
    1/2 msr creme de banane
    1 msr passion fruit juice
    1 msr mango juice
    1 teaspoon grenadine

Shake and strain.   C

Caruso

Mint flavour   *Alcohol 1.6*

Named after the great Italian tenor Caruso. It was created for him in the
1920s during his stay at the Hotel Sevilla, Cuba.

    1 msr gin
    1 msr dry vermouth
    1/3 msr green creme de menthe

Add to glass half filled with broken ice,
add cherry on a stick. Originally a full measure
of green creme de menthe was used.   R

If white creme de menthe is used, this is a Caruso Blanco.

Centenario

Fruit rum flavour   *Alcohol 2.0*

Courtesy of Cinco Dias & Co, Havana Club Rum.

    1 msr Havana Club Old Gold (golden rum)
    1/2 msr Havana Club Extra Aged (aged golden rum)
    1/2 msr triple sec
    1/4 msr coffee liqueur
    1 teaspoon grenadine
    1/2 teaspoon lime juice

Stir and strain into glass filled with broken ice.
Garnish: mint sprig and fruit in season.   R

César Ritz

Subtle fruit flavour   *Alcohol 2.8*

Created at Hotel Ritz, Paris.

    2 msr gin
    2/3 msr dry vermouth
    1/3 msr Peter Heering (cherry brandy)
    1/3 msr kirsch

Stir and strain. Garnish: red cherry
soaked in eau de vie.

C

Chandos Club

Orange / Lemon flavour   *Alcohol 2.0*

    1 msr cognac
    1 msr Grand Marnier
    2 msr sparkling bitter lemon

Add to glass three-quarters filled with broken ice.

R

Chaos Calmer

Orange gin flavour   *Alcohol 1.8*

    1 1/2 msr Plymouth gin
    1/4 msr triple sec
    1 1/2 msr orange juice
    3/4 msr lime juice
    1 teaspoon grenadine

Shake with a glassful of broken ice and pour
unstrained. Garnish: fruit in season.

G

Charles's Nightcap

Pear brandy flavour   *Alcohol 1.8*

    1 1/2 msr armagnac
    1/2 msr pear liqueur

Stir and strain.

B

Chartreuse Cocktail

Herb flavour   *Alcohol 2.2*

    1 msr Yellow Chartreuse
    1 msr cognac
    1/2 msr dry vermouth

Stir and strain. Garnish: cherry.

L

Cheese Sandwich
Melon flavour

Alcohol 1.5

   1¹/₂ msr melon liqueur
   ¹/₂ msr triple sec
   1 teaspoon dark rum
   ¹/₄ msr lemon juice
   2 msr lemonade

Add to glass three-quarters filled with broken ice.   R

Cherry Blossom
Cherry flavour

Alcohol 2.0

   1¹/₂ msr cherry brandy
   1 msr brandy
   ¹/₄ msr triple sec
   ¹/₄ msr lemon juice
   ¹/₃ msr egg white
   1 teaspoon grenadine
   ¹/₄ msr sugar syrup

Rim glass with grenadine/caster sugar.
Shake well and strain. Garnish: slice of orange
speared with red cherry.   CS

Chinatown
Lychee flavour

Alcohol 1.7

   1 msr lychee wine
   1 msr gin
   ¹/₃ msr kirsch
   ¹/₂ msr pineapple syrup
   2 stoned lychees

Blend until smooth, add a glassful of crushed ice
and blend again briefly, add straws.   R

Chocolate Soldier
Chocolate / Herb flavour

Alcohol 2.8

   2 msr dark creme de cacao
   1 msr cognac
   1 msr dry vermouth
   1 teaspoon triple sec

Shake and strain. Garnish: chocolate stick/flake.   C

Chop Nut

Coconut / Orange flavour   *Alcohol 1.8*

    1 msr white rum
    3/4 msr coconut rum
    1/2 msr white creme de cacao
    1 teaspoon Frangelico
    1 1/2 msr mandarin juice
    1 teaspoon egg white

Shake well and strain into glass filled
with broken ice.   D

Citrus Cactus

Lemon flavour   *Alcohol 2.2*

    2 msr silver tequila
    1 teaspoon Pernod
    1/2 msr lemon juice
    1/2 msr lime juice
    1/2 msr sugar syrup
    1 teaspoon egg white
    1 teaspoon grenadine

Shake and strain into glass filled with crushed ice.   D

Cloud Walker

Fruit scotch flavour   *Alcohol 1.3*

    1 msr Lakka Cloudberry Liqueur
    3/4 msr Johnnie Walker scotch
    1/3 msr lime juice
    2 msr lemonade

Add to glass filled with broken ice and lime slice.   R

Clover Club

Rich lemon flavour   *Alcohol 1.5*

First appeared around 1925 and takes its name from the famous
American nightspot.

    1 1/2 msr gin
    3/4 msr lemon juice
    1/2 msr grenadine
    1 egg white

Shake well and strain.   CS

If 4–5 mint leaves are included before shaking and a sprig of
mint is used as a garnish, this is a Clover Leaf.

Clover Club Royal

Lemon / Advocaat flavour Alcohol 2.0

2 msr gin
3/4 msr lemon juice
1/4 msr grenadine
1 egg yolk

Shake well and strain into glass filled with
crushed ice. Garnish: slice of lemon.

D

Cock-a-bendy

Vermouth flavour Alcohol 2.5

Old Scottish term for a sprightly youth.

2 msr single grain scotch
3/4 msr rosso vermouth
1 teaspoon Campari

Shake with a glassful of broken ice and
pour unstrained; add lemon twist.

R

Coconut Gin

Coconut flavour Alcohol 1.5

1 1/2 msr gin
1/2 msr lime juice
1 msr coconut cream

Shake and strain into glass filled with crushed ice.

CS

If gold tequila is used in place of gin, this is a Coconut Tequila.

Coconut Monkey

Coconut / Fruit flavour Alcohol 1.5

1 msr white rum
1 msr apricot brandy
3/4 msr coconut cream
1 1/2 msr pineapple juice

Shake and strain into glass filled with
crushed ice.

D

Columbus Cocktail

Fruit rum flavour   *Alcohol 1.9*

    1½ msr golden rum
    ¾ msr apricot brandy
    1 msr lime juice

Shake briefly with a glassful of crushed ice,
add slice of lime.   D

Commonwealth

Orange flavour   *Alcohol 2.3*

    1¾ msr Canadian whisky
    ½ msr Van der Hum (substitute: Mandarine Napoléon)
    ¼ msr lemon juice

Stir and strain.   B

Connecticut Bullfrog

Lemon flavour   *Alcohol 1.5*

    1 msr gin
    ½ msr dark rum
    ½ msr maple syrup
    ½ msr lemon juice

Shake and strain into glass filled
with crushed ice.   CS

Connoisseur's Treat

Orange brandy flavour   *Alcohol 2.5*

    1½ msr cognac
    ½ msr Galliano
    ½ msr Grand Marnier

Stir and strain.   B

Corcovado

Herb flavour   *Alcohol 2.0*

    1 msr gold tequila
    ¾ msr Drambuie
    ¼ msr blue curacao
    2 msr lemonade

Add to glass and fill up with crushed ice.
Garnish: slice of lime and a cherry, add short straws.   D

Corkscrew

Peach flavour   *Alcohol 2.0*

   1½ msr white rum
   ½ msr peach brandy
   ½ msr dry vermouth

Fill glass with broken ice and spiral of lemon.
Shake and strain into prepared glass.   R

Corniche

Strawberry flavour   *Alcohol 1.5*

In eighteenth century Russia, innkeepers offered a multitude of flavoured
vodkas, often one for every letter of the alphabet, and each with a
distinctive fruit or herb flavour.

   1½ msr Russian vodka
   1 msr clear strawberry juice
   1 teaspoon caster sugar

Shake and strain into glass three-quarters filled
with broken ice. Garnish: half a sugar-dipped
strawberry.   R

Cosmopolitan

Fruity flavour   *Alcohol 1.6*

H. Klein, The Selfridge Hotel, London. Courtesy of Gordon's London Dry Gin.

   1 msr gin
   ½ msr Southern Comfort
   ½ msr blackcurrant cordial or syrup
   1 msr lime juice
   1 teaspoon egg white

Shake and strain into glass filled with crushed ice.
Garnish: slice of star-fruit and sprig of mint.   CS

Coterie

Herb flavour   *Alcohol 2.0*

   1 msr cognac
   ½ msr Izarra or Yellow Chartreuse
   ½ msr gin
   1 teaspoon lemon syrup

Stir and strain.   L

Cracklin' Rosie

Fruity flavour *Alcohol 1.8*

Virgil Jones, USA. Courtesy of Bols International B.V.

    1½ msr white rum
    ½ msr Bols Creme de Bananes
    ¾ msr passion fruit juice
    ½ msr pineapple juice
    ½ msr lime juice

Shake and strain, add cherry on a stick.   C

Crater Face

Wine flavour *Alcohol 2.1*

    1½ msr madeira
    1 msr bourbon
    1 teaspoon creme de banane
    1 teaspoon grenadine

Add to glass three-quarters filled with broken ice.   R

Crimean Cocktail

Citrus wine flavour *Alcohol 1.4*

    2 msr dry white wine
    ⅔ msr Cointreau
    grated zest of one lemon
    1 msr soda water

Stir and strain through fine filter, add the
soda and two cherries on a stick.   C

Crooked Sister

Chocolate / Orange flavour *Alcohol 2.6*

    1 msr Cointreau
    1 msr gin
    1 msr white creme de cacao

Stir and strain into glass three-quarters filled
with broken ice. Garnish: cherry and
slice of orange.   R

Crow's Nest

Sherry flavour   *Alcohol 1.5*

1 msr gin
1 msr sweet sherry

Add to glass filled with broken ice and lemon twist.   R

CRUSTAS

Said to have been invented around 1850 by Santina, the proprietor of Santina's Saloon, a Spanish cafe in New Orleans, USA. A Crusta is served in a large sugar-rimmed wine glass lined with a spiral of lemon peel. Any spirit base can be used, and a small amount of lemon juice should be included.

Brandy Crusta

Sour brandy flavour   *Alcohol 2.9*

2 msr brandy
1 msr triple sec
1/4 maraschino
1/3 msr lemon juice

Rim glass with lemon/caster sugar. Fill glass
with lemon spiral and broken ice. Shake and
strain into glass, add cherry on a stick.   R

Simply replace the brandy in the following popular Crustas:

Bourbon Crusta	2 msr bourbon
Gin Crusta	2 msr gin
Rum Crusta	2 msr dark rum

Cubano

Pineapple flavour   *Alcohol 2.0*

2 msr white rum
1 msr pineapple juice
1 msr lime juice
1 level teaspoon caster sugar

Shake and strain.   C

DAIQUIRIS

The original Daiquiri of rum, lime and sugar was created in Cuba by
American mining engineer Jennings Cox in 1896. His colleague Mr
Pagliuchi suggested naming it after the nearby town of Daiquiri.

Daiquiri (Original)

Citrus / Sour flavour   *Alcohol 2.0*

    2 msr white rum
    2/3 msr lime juice
    1 teaspoon caster sugar

Shake and strain into frosted glass. Garnish: slice lime. CS

When served in a rocks glass over ice this is a
Daiquiri on the Rocks.

Orange Daiquiri

Orange flavour   *Alcohol 2.0*

    2 msr white rum
    2 msr orange juice
    1/2 msr lime juice
    1 teaspoon caster sugar

Dissolve sugar, shake and strain into frosted glass.
Garnish: slice of orange. CS

Frozen Daiquiris

See also Frozen Fruit Daiquiris, in Long Drinks section.
The original Frozen Daiquiri is credited to Constantino 'Constante'
Ribailagua of La Floridita Bar, 'La Catedral del Daiquiri', on the corner
of Monserrate Street, in Havana, Cuba, where he worked from 1912
until his death in 1952.
The critical difference he made to this drink was not merely to serve it
with crushed ice, but to add the professional touch of squeezing the lime
juice by hand directly into the mixer, thus releasing an all-important
spray of lime oil. This gives the drink both flavour and bouquet.

Derby Daiquiri

Orange / Lime flavour   *Alcohol 1.5*

    1 1/2 msr white rum
    juice of 1/2 a lime
    1 msr orange juice
    1 level teaspoon caster sugar

Shake and strain into glass filled with crushed ice. CS

Frozen Daiquiri (Original)

Citrus flavour **Alcohol 2.0**

   2 msr white rum
   juice of ½ a fresh lime
   1 heaped teaspoon caster sugar

Squeeze juice directly into blender. Add remaining
ingredients and blend briefly with a glassful of
crushed ice and pour into frosted glass.
Garnish: slice of lime.

D

If ¼ msr grenadine is added, this is a Pink Daiquiri.

If ¼ msr creme de cassis is added, this is a   *Alcohol 2.1*
French Daiquiri – as created by Ernest Luthi of the
Stork Club, New York, around 1935.

Galliano Daiquiri

Herb flavour **Alcohol 1.8**

   1 msr golden rum
   ¾ msr Galliano
   juice of ½ a lime
   ½ msr sugar syrup

Shake briefly with a glassful of crushed ice,
add to frosted glass. Garnish: slice of lime
and cherry on a stick.   D

Hemingway Special

Citrus flavour **Alcohol 2.3**

Created by 'Constante' at La Floridita and named after his regular
customer and Daiquiri enthusiast Ernest Hemingway. It is a form of
Daiquiri but wholly unsweetened.

   2 msr white rum
   ¼ msr maraschino
   juice of ½ a lime
   1 msr grapefruit juice

Squeeze lime juice into shaker, add remaining
ingredients and shake briefly with a glassful of
crushed ice. Serve in frosted glass.   D

If sweetened with ⅔ msr sugar syrup, this is a
Florida Daiquiri – also created at La Floridita.

La Floridita Daiquiri

Lime flavour   *Alcohol 2.2*

Also created at La Floridita Bar, Cuba.

    2 msr white rum
    1/4 msr maraschino
    juice of 1 lime
    2/3 msr sugar syrup

Shake briefly with a glassful of crushed ice.
Serve in frosted glass.   D

Mandarin Daiquiri

Mandarin flavour   *Alcohol 2.3*

    1 1/2 msr golden rum
    3/4 msr Mandarine Napoléon
    juice of 1/2 a lime
    1/2 msr sugar syrup

Shake and strain into glass filled with crushed ice,
add cherry and slice of orange on a stick. CS

DAISIES

An American drink in existence since the 1850s, the Daisy should be
served very cold, in a tankard, though now more commonly a rocks glass
is used. They should be shaken and augmented with ample broken or
crushed ice – though it was originally strained and served straight up.
Any base spirit can be used, but only a small quantity of soda water, if
any, should be added – no more than half the quantity of spirits. Lemon
or lime juice and a small amount of a fruit syrup should be included, and
a little fruit in season used as a garnish.

Brandy Daisy

Lemon flavour   *Alcohol 2.0*

    2 msr brandy
    1 msr lemon juice
    1 level teaspoon caster sugar
    1 teaspoon grenadine
    1 msr soda water (optional)

Shake well and strain into glass filled with
broken ice, add the soda if desired.
Garnish: fruit in season and a sprig of mint.   R

Simply replace the brandy in the following popular Daisies:

Bourbon Daisy	2 msr bourbon
Gin Daisy	2 msr gin
Scotch Daisy	2 msr scotch
Vodka Daisy	2 msr vodka

Rum Daisy

Sour lime flavour   *Alcohol 1.5*

> 1½ msr white rum
> 1 msr lime juice
> 1 teaspoon grenadine
> twists of lime and orange

Shake with a glassful of crushed ice and pour into frosted
glass. Garnish: fruit in season, add short straws.   R

Dawn Chorus

Wine flavour   *Alcohol 1.7*

> 1 msr Southern Comfort
> ³/₄ msr LBV port
> ½ msr Punt e Mes
> ⅓ msr lemon juice
> 1 teaspoon grenadine
> 2 msr cold cola

Shake and strain into glass three-quarters
filled with broken ice, add the cola.   R

Dempsey

Subtle herb flavour   *Alcohol 2.1*

Created in 1921 to celebrate Jack Dempsey's world championship boxing
victory.

> 1 msr gin
> 1 msr apple brandy
> ½ teaspoon Pernod
> ½ teaspoon grenadine

Shake and strain into glass three-quarters
filled with broken ice.   R

Derby
Gin flavour   *Alcohol 2.1*

    2 msr gin
    1 teaspoon peach bitters (substitute: peach brandy)
Stir and strain, add olive and mint leaf.

L

Devon Air
Apple flavour   *Alcohol 2.1*

    1 msr apple brandy
    1/2 msr gin
    2 msr dry cider
    1 teaspoon grenadine
Add to glass half filled with broken ice,
add cherry on a stick.

R

Devon Gin
Cider flavour   *Alcohol 1.5*

    3 msr sweet cider
    3/4 msr gin
    1 teaspoon triple sec
Add to glass half filled with ice.

R

Diablo
Subtle fruit flavour   *Alcohol 1.4*

    2 msr white port
    3/4 msr dry vermouth
    1 teaspoon pineapple syrup
    1 teaspoon lemon juice
Add to glass three-quarters filled with broken ice.

R

Dick Swiveller
Subtle fruit flavour   *Alcohol 1.5*

A heavy drinker in Dickens' *The Old Curiosity Shop*.
    1 msr Geo. A. Dickel whiskey
    1/2 msr sloe gin
    1/4 msr Campari
    1 teaspoon passion fruit syrup
    2 msr 7UP
Add to glass filled with broken ice and mint sprig.

G

Downhill Cocktail

Wine flavour   *Alcohol 1.7*

    1 msr sweet sherry
    1/2 msr gin
    1/2 msr dry vermouth
    1/2 msr dry orange curacao
    1 teaspoon cognac

Stir and strain into glass filled with broken ice.
Garnish: slice of orange and a cherry, add straws.   R

Dubonnet Cocktail

Vermouth / Spirit flavour   *Alcohol 2.2*

    1 1/2 msr Dubonnet
    1 1/2 msr gin

Stir and strain into glass half filled with
broken ice, add lemon twist.   R

Duck Soup

Fruit bourbon flavour   *Alcohol 2.3*

    2 msr bourbon
    1/2 msr apricot brandy
    3/4 msr lemon juice
    3/4 msr pineapple juice
    1/2 teaspoon caster sugar

Shake and strain into glass three-quarters
filled with broken ice.   R

Duke of Cornwall

Apple flavour   *Alcohol 1.5*

    1 msr apple brandy
    1 msr sweet sherry
    2 msr sparkling apple juice

Add to glass half filled with broken ice.   R

Earls Court

Orange / Peach flavour Alcohol 1.9

    1 1/3 msr Bundaberg (substitute: dark rum)
    2/3 msr peach schnapps
    1/3 msr Pimm's No.1
    1 msr mandarin juice
    1 msr lemonade

Shake and strain into glass half filled with
broken ice, add the lemonade. Garnish: cherry
and orange slice, add short straws.   R

East West Cocktail

Bourbon / Peach flavour Alcohol 2.1

    1 msr vodka
    1 msr bourbon
    1/4 msr peach schnapps
    1/4 msr lemon juice

Shake and strain into glass containing
two large ice cubes.   R

Easy Action

Apricot flavour Alcohol 1.4

    1 msr dry vermouth
    3/4 msr apricot brandy
    1/2 msr single grain scotch
    1 teaspoon lemon juice

Shake with a glassful of broken ice and
pour unstrained, add slice of lemon.   R

Eclipse

Fruity flavour Alcohol 1.5

    1 1/2 msr sloe gin
    1/2 msr gin
    approximately 1/2 msr grenadine
    1 red cherry

Shake and strain the gins into glass containing
the cherry. Gently add/sink sufficient grenadine
to just cover the cherry at the bottom of the glass –
but do not mix it with the gins. Garnish: half
slice of orange.   L

Eden Cocktail

Mandarin flavour

Alcohol 1.8

    1½ msr pisco
    ½ msr apricot brandy
    1½ msr mandarin juice
    1 teaspoon lime juice

Shake and strain into glass filled with
crushed ice, add short straw.

D

Egril

Fruity flavour

Alcohol 1.9

    ½ msr dark rum
    ½ msr white rum
    ½ msr Irish Mist
    1½ msr pineapple juice
    ½ a fresh lime
    1 teaspoon caster sugar

Cut lime into eight segments and place in glass,
add sugar and crush until the juice is released.
Add remaining ingredients and ensure sugar has
dissolved, fill up with broken ice. Garnish: slice
of lime and a cherry, add short straw.

R

Emerald Star

Fruity flavour

Alcohol 1.7

    1 msr white rum
    ⅔ msr melon liqueur
    ⅓ msr apricot brandy
    ⅓ msr lime juice
    1 msr passion fruit juice

Shake and strain.

C

Evergreen

Fruity flavour

Alcohol 1.5

    1 msr creme de banane
    ½ msr melon liqueur
    ½ msr blue curacao
    ½ msr gin
    2 msr white grape juice

Shake and strain, add green cherry.

C

Exterminator

Herb flavour

Alcohol 2.5

    1 msr Green Chartreuse
    1 msr overproof white rum

Add to glass filled with broken ice. Garnish: green cherry. **R**

FANCIES

Fancy Brandy

Brandy flavour

Alcohol 2.1

    2 msr brandy
    1 teaspoon triple sec
    1 teaspoon sugar syrup
    1 dash Angostura

Shake and strain into glass three-quarters filled
with broken ice, add twist of lemon. **R**

Replace the brandy in the following Fancies:

Fancy Bourbon	2 msr bourbon
Fancy Gin	2 msr gin
Fancy Scotch	2 msr scotch

Fantaisie

Apricot wine flavour

Alcohol 1.4

    4 msr cold medium white wine
    ¾ msr apricot brandy

Add to frosted glass. **W**

Federal Punch

Lemon flavour

Alcohol 1.9

    1 msr bourbon
    ½ msr dark rum
    ¼ msr cognac
    ¼ msr triple sec
    1 msr lemon juice
    1 teaspoon caster sugar

Shake and strain into glass filled with
crushed ice, add cherry on a stick. **D**

Firebird

Lemon flavour

Alcohol 1.8

1½ msr silver tequila
½ msr creme de banane
½ msr lime juice
2 msr lemonade

Add to glass three-quarters filled with broken ice.　　R

FIXES

An American mix which first appeared in the early nineteenth century. A smaller version of a Cobbler, the Fix is made by adding a spirit-based mixture to crushed ice. A fruit syrup and/or sugar syrup should be included, as should citrus juice. It is decorated with ample fruit in season, and usually served with a twist of lemon and straws.

Originally plain sugar syrup was used, but by 1900 raspberry or pineapple syrup was the norm. Today fruit syrups are less common but are always an option.

Gin Fix

Lemon flavour

Alcohol 2.0

2 msr gin
¾ msr lemon juice
⅓ msr sugar syrup (substitute: pineapple or raspberry syrup)

Combine in mixing glass without ice, then pour into serving glass filled with crushed ice.
Garnish: fruit in season, add short straws
and twist of lemon.　　R

Simply replace the gin in the following popular Fixes:

Bourbon Fix	2 msr bourbon
Brandy Fix	2 msr brandy
Scotch Fix	2 msr scotch
Rum Fix	1 msr dark rum and 1 msr white rum

Santa Cruz Fix

Cherry rum flavour

Alcohol 1.3

  2 msr Santa Cruz rum (substitute: dark rum)
  1 msr cherry brandy
  1 msr lemon juice
  3/4 msr sugar syrup

Add to glass filled with crushed ice.
Garnish: fruit in season, add short straws
and twist of lemon.

R

Flamenco

Sherry brandy flavour

Alcohol 2.1

  1 msr medium sherry
  1 msr armagnac
  1 teaspoon Campari
  1 msr mandarin juice
  1 msr sparkling bitter lemon

Add to glass half filled with broken ice.

R

Flame Thrower

Peach flavour

Alcohol 1.6

  3/4 msr Grappa/Marc
  3/4 msr Southern Comfort
  1 teaspoon overproof white rum

Add to glass, heat and ignite rum in teaspoon and
add flaming to glass. Blow out flame. Shooter.

S

FLIPS

Flips take their name from the old method of flipping them over and over
between two vessels to obtain smoothness. In the 1690s a typical flip
would consist of beaten eggs, sugar, spices, rum and a quantity of hot ale.
This was mulled with a hot iron 'loggerhead' before serving. Today, fully
Americanised, they are invariably served short, cold and sprinkled with
nutmeg.

Flips are now made with any type of liquor, contain egg yolk or whole eggs,
with a dash of light cream optional. Milk cannot be used or they would
become Egg Noggs. Do not be put off by the thought of drinking raw egg;
after mixing it is unrecognisable.

Sherry Flip

Sherry flavour   *Alcohol 1.4*

    2 msr cream sherry
    1/2 msr sugar syrup
    1 small beaten egg

Shake and strain, sprinkle with grated nutmeg.   CS

Replace the sherry in the following popular Flips:

Amaretto Flip	1 1/2 msr amaretto 1/2 msr vodka	*Alcohol 1.5*
Apricot Flip	2 msr apricot brandy	*Alcohol 1.1*
Banana Flip	1 1/2 msr creme de banane 1/2 msr vodka	*Alcohol 1.5*
Blackberry Flip	1 1/2 msr blackberry brandy	*Alcohol 1.2*
Bourbon Flip	2 msr bourbon	*Alcohol 2.0*
Brandy Flip	2 msr brandy/cognac	*Alcohol 2.0*
Chocolate Flip	2 msr Mozart 1/2 msr vodka	*Alcohol 1.3*
Coffee Flip	1 1/2 msr Kahlua 1/2 msr vodka	*Alcohol 1.5*
Comfortable Flip	2 msr Southern Comfort	*Alcohol 2.0*
Gin Flip	2 msr gin	*Alcohol 2.0*
Melon Flip	2 msr Midori	*Alcohol 1.2*
Orange Flip	2 msr dry orange curacao	*Alcohol 1.8*
Peach Flip	2 msr peach schnapps	*Alcohol 1.2*
Pineau Flip	1 1/2 msr pineau des charentes 3/4 msr cognac	*Alcohol 1.5*
Raspberry Flip	2 msr Chambord	*Alcohol 0.9*
Rum Flip	1 msr white rum 1 msr dark rum	*Alcohol 2.0*
Scotch Flip	2 msr scotch whisky	*Alcohol 2.0*
Slow Comfortable Flip	1 msr sloe gin 1 msr Southern Comfort	*Alcohol 1.7*
Slow Flip	2 msr sloe gin	*Alcohol 1.3*
Strawberry Flip	1 1/2 msr creme de fraise 1/2 msr vodka	*Alcohol 1.3*
Tequila Flip	2 msr gold tequila	*Alcohol 2.0*
Vodka Flip	2 msr vodka	*Alcohol 2.0*

Wild Flip   2 msr Wild Turkey   ♈♈♈ *Alcohol 2.0*

Mocha Flip
Chocolate coffee flavour   *Alcohol 1.2*
  1 msr coffee liqueur
  1 msr Mozart
  1 beaten egg yolk
Shake well and strain into glass three-quarters filled with
crushed ice; sprinkle with grated nutmeg.   W

Norman Porto Flip
Wine / Advocaat flavour   *Alcohol 1.7*
  1 msr calvados
  1 msr LBV port
  1 beaten egg yolk
  1 teaspoon caster sugar
Shake well and strain into glass filled with
broken ice, sprinkle with grated nutmeg.   W

Flying Grasshopper
Mint flavour   *Alcohol 2.0*
  1 msr white creme de cacao
  1 msr vodka
  1/3 msr green creme de menthe
Shake briefly with three-quarters
of a glassful of crushed ice, add short straw.   R

Fog Cutter
Orange wine flavour   *Alcohol 1.7*
  1/2 msr brandy
  1/2 msr white rum
  1/2 msr gin
  1/3 msr sweet sherry
  1 msr orange juice
  1/2 msr lemon juice
  1/2 msr sugar syrup
  1 teaspoon orgeat / almond syrup
Shake and strain into glass filled with broken ice.   R

Fondaudège

Lemon / Aniseed flavour

Alcohol 1.9

Courtesy of Marie Brizard Liqueurs, France.

    1 msr Anisette Marie Brizard
    1 msr vodka
    ¹/₃ msr Creme de Mure Marie Brizard
    1 msr lemon juice

Shake and strain into glass half filled with
broken ice, or serve straight up.

R

Forget-Me-Not

Cherry flavour

Alcohol 2.0

    1 msr schnapps
    ³/₄ msr cherry brandy
    ¹/₄ msr kirsch

Add to glass filled with broken ice, add lime twist.

R

Francine

Raspberry flavour

Alcohol 1.5

    ³/₄ msr raspberry liqueur
    ³/₄ msr cognac
    ³/₄ msr rosso vermouth
    2 msr lemonade

Shake and strain into glass half filled with
broken ice, add the lemonade. Garnish: lemon
slice and sugar-dipped raspberry.

R

FRAPPÉS

A short drink simply poured over crushed ice in the serving glass and
served with short straws. Any liqueur or spirit can be used.

Amaretto Frappé

Almond flavour

Alcohol 1.6

    2¹/₂ msr amaretto

Add to glass filled with crushed ice.
Garnish: cherry on a stick, add short straws.

CS

Replace the amaretto in the following popular Frappés:

Apricot Frappé   2¹/₂ msr apricot brandy

Alcohol 1.3

Banana Frappé	2½ msr creme de banane	Alcohol 1.3
Blackberry Frappé	2½ msr blackberry brandy	Alcohol 1.3
Cherry Frappé	2½ msr cherry brandy	Alcohol 1.6
Chocolate Frappé	2½ msr white creme de cacao	Alcohol 1.5
Coffee Frappé	2½ msr coffee liqueur	Alcohol 1.7
Melon Frappé	2½ msr Midori	Alcohol 1.2
Orange Frappé	2½ msr triple sec	Alcohol 1.9
Peach Frappé	2½ msr peach schnapps	Alcohol 1.9
Pernod Frappé	2 msr Pernod ⅔ msr anisette 1 msr cold water	Alcohol 2.5
Raspberry Frappé	2½ msr Chambord	Alcohol 1.0
Sloe Frappé	2½ msr sloe gin	Alcohol 1.7
Strawberry Frappé	2½ msr creme de fraise	Alcohol 1.3
Tiger's Eye Frappé	1¾ msr Pernod ½ msr peppermint schnapps	Alcohol 2.2

All White Frappé

Alcohol 1.5

Sweet herb flavour

1 msr white creme de cacao
1 msr anisette
½ msr white creme de menthe
⅓ msr lime juice

Mix and add to glass filled with crushed ice.
Garnish: cherry on a stick, add short straws.

D

Brandied Apricot Frappé

Apricot flavour

Alcohol 1.7

    1 msr cognac
    1 msr apricot brandy
    1 teaspoon amaretto
    1 msr apricot juice

Mix and add to glass filled with crushed ice.
Garnish: cherry on a stick, add short straws.

D

Cafe Royal Frappé

Coffee flavour

Alcohol 1.0

    1 msr cognac
    3 msr cold black coffee

Mix and add to glass filled with crushed ice.
Garnish: cherry on a stick, add short straws.

D

Chocolate Orange Frappé

Chocolate / Orange flavour

Alcohol 1.7

    1 1/2 msr dark creme de cacao
    3/4 msr Mandarine Napoléon
    1 msr orange juice

Mix and add to glass filled with crushed ice,
add short straw.

CS

Cognac Mint Frappé

Mint brandy flavour

Alcohol 2.0

    1 1/2 msr cognac
    3/4 msr white creme de menthe

Mix and add to glass filled with crushed ice.
Garnish: mint sprig, add short straw.

CS

Fruit Frappé

Fruity flavour

Alcohol 1.4

    1 msr white rum
    1/2 msr creme de banane
    1/4 msr creme de cassis
    1 msr mandarin juice

Mix and add to glass filled with crushed ice,
add short straw.

CS

French Bite
Mandarin flavour

Alcohol 1.8

    1 msr cognac
    ³/₄ msr Mandarine Napoléon
    2 msr sparkling apple juice
Add to ice-filled glass.

R

French Horn
Sour raspberry flavour

Alcohol 1.3

    1 msr vodka
    ³/₄ msr Chambord
    ¹/₂ msr lemon juice
Stir and strain. Garnish: cherry on a stick.

L

Frozen Aquavit
Caraway flavour

Alcohol 2.0

    1³/₄ msr aquavit
    ¹/₄ msr kirsch
    ¹/₂ msr lime juice
    1 teaspoon egg white
    ¹/₃ msr sugar syrup
Shake well and strain into glass
heaped with crushed ice.

CS

Frozen Melon Ball
Fruity flavour

Alcohol 1.6

    1¹/₂ msr Midori
    ¹/₂ msr vodka
    2 msr pineapple juice
    1 teaspoon lime juice
Shake and strain into glass filled with crushed ice.
Garnish: melon ball and slice of lime on a stick,
add short straw.

D

Frozen Southern Comfort

Lime / Peach flavour

Alcohol 2.1

    2 msr Southern Comfort
    1 teaspoon maraschino
    juice of ½ a lime
    ½ teaspoon caster sugar

Blend briefly with a glassful of crushed ice,
add short straws.

D

Fruits of the Desert

Grapefruit flavour

Alcohol 1.9

    1½ msr gold tequila
    ½ msr triple sec
    2 msr grapefruit juice
    1 teaspoon caster sugar

Shake and strain into glass half filled
with broken ice, add cherry.

R

Garden Fresh

Grapefruit flavour

Alcohol 1.4

    1 msr golden rum
    ½ msr melon liqueur
    1 teaspoon pear liqueur
    1½ msr grapefruit juice
    ¾ msr pineapple juice
    1 teaspoon kiwi syrup

Shake and strain, add cherry.

C

Gemini

Orange wine flavour

Alcohol 2.0

    ¾ msr Galliano
    ¾ msr Grand Marnier
    ½ msr cognac
    1 msr lemonade

Add to glass three-quarters filled with
broken ice, add orange twist.

R

German Bight

Fruity flavour   *Alcohol 1.5*

    1 msr apple schnapps
    1/2 msr Barenfang
    1/3 msr rosso vermouth
    1/3 msr dry vermouth
    2 msr pineapple juice

Shake and strain.   C

GIMLETS

A gimlet is a small, sharp, hand tool used to bore holes in wood. Gimlets were commonly used in bars to tap into barrels, and the term eventually came to describe a small sharp cocktail.

The standard gimlet recipe appeared around 1930, and appears to be a cross between these two recipes, which were popular just after the First World War. Gimblet – 1½ msr dry gin, ½ msr lime juice. Shake and strain, add 2 msr soda – no ice. Gimlet – 1 msr Plymouth Gin, 1 msr Rose's Lime Cordial. Stir and strain into ice-filled glass – no soda.

Rose's Lime Cordial is now accepted as being the correct ingredient to use in a Gimlet, as it was virtually the only brand available when the recipe appeared. Some traditionalists also insist on the use of Plymouth Gin, but this is not entirely justified.

Gimlet

Lime flavour   *Alcohol 2.0*

    2 msr gin
    3/4 msr Rose's Lime Cordial
    1 msr cold soda water (optional)

Shake and strain into glass filled with broken ice,
add the soda. Garnish: wedge of lime.   R

Replace the gin in the following popular Gimlets:

Rum Gimlet	2 msr white rum
Tequila Gimlet	2 msr gold tequila
Vodka Gimlet	2 msr vodka

Gloom Raiser

Aniseed gin flavour   *Alcohol 2.6*

Created by Robert Vermeire in 1915 at the Royal Automobile Club, Pall Mall, London.

    2 msr gin

1 msr Noilly Prat (dry vermouth)
1 teaspoon Pernod
1 teaspoon grenadine
Stir and strain, squeeze lemon twist and discard.   CS

Godchild

Almond flavour   *Alcohol 1.7*

    1 msr brandy
    1 msr amaretto

Add to glass three-quarters filled with broken ice.   R

If only 1/3 msr amaretto is used, this is a   *Alcohol 1.3*
Weave and Skid.

Godmother

Almond flavour   *Alcohol 2.0*

    1 1/2 msr vodka
    3/4 msr amaretto

Add to glass three-quarters filled with broken ice.   R

Goin' Home

Peach / Apple flavour   *Alcohol 1.8*

    1 msr gin
    1 msr peach schnapps
    1/2 msr dry vermouth
    1/3 msr lime juice
    1 1/2 msr sparkling apple juice

Shake and strain into glass half filled with
broken ice; add the apple juice.   R

Gold Mine

Lime flavour   *Alcohol 1.2*

    1/2 msr scotch
    1/2 msr Galliano
    1/2 msr sweet sherry
    1 teaspoon egg white
    1 msr lime juice
    1 msr lemonade

Shake well and strain into glass three-quarters
filled with broken ice, add the lemonade.
Garnish: orange slice and cherry.   R

Golden Dawn

Fruity flavour

Alcohol 2.0

    1½ msr applejack
    ½ msr gin
    ¾ msr apricot brandy
    1½ msr orange juice
    1 teaspoon grenadine

Shake and strain. Add grenadine last,
allowing it to sink to bottom.

W

When calvados is used in place of applejack, this is a Normandy Dawn.

Golden Russian

Aniseed flavour

Alcohol 2.5

    1½ msr vodka
    1 msr Galliano
    1 teaspoon lime juice

Add to glass three-quarters filled with broken ice.
Garnish: slice of lime.

R

If Strega is used in place of Galliano, this is a Warlock.

Goodbye Sigh

Fruit brandy flavour

Alcohol 1.8

    1 msr peppermint schnapps
    1 msr apricot brandy
    ½ msr cognac

Shake and strain into glass filled with
crushed ice, add cherry.

CS

Goodness Gracious

Cherry brandy flavour

Alcohol 2.1

    1 msr cherry brandy
    1 msr white creme de cacao
    1 msr cognac
    1 teaspoon egg white

Shake well and strain into glass three-quarters
filled with broken ice.

R

Grand Pear

Orange / Pear flavour — Alcohol 1.3

    1 msr pear liqueur
    1/2 msr Grand Marnier
    1/4 msr poire william
    1 msr mandarin juice
    1 msr pear juice

Shake and strain into glass half
filled with broken ice.

R

Grapevine

Wine flavour — Alcohol 1.5

    1 msr gin
    1/2 msr sweet sherry
    1/2 msr dry sherry
    2 msr red grape juice

Shake and strain into glass filled with broken ice.
Garnish: mint sprig, add short straw.

D

Greek Manhattan

Brandy / Wine flavour — Alcohol 2.5

    2 msr Metaxa brandy
    2 msr red Greek wine (originally Mavrodaphne)

Stir and strain into glass three-quarters filled with
broken ice. Garnish: orange slice and cherry.

C

Grimaldi

Exotic fruit flavour — Alcohol 1.2

Guiseppe Novena, France. Courtesy of Bols International B.V.

    1 msr Safari
    1 msr Pecher Mignon
    1/3 msr Bols Blue Curacao
    1 msr pineapple juice

Shake and strain. Garnish: cherry.

C

Guesswork Cocktail

Fruity flavour   *Alcohol 1.5*

     1 msr peach schnapps
     3/4 msr gin
     1/3 msr dry sherry
     1 msr passion fruit juice
     1 msr pineapple juice
     1/2 msr lime juice

Shake and strain into frosted glass.   C

Hara Kiwi

Kiwi flavour   *Alcohol 1.6*

     1 msr kiwi liqueur
     1 msr Canadian whisky
     1/3 msr lemon juice
     1 msr lemonade

Add to glass half filled with broken ice.
Garnish: kiwi slice and cherry.   R

Harbor Light

Coffee flavour   *Alcohol 2.2*

     1 msr Kahlua
     1 msr triple sec
     1/2 msr cognac
     1 teaspoon overproof white rum

Make pousse-café. Ignite rum in teaspoon
before floating on top.   L

Hard Case

Fruit brandy flavour   *Alcohol 1.8*

     1 1/2 msr cognac
     1/2 msr creme de cassis
     1/4 msr lemon juice

Stir and strain.   B

Hay Fever Remedy

Fruity flavour
Alcohol 1.0

½ msr vodka
¼ Southern Comfort
¼ amaretto
½ msr pineapple juice
1 teaspoon grenadine

Shake and strain. Shooter.
S

Haymaker

Lime bourbon flavour
Alcohol 1.7

The word whisky comes from the Latin *aquae vitae* meaning 'water of life'. Scottish and Canadian producers spell it whisky, American and Irish, whiskey.

There is an exception. The founder of the Maker's Mark bourbon distillery, Mr Samuels, dropped the 'e' from his label, partly in deference to his Scottish ancestry.

¾ msr Maker's Mark bourbon whisky
¾ msr triple sec
¾ msr dry vermouth
¾ msr lime juice

Shake and strain into glass three-quarters filled with broken ice.
R

Hell Frozen Over

Orange / Sloe flavour
Alcohol 1.9

1 msr sloe gin
1 msr dry vermouth
½ msr apricot brandy
½ msr Mandarine Napoléon

Shake and strain into glass filled with crushed ice, add cherry on a stick.
CS

Hen Night Zipper-Ripper

Tart fruit flavour
Alcohol 2.0

1½ msr white rum
1 msr advocaat
¾ msr mandarin juice
¾ msr lime juice
¼ msr grenadine

Shake and strain. Garnish: slice of lime and a cherry.
C

High Road

Scotch flavour

Alcohol 2.2

1½ msr scotch
½ msr Drambuie
½ msr dry sherry
1 teaspoon lemon juice

Shake with a glassful of broken ice and
pour unstrained; add lemon twist.

R

Hollywood Nuts

Nut flavour

Alcohol 1.9

1 msr white rum
½ msr amaretto
½ msr dark creme de cacao
½ msr Frangelico
1 teaspoon egg white
1 msr 7UP

Shake and strain into ice-filled glass,
add the 7UP.

R

Honolulu Shooter

Fruity flavour

Alcohol 1.0

1 msr gin
1 teaspoon pineapple juice
1 teaspoon orange juice
1 teaspoon lemon juice
1 teaspoon pineapple syrup
1 drop Angostura

Shake and strain. Shooter.

S

Hopeless Case

Herb cola flavour

Alcohol 1.1

1 msr sloe gin
½ msr peppermint schnapps
3 msr cold cola

Add to ice-filled glass. Garnish: lime slice.

R

Hustler

Passion fruit flavour   *Alcohol 2.0*

    1 msr golden rum
    1 msr white rum
    1 msr passion fruit juice
    1 msr lime juice
    1 teaspoon caster sugar
Shake and strain into glass filled with broken ice.
Garnish: sprig of mint.   R

Incredible Cocktail

Herb brandy flavour   *Alcohol 2.0*

The original recipe for Chartreuse, using 130 herbs and spices, was
probably produced by an alchemist experimenting with alcoholic
infusions as early as the sixteenth century. In 1605 the 'Elixir of Long
Life' was passed to Carthusian monks – Les Peres Chartreux – and later
on, to the Monastery of La Grande Chartreuse in the French Alps. By
around 1740 the production technique was perfected and Green
Chartreuse appeared. The less alcoholic yellow version appeared in 1838.
In 1876 the Procurator of the monastery obtained an order preventing
any other distiller from using the word Chartreuse on their label. Today
there is only one Chartreuse.

The production facility is now at Voiron; only three monks know the
precise formula.

    1 msr cognac
    1/2 msr Green Chartreuse
    1/2 msr cherry brandy
Stir and strain.   B

Inedible Cocktail

Subtle herb flavour   *Alcohol 2.2*

    1 1/2 msr Canadian whisky
    1/2 msr Glayva
    1/4 msr Punt e Mes
Shake with a glassful of broken ice and pour unstrained.   R

Irish Shillelagh

Fruit whiskey flavour   *Alcohol 2.0*

    1 1/2 msr Irish whiskey
    1/2 msr sloe gin
    1 teaspoon overproof white rum
    1 teaspoon peach schnapps
    1 teaspoon lemon juice
    1 teaspoon sugar syrup
Shake with a glassful of broken ice and pour
unstrained.   R

Italia

Fruity flavour   *Alcohol 2.0*

    3 teaspoons grenadine
    1 teaspoon cherry brandy – mixed

    3 teaspoons anisette
    1 teaspoon white creme de cacao – mixed

    3 teaspoons Yellow Chartreuse
    1 teaspoon blue curacao – mixed

Make pousse-café to produce the colours of the Italian flag.
Difficult but charming, very Italian!   L

Jack Frost

Fruity flavour   *Alcohol 1.5*

    1 msr Jack Daniel's
    3/4 msr dry vermouth
    1/3 msr creme de banane
    1 msr passion fruit juice
    1/3 msr pineapple syrup
Shake and strain into glass filled with crushed ice.   D

Jack Rose

Sharp / Fruity flavour   *Alcohol 2.0*

An old recipe apparently named after the New York gangster.

    2 msr applejack/apple brandy
    1 msr lime juice
    1/2 msr grenadine

Rim glass with grenadine/caster sugar
Shake and strain.   CS

Jamaica Sunday

Lime rum flavour　　　　　　　　Alcohol 2.0

    2 msr dark rum (preferably Jamaican)
    1 teaspoon honey
    1/2 msr lime juice
    2 msr lemonade

Dissolve honey in rum. Add to glass half filled with broken ice.

R

Japanese Slipper

Medium sour flavour　　　　　　　Alcohol 1.8

    1 1/3 msr vodka
    1 1/3 msr melon liqueur
    3/4 msr lemon juice

Shake and strain. Garnish: slice of lemon.

CS

Jerez Cocktail

Fruit wine flavour　　　　　　　Alcohol 1.5

    2 msr dry sherry
    1 teaspoon peach brandy
    1 teaspoon triple sec

Add to glass half filled with broken ice.

R

Jockey Club

Fruit gin flavour　　　　　　　Alcohol 2.4

Created in the 1920s at the Jockey Club, in Havana, Cuba.

    2 msr gin
    1/3 msr amaretto
    1 teaspoon triple sec
    1 dash Angostura
    1/3 msr lemon juice

Shake and strain into glass filled with broken ice.

R

Josephine

Honey cognac flavour　　　　　　Alcohol 1.5

    1 msr cognac
    1/2 msr Irish Mist

Add to glass.

B

245

Juliet

Pineapple flavour

Alcohol 1.6

John Hansen, Denmark. Courtesy of Bols International B.V.

    1 msr gold tequila
    1 msr Pisang Ambon
    1 1/2 msr pineapple juice
    1/2 teaspoon grenadine

Shake and strain. Garnish: pineapple slice
and a cherry.

C

July Passion

Fruity flavour

Alcohol 0.5

    1 msr strawberry liqueur
    1 msr passion fruit juice
    1 msr pineapple juice
    1 msr lemonade

Shake and strain into glass three-quarters filled
with broken ice, add the lemonade.
Garnish: sugar-dipped strawberry.

R

Jungle Frost

Passion fruit flavour

Alcohol 1.5

    3/4 msr gin
    3/4 msr Pisang Ambon
    3/4 msr dry vermouth
    3/4 msr passion fruit juice
    1/2 teaspoon caster sugar

Shake and strain into glass filled with crushed ice.

CS

Jungle Spice

Tropical fruit flavour

Alcohol 1.5

    1 1/2 msr white rum
    1 msr guava juice
    1 msr mandarin juice
    1/2 msr lime juice

Shake and strain into glass filled with crushed ice.
Sprinkle with grated nutmeg, add short straws.

D

Kahlua Cognac

Coffee flavour

Alcohol 1.7

   1 msr Kahlua
   1 msr cognac

Add to glass.

B

Katinka

Sharp apricot flavour

Alcohol 2.3

   1³/₄ msr vodka
   1 msr apricot brandy
   ¹/₂ msr lime juice

Shake and strain into glass filled with crushed ice.
Garnish: sprig of mint.

CS

Kentucky Kernel

Fruit bourbon flavour

Alcohol 1.8

   1¹/₂ msr bourbon
   ¹/₂ msr apricot brandy
   1 msr grapefruit juice
   1 teaspoon Grenadine

Shake with a glassful of broken ice
and pour unstrained.

R

Killarney

Sweet herb flavour

Alcohol 2.5

   1 msr Irish Mist
   1 msr gin
   ³/₄ msr dry vermouth
   ¹/₄ msr rosso vermouth

Shake with a glassful of broken ice and
pour unstrained, add lemon slice.

R

Kir

Blackcurrant flavour   *Alcohol 1.7*

Created by French farm workers in Burgundy, France. They added cassis
to their Bourgogne Aligote wine to make it even more drinkable, and
named the mix after the colourful war hero and Mayor of Dijon, Canon
Felix Kir (1876–1968).

> ¹/₂ msr creme de cassis
> 4 msr cold dry white wine (preferably burgundy)

Add to chilled glass.   W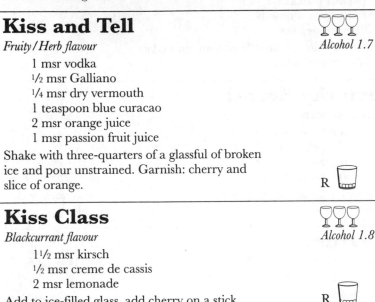

Kiss and Tell

Fruity / Herb flavour   *Alcohol 1.7*

> 1 msr vodka
> ¹/₂ msr Galliano
> ¹/₄ msr dry vermouth
> 1 teaspoon blue curacao
> 2 msr orange juice
> 1 msr passion fruit juice

Shake with three-quarters of a glassful of broken
ice and pour unstrained. Garnish: cherry and
slice of orange.   R

Kiss Class

Blackcurrant flavour   *Alcohol 1.8*

> 1¹/₂ msr kirsch
> ¹/₂ msr creme de cassis
> 2 msr lemonade

Add to ice-filled glass, add cherry on a stick.   R

Kretchma

Sweet lemon flavour   *Alcohol 1.7*

> 1 msr vodka
> 1 msr white creme de cacao
> ¹/₃ msr lemon juice
> 1 teaspoon grenadine

Shake with a glassful of broken ice and pour
unstrained, add slice of lemon.   R

If no grenadine and only ¹/₂ msr cacao is used,   *Alcohol 1.4*
this is a Ninotchka.

La Paz

Orange cola flavour   *Alcohol 2.3*

Named after La Paz in Bolivia. It comes from California.

1 msr white rum
½ msr russo vermouth
½ msr Grand Marnier
1 teaspoon lime juice
2 msr cold cola

Add to glass half filled with broken ice
and lime twist.   R

Lady's Mango

Grapefruit flavour   *Alcohol 1.5*

Courtesy of Marie Brizard Liqueurs, France.

1 msr gin
1 msr Mango Passion Marie Brizard
2½ msr grapefruit juice
1 teaspoon grenadine

Shake and strain.   C

Last Chance

Lime flavour   *Alcohol 1.9*

1¾ msr gold tequila
¼ msr apricot brandy
1 msr lime juice
1 teaspoon honey

Shake with a glassful of broken ice and pour
unstrained, add lime wedge.   R

Last Goodbye

Fruit brandy flavour   *Alcohol 1.7*

1 msr cognac
¾ msr cherry brandy
¼ msr triple sec
½ msr lime juice
1 teaspoon grenadine

Add to glass half filled with broken ice.   R

Laugh a Minute

Cherry flavour   *Alcohol 1.8*

Perhaps inspired by Philemon, a Greek comic poet who is said to have died laughing at his own jokes.

    1 msr cherry vodka
    1 msr rosso vermouth
    1/2 msr amaretto
    2 msr lemonade

Shake and strain into glass half filled with broken ice, add the lemonade.

R

Lawnmower

Sweet grass flavour   *Alcohol 1.1*

    1 msr bison grass vodka
    1 teaspoon sweet sherry
    3 msr lemonade

Add to glass filled with broken ice.

R

Lazy Lover

Fruity flavour   *Alcohol 2.0*

    1 1/2 msr Southern Comfort
    1/2 msr armagnac
    1 msr pineapple juice
    3/4 msr lime juice
    1/2 msr passion fruit syrup

Shake and strain, add cherry on a stick.

C

Le '333'

Sour fruit flavour   *Alcohol 1.8*

Courtesy of Père Magloire Calvados.

    1 msr calvados
    1 msr dry orange curacao
    1 msr grapefruit juice

Shake and strain into glass three-quarters filled with crushed ice. Garnish: slice of lemon, cherry and sprig of mint. Add a straw.

F

Le Saintongeais

Subtle herb flavour   *Alcohol 1.2*

Pierre-Jean Baillard, France.

>   3 msr pineau des charentes white
>   1 teaspoon triple sec
>   1 dash Angostura

Shake and strain into glass filled with
broken ice, add twist of lemon.   R

Leap Year

Orange gin flavour   *Alcohol 2.7*

Created on 29 February 1928 during leap year celebrations by Harry
Craddock, head barman at the American Bar, at the Savoy Hotel,
London.

Craddock was a leading American bartender in his day, and became
something of a celebrity. In 1930 he published the now highly collectable
Savoy Cocktail Book. In 1939 he moved to the Dorchester Hotel, and in
1951 opened a new cocktail bar at Brown's Hotel.

>   1½ msr gin
>   ¾ msr Grand Marnier
>   ¾ msr rosso vermouth
>   1 teaspoon lemon juice

Shake and strain into glass filled with
broken ice, squeeze lemon twist and discard.
Originally served straight up.   R

Leg Spreader

Sweet herb flavour   *Alcohol 1.2*

>   ¾ msr sambuca
>   ¾ msr Tia Maria

Add to glass. Shooter.   S

Lemon Lady

Lemon flavour   *Alcohol 1.4*

>   1 msr brandy
>   ½ msr triple sec
>   3 msr lemon sherbet/sorbet

Shake without ice and pour into frosted glass.
Garnish: cherry and slice of lemon, add short straw.   CS

Liberator

Mango flavour

Alcohol 1.8

    1¹/₂ msr vodka
    ¹/₂ msr melon liqueur
    2 msr mango juice
    ¹/₂ msr lime juice

Shake and strain, add slice of lime.

C

Lime Passion

Tropical fruit flavour

Alcohol 2.0

Courtesy of Marie Brizard Liqueurs, France.

    2 msr Lime Citron Marie Brizard
    1 msr Coconut Passion Marie Brizard
    ¹/₂ msr white rum
    1 msr orange juice
    ¹/₂ msr soda water

Shake and strain, add the soda. Garnish: lime slice.
Sometimes served on the rocks.

C

Little Red Riding Hood

Red fruit flavour

Alcohol 1.8

    1 msr gin
    ³/₄ msr creme de mure
    ³/₄ msr wild strawberry liqueur
    1¹/₂ msr orange juice

Shake and strain into glass filled with
crushed ice. Garnish: berries, add short straw.

D

Little White Lie

Tropical fruit flavour

Alcohol 1.9

    1¹/₂ msr white rum
    1 msr lychee wine
    ¹/₂ msr lime juice
    ¹/₂ msr passion fruit juice

Shake and strain into glass filled with
crushed ice, add short straw.

D

London Fog

Aniseed flavour *Alcohol 2.7*

   1³/₄ msr gin
   1³/₄ msr anisette
Shake and strain into glass filled with crushed ice,
add lemon slice.

CS

Lost Bikini

Mandarin / Herb flavour *Alcohol 1.8*

   ³/₄ msr Galliano
   ³/₄ msr amaretto
   ¹/₂ msr white rum
   ¹/₂ msr lime juice
   2 msr mandarin juice
Shake and strain. Garnish: two cherries.

C

Luigi

Mandarin flavour *Alcohol 2.3*

Created around 1925 by Luigi Naintré, a famous restaurateur, whilst
working at the Criterion, London.

   1¹/₂ msr gin
   1¹/₂ msr dry vermouth
   ¹/₂ teaspoon Cointreau
   1 teaspoon grenadine
   1 msr mandarin juice
Shake and strain. Garnish: cherry and slice of orange.

C

Luxury

Fruity flavour *Alcohol 2.5*

Walter Simpson, USA. Courtesy of Bols International B.V.

   1¹/₃ msr gin
   ²/₃ msr Bols Creme de Bananes
   ²/₃ msr rosso vermouth
   ²/₃ msr Pimm's No.1
   ²/₃ msr Rose's Lime Cordial
   1 dash Angostura
Shake and strain.

C

Mach 1

Sloe flavour   *Alcohol 0.7*

    1 msr sloe gin
    1 msr cold 7UP
Add to glass. Shooter.   S

Mackinnon Spice

Lime flavour   *Alcohol 1.8*

Drambuie is made from fine Scotch whisky, heather honey and herbs. It
has been made by the Mackinnon family since 1745 and was enjoyed by
Bonnie Prince Charlie. The precise recipe is passed down and known
only to the female members of the family.

    1 msr Drambuie
    3/4 msr spiced rum
    1/2 msr lime juice
    1 msr lemonade
Add to glass three-quarters filled with broken ice.   R

Maggie May

Fruit wine flavour   *Alcohol 1.4*

    2/3 msr raspberry liqueur
    1 msr dry vermouth
    3 msr red lambrusco wine
Add to frosted glass.   F

Maiden's Kiss

Herb flavour   *Alcohol 1.4*

    1/3 msr creme de roses (substitute: Licor 43)
    1/3 msr maraschino
    1/3 msr triple sec
    1/3 msr Yellow Chartreuse
    1/3 msr Benedictine
Stir and strain. Originally made pousse-café style.   L

Major Bailey

Mint gin flavour   *Alcohol 2.0*

    2 msr gin
    1 teaspoon lemon juice
    1 teaspoon lime juice

1 teaspoon caster sugar
2 mint sprigs

Add to glass, gently crush mint and fill up with
crushed ice. Garnish: cherry and fresh mint sprig.   D

Malayan Gold

Tropical fruit flavour   *Alcohol 1.5*

   1 msr Pisang Ambon
   1 msr anisette
   1 msr mandarin juice
   1/2 msr pomegranate juice
   1/2 teaspoon caster sugar

Shake and strain into glass filled with crushed ice.   D

Man Overboard

Pomegranate flavour   *Alcohol 2.0*

   1 msr cognac
   3/4 msr triple sec
   1/2 msr Galliano
   2 msr pomegranate juice
   1 heaped teaspoon caster sugar

Dissolve sugar, shake and strain. Garnish: cherry.   C

Maragato Special

Orange / Lime flavour   *Alcohol 2.1*

Invented by Emilio 'Maragato' González, Florida Hotel Bar, Cuba,
around 1920. His famous recipe only became widely available after his
death in 1935.

   1 msr white rum
   3/4 msr dry vermouth
   3/4 msr rosso vermouth
   1/2 teaspoon maraschino
   juice of 1/3 orange
   juice of 1/2 lime

Shake and strain into glass filled with crushed ice.
Garnish: slices of orange and lime.   D

MARGARITAS

Actress Marjorie King was the inspiration for this world famous cocktail in 1948. She was a regular guest at Rancho La Gloria, a restaurant owned by Mr Danny Herrera near Tijuana, Mexico. As she was allergic to most spirits except tequila, Herrera mixed this specially for her and named it Margarita – Mexican for Marjorie.

Margarita

Citrus flavour   *Alcohol 2.9*

> 2 msr silver tequila
> 1¼ msr triple sec
> ¾ msr lemon juice

Rim chilled glass with lemon juice/salt.
Few people like much salt. Shake and strain,
add thin wedge of lemon.   CS

Replace the triple sec in the following popular Margaritas:

Blue Margarita	¾ msr blue curacao	*Alcohol 2.3*
Galliano Margarita	¾ msr Galliano	*Alcohol 2.5*

FROZEN MARGARITAS

Frozen Margarita

Citrus flavour   *Alcohol 2.7*

> 1¾ msr silver tequila
> 1¼ msr triple sec
> ¾ msr lemon juice

Rim glass with lemon juice/salt. Shake and strain
into glass filled with crushed ice. Garnish: slice
of lemon.   D

Replace the triple sec in the following popular Frozen Margaritas:

Frozen Blue Margarita	¾ msr blue curacao	*Alcohol 2.2*
Frozen Pink Margarita	½ msr grenadine	*Alcohol 1.8*

Golden Margarita

Orange flavour Alcohol 2.8

  1³/₄ msr gold tequila
  ¹/₂ msr Cointreau
  ¹/₂ msr Grand Marnier
  ³/₄ msr lemon juice

Rim glass with lemon juice/salt. Shake and
strain into glass filled with crushed ice.
Garnish: slice of lime.   D

If the Cointreau is omitted, this becomes a Granrita.

FROZEN FRUIT MARGARITAS

Strawberry Margarita

Strawberry flavour Alcohol 2.3

  1¹/₂ msr gold tequila
  ³/₄ msr strawberry liqueur
  ¹/₂ msr triple sec
  1 msr strawberry puree
  ³/₄ msr lemon juice

Rim frosted glass with lemon/caster sugar.
Blend briefly with a glassful of crushed ice.
Garnish: half a strawberry.   D

Simply replace the strawberry liqueur and puree in the following popular
Frozen Fruit Margaritas:

Mandarin Margarita	²/₃ msr Mandarine Napoléon	
	Garnish: orange slice	Alcohol 2.5
Melon Margarita	1 msr melon liqueur	
	Garnish: lemon wedge	Alcohol 2.4

Banana Margarita

Banana flavour Alcohol 1.9

  1 msr creme de banane
  1 msr gold tequila
  ¹/₂ msr triple sec
  ³/₄ msr lemon juice
  ¹/₄ of a banana – mashed

Rim frosted glass with lemon/caster sugar.
Blend briefly with a glassful of crushed ice.
Garnish: lemon juice-dipped slice of banana.   D

Peach Margarita

Peach flavour　　　　　　　　　　　*Alcohol 1.9*

　　　1 msr peach schnapps
　　　1 msr gold tequila
　　　1/2 msr triple sec
　　　1/3 of a ripe peach – peeled and mashed
　　　3/4 msr lemon juice

Rim glass with lemon/caster sugar. Blend briefly
with a glassful of crushed ice until smooth.
Garnish: slice of peach.　　　　　　D

Marimba

Tropical fruit flavour　　　　　　　*Alcohol 1.7*

　　　1 msr Southern Comfort
　　　1/2 msr gin
　　　1/4 msr amaretto
　　　1 msr pineapple juice
　　　1 msr mango juice
　　　1/4 msr lime juice

Shake and strain. Garnish: orange and pineapple slices.　C

Martian Cherry

Fruit/Herb flavour　　　　　　　　*Alcohol 2.0*

　　　1 msr cherry vodka
　　　1 msr dry vermouth
　　　3/4 msr sloe gin
　　　1 msr pineapple juice

Shake and strain into glass three-quarters
filled with broken ice.　　　　　　R

Mary Pickford

Pineapple flavour　　　　　　　　*Alcohol 1.6*

Created in the 1920s at the Hotel Sevilla Bar, Cuba, and named after the
popular actress.

　　　1 1/2 msr white rum
　　　1 teaspoon maraschino
　　　1 1/2 msr pineapple juice
　　　1 teaspoon grenadine

Shake and strain into glass filled with crushed ice,
add cherry on a stick and short straw.　　　D

Mayfair

Orange flavour

Alcohol 2.0

Created by Robert Vermeire, Embassy Club, London, 1921.

    2 msr gin
    1/4 msr apricot brandy
    2 msr orange juice
    1 teaspoon syrup of cloves

Shake and strain.   C

Melonade

Melon flavour

Alcohol 1.0

    1 1/2 msr Midori
    2 msr lemonade

Add to glass filled with broken ice.
Garnish: green cherry.   R

Melon Tree

Melon flavour

Alcohol 2.1

    1 1/2 msr melon liqueur
    1 msr white rum
    1 teaspoon Southern Comfort
    1/2 msr lime juice
    1 msr lemonade

Add to glass three-quarters filled with broken ice.   R

Merlin's Love Potion

Fruity flavour

Alcohol 1.9

    2 msr watermelon schnapps
    1/2 msr lemon vodka
    1/4 msr strawberry brandy

Shake and strain into glass filled with crushed ice.
Garnish: lemon slice and sugar-dipped strawberry.   CS

Mexican Flag

Herb flavour

Alcohol 1.5

    2/3 msr grenadine
    2/3 msr white creme de menthe
    2/3 msr Green Chartreuse

Make pousse-café. Shooter.   S

Mexican Strawberry

Strawberry flavour

Alcohol 2.0

> 2 msr gold tequila
> 1 msr orange juice
> 1 msr strawberry puree
> 1/4 msr strawberry syrup
> 1/4 msr lemon juice

Shake and strain into glass filled with crushed ice.
Garnish: sugar-dipped strawberry.

D

Millionaire

Subtle fruit flavour

Alcohol 2.0

Created around 1910 in New York.

> 1 1/2 msr Canadian whisky
> 1/2 msr triple sec
> 1/3 msr grenadine
> 1/2 msr egg white
> 1 teaspoon pastis/Pernod

Shake well and strain into a glass filled with broken ice.

D

Mint Gin

Mint gin flavour

Alcohol 2.0

> 1 1/2 msr gin
> 3/4 msr white creme de menthe
> 1 teaspoon green creme de menthe
> 1/2 msr egg white
> 1 teaspoon lemon juice

Shake well and strain into glass three-quarters
filled with broken ice. Garnish: mint sprig.

R

Missile Rider

Sweet herb flavour

Alcohol 2.0

> 1 1/2 msr vodka
> 1/3 Yellow Chartreuse
> 1/2 teaspoon Pernod
> 2/3 msr lime juice
> 1/2 teaspoon caster sugar

Shake and strain into glass three-quarters
filled with broken ice.

R

Missile Stopper

Fruity flavour *Alcohol 1.3*

 1 msr cognac
 ½ msr strawberry liqueur
 1 msr grapefruit juice
 1 msr pineapple juice
 1 teaspoon grenadine

Shake and strain into glass three-quarters
filled with broken ice. R

MISTS

Scotch Mist

Whisky flavour *Alcohol 2.0*

 2 msr scotch whisky

Shake briefly with a glassful of crushed ice
and pour, add twist of lemon peel. R

Substitute the scotch in the following popular Mists:

Bourbon Mist	2 msr bourbon Replace lemon with cherry	*Alcohol 2.0*
Brandy Mist	2 msr brandy/cognac Replace lemon with cherry	*Alcohol 2.0*
Canadian Mist	2 msr Yukon Jack Replace lemon with cherry	*Alcohol 2.0*
Comfortable Mist	2 msr Southern Comfort Replace lemon with cherry	*Alcohol 2.0*
Gin Mist	2 msr gin Replace lemon with twist of lime peel	*Alcohol 2.0*
Rum Mist	2 msr dark rum Replace lemon with twist of lime peel	*Alcohol 2.0*
Russian Mist	2 msr vodka Replace lemon with twist of lime peel	*Alcohol 2.0*
Rye Mist	2 msr rye/Canadian whisky Replace lemon with cherry	*Alcohol 2.0*
Sloe Comfortable Mist	1 msr Southern Comfort 1 msr sloe gin Replace lemon with cherry	*Alcohol 1.8*

Tequila Mist	2 msr gold tequila Replace lemon with twist of lemon peel	 *Alcohol 2.0*

Modern Cocktail

Scotch flavour *Alcohol 2.7*

This was modern in the 1920s.

> 2 msr scotch
> 1/3 msr dark rum
> 1 teaspoon Pernod
> 1 teaspoon triple sec
> 1/3 msr lemon juice

Shake and strain.

C

Monkey Gland

Fruity flavour *Alcohol 2.1*

Created by Harry MacElhone around 1920 at Ciro's Club, London.

> 2 msr gin
> 2 msr orange juice
> 1 teaspoon Pernod
> 2 teaspoons grenadine

Shake and strain. Garnish: slice of orange wrapped around a cherry.

C

Monkey Tree

Mango flavour *Alcohol 1.5*

> 1 msr gold tequila
> 1/2 msr Rum Tree
> 1/2 msr creme de banane
> 1/3 msr lime juice
> 2 msr mango juice

Rim frosted glass with grenadine/caster sugar. Shake and strain.

C

Moon Drops

Beer flavour *Alcohol 1.3*

> 1 msr sweet sherry
> 4 msr cold lager

Add to glass. Garnish: two melon balls.

W

Morticia

Herb flavour

Alcohol 2.1

1 msr gin
1/2 msr Pernod
1/2 msr dry vermouth
1/2 msr sloe gin
1 teaspoon lemon juice
1/4 msr sugar syrup

Shake with a glassful of broken ice
and pour unstrained.

R

Mulata

Lime flavour

Alcohol 1.9

Created in the 1940s by Cuban barman José Maria Vázquez.

13/4 msr golden rum
1/4 msr dark creme de cacao
juice of 1/2 lime

Shake briefly with a glassful of crushed ice.

D

Mule's Hind Leg

Fruit / Herb flavour

Alcohol 1.5

1/2 msr gin
1/2 msr apple brandy
1/3 msr Benedictine
1/3 msr apricot brandy
1/3 msr maple syrup

Shake and strain into glass three-quarters
filled with broken ice.

R

Narragansett

Bourbon / Herb flavour

Alcohol 2.2

2 msr bourbon
1/3 msr rosso vermouth
1 teaspoon anisette

Add to glass filled with broken ice.
Add twist of lemon.

R

New York

Lime / Whisky flavour

Alcohol 2.0

    2 msr Canadian whisky
    3/4 msr lime juice
    1/2 msr sugar syrup
    1 teaspoon grenadine

Shake and strain into glass three-quarters filled with broken ice, add twist of orange.

R

If bourbon is used in place of Canadian and the sugar syrup is omitted, this is a New Yorker.

Night Skies Over London

Port flavour

Alcohol 1.5

    1 msr gin
    1 msr LBV port
    1/4 msr lime juice
    1 teaspoon sloe gin
    2 msr lemonade

Add to glass half filled with broken ice.

R

Nightie Lifter

Blackberry flavour

Alcohol 2.0

    1 1/2 msr bourbon
    3/4 msr blackberry brandy
    1 teaspoon peach schnapps

Shake with a glassful of broken ice and pour unstrained.

R

Noblesse

Strawberry flavour

Alcohol 2.4

Courtesy of Reynac Pineau.

    1 1/3 msr pineau des charentes white
    1 msr gin
    2/3 msr strawberry liqueur
    1/3 msr Yellow Chartreuse

Shake and strain into glass filled with broken ice. Garnish: a seedless grape.

R

Novocaine

Bitter lemon flavour   *Alcohol 1.9*

    1½ msr Pisang Ambon
    ¾ msr gin
    ¼ msr Green Chartreuse
    2 msr sparkling bitter lemon

Shake with half a glassful of broken ice
and pour unstrained, add the lemon.   R

O.D.

Fruity flavour   *Alcohol 1.0*

    ⅓ msr Southern Comfort
    ⅓ msr vodka
    ⅓ msr amaretto
    ⅓ msr orange juice
    ⅓ msr pineapple juice

Add to glass. Shooter.   S

One Exciting Night

Herb flavour   *Alcohol 2.0*

    1 msr Plymouth gin
    1 msr dry vermouth
    1 msr rosso vermouth
    1 teaspoon orange juice
    1 teaspoon grenadine

Shake and strain into glass filled with
broken ice, add orange twist.   D

Operation Recoverer

Fruity flavour   *Alcohol 1.6*

    1 msr lemon vodka
    1 msr peach schnapps
    2 msr mandarin juice
    1 teaspoon grenadine

Shake and strain into glass three-quarters
filled with broken ice, or serve straight up.
Garnish: fruit in season, add short straw.   R

Operator

Ginger wine flavour   *Alcohol 0.7*

> 2 msr cold dry white wine
> 2 msr dry ginger ale
> 1 teaspoon lime juice

Add to ice-filled glass, add half slice of lime.   R

Orange Blossom

Orange flavour   *Alcohol 1.5*

During the Second World War, President Roosevelt shook one of these for Winston Churchill. The Prime Minister broke the habit of a lifetime by refusing a second drink.

> 1½ msr gin
> 1½ msr orange juice
> ½ teaspoon caster sugar

Dissolve sugar, shake and strain into glass filled with crushed ice. Garnish: orange slice and cherry. Originally served straight up.   D

If gin is replaced with peach brandy, this is a Peach Blossom.   *Alcohol 0.8*

Orange Comfort

Orange / Peach flavour   *Alcohol 1.5*

> 1½ msr Southern Comfort
> 3 msr orange juice
> ¼ msr lemon juice

Shake and strain into glass half filled with broken ice.   R

Orange Tree

Orange flavour   *Alcohol 1.7*

> ⅔ msr Mandarine Napoléon
> ⅔ msr cognac
> ⅔ msr apricot brandy
> ⅔ msr mandarin juice
> 2 msr lemonade

Add to glass filled with broken ice and orange slice.   R

Ozone

Fruit wine flavour   *Alcohol 1.3*

   3/4 msr sweet sherry
   3/4 msr bourbon
   1 teaspoon Campari
   1 msr pineapple juice
   1/2 msr lime juice
   1 teaspoon grenadine

Shake with a glassful of broken ice
and pour unstrained.

R

Palmera

Pineapple flavour   *Alcohol 1.9*

Courtesy of Cinco Dias & Co, Havana Club Rum.

   1 1/2 msr Havana Club light dry rum (white rum)
   1 1/2 msr medium white wine
   3/4 msr pineapple juice
   1/2 teaspoon grenadine
   1/2 teaspoon lime juice

Shake and strain over large single ice cube.

W

Pamplemousse

Grapefruit flavour   *Alcohol 2.0*

   1 1/2 msr Canadian whisky
   1/2 msr Southern Comfort
   2 msr grapefruit juice
   1 teaspoon pineapple syrup

Shake with a glassful of broken ice and
pour unstrained, add small grapefruit
slice and a cherry.

R

Pan-Galactic Gargle Blaster

Melon flavour   *Alcohol 1.8*

   1 1/2 msr melon liqueur
   1/2 msr overproof white rum
   1/2 msr lime juice
   1/4 msr pineapple syrup
   1 1/2 msr lemonade

Shake and strain, add the lemonade.

F

Paradise

Apricot / Orange flavour

Alcohol 2.0

1 1/2 msr gin
1 msr apricot brandy
2 msr orange juice

Shake and strain. Garnish: blossom of a flower
(preferably white orchid) and cherry on a stick.

CS

Parrot

Sweet herb flavour

Alcohol 2.2

1 msr Yellow Chartreuse
1 msr dry vermouth
1 msr apricot brandy
1 teaspoon anisette

Stir and strain into glass filled with broken ice.
Garnish: red, green and yellow cherries on a stick.

W

Passion Punch

Fruity flavour

Alcohol 1.5

1 1/2 msr golden rum
1 msr red grape juice
1 msr passion fruit juice
1 teaspoon pineapple syrup

Shake with a glassful of broken ice and pour unstrained.

R

Peach Picnic

Peach flavour

Alcohol 1.4

1 msr peach schnapps
1 msr apple schnapps

Add to glass. Shooter.

S

Peacock's Tail

Sweet herb flavour

Alcohol 1.4

1 msr Green Chartreuse

Add to frosted glass and half fill with crushed ice. Damp down
slightly with flat end of barspoon. Add 3/4 msr semi-frozen
grenadine to form a layer. Fill up with lemon sherbet/sorbet
and sprinkle 1 teaspoon Strega on top.
Garnish: mint leaf and cherry, add straw.

F

Pepper Eater

Orange flavour

Alcohol 1.8

   1 msr gold tequila
   1 msr triple sec
   1 teaspoon pepper vodka
   1 msr orange juice
   1 msr cranberry juice

Shake and strain into glass three-quarters filled
with broken ice; add a red pepper.

R

Perfect Lady

Light / Sour flavour

Alcohol 1.3

   1 msr gin
   1/2 msr peach brandy
   1/2 msr lemon juice
   1 msr egg white

Blend briefly with a glassful of crushed ice.
Garnish: peach slice.

D

Petite Fleur

Citrus flavour

Alcohol 2.4

   1 1/3 msr Cointreau
   1 msr white rum
   1 1/3 msr grapefruit juice
   1/3 msr sugar syrup (optional)

Shake and strain, add cherry on a stick.

C

Pineapple Hornblower

Pineapple flavour

Alcohol 1.5

   1 1/2 msr gin
   1 1/2 msr pineapple juice
   1/2 msr lemon juice
   1/2 msr sugar syrup
   1 teaspoon Baileys

Shake and strain into glass filled with crushed ice.

D

Pineau-cchio

Orange wine flavour

Alcohol 1.4

1½ msr pineau des charentes white
½ msr cognac
½ msr triple sec

Rim glass with orange/caster sugar.
Add to glass filled with broken ice.
Garnish: slice of orange.

W

Pink Almond

Fruity flavour

Alcohol 1.8

1 msr scotch whisky
½ msr kirsch
½ msr Amaretto di Saronno
½ msr lemon juice
½ msr orgeat/almond syrup
¼ msr grenadine

Shake and strain into glass filled with crushed ice.
Garnish: fruits in season.

D

Pink Elephant

Lemon whisky flavour

Alcohol 2.0

2 msr bourbon
¾ msr lemon juice
⅓ msr grenadine
1 teaspoon egg white

Shake well and strain into glass filled with crushed
ice. Garnish: slice of lemon and cherry on a stick.

C

Pink Gin

Spirity flavour

Alcohol 2.0

In 1824 Dr Johan G. B. Siegert perfected his bitter-tasting formula using various local plant extracts, as a remedy for stomach complaints suffered by the Venezuelan army. He named it after the town on the Orinoco River where he had worked – Angostura.

The British Navy added this product to its medicine chest, but soon discovered it added a whole new dimension to Plymouth gin, and thus created a 'Pink Gin'.

2 msr Plymouth gin

4 dashes Angostura
iced water

Coat interior bottom half of frosted glass
with Angostura, discard the excess. Stir and
strain gin into glass and serve with the water.

W

If served with soda water, not plain, this is a Coaster.

Pinko

Fruity flavour   *Alcohol 1.6*

    1 msr vodka
    1 msr apricot brandy
    2 msr pineapple juice
    1 teaspoon grenadine

Shake and strain into glass filled with
broken ice. Garnish: cherry.

D

Pino Frio

Pineapple flavour   *Alcohol 1.5*

A Cuban speciality.

    1½ msr white rum
    2 heaped tablespoons pineapple chunks or pieces
    1 teaspoon caster sugar

Blend until smooth, add three-quarters of
a glassful of crushed ice and blend again briefly.

R

Pit Stop

Cherry flavour   *Alcohol 1.9*

    1 msr kirsch
    1 msr cherry brandy
    1 teaspoon amaretto
    2 msr lemonade

Add to glass half filled with broken ice.

R

Plank Walker

Scotch / Herb flavour   *Alcohol 2.3*

    1½ msr Johnnie Walker scotch
    ½ msr rosso vermouth
    ½ msr Yellow Chartreuse

Add to glass three-quarters filled with broken ice.

R

Pomegranate Polecat

Pomegranate flavour   *Alcohol 2.0*

    1¹/₃ msr white rum
    ¹/₂ msr amaretto
    ¹/₂ msr sweet sherry
    1¹/₂ msr pomegranate juice
    1 teaspoon caster sugar
Shake and strain into glass three-quarters
filled with broken ice.

R

Pompanski

Grapefruit flavour   *Alcohol 1.4*

Poland and Russia both claim to have invented vodka. The word vodka is
either derived from 'voda', meaning 'water' in Russian, or from 'wodka',
meaning vodka in Polish, itself taken from their word 'woda' meaning
'little water'.

    1 msr Polish vodka
    ¹/₂ msr dry vermouth
    1 teaspoon triple sec
    1 msr grapefruit juice

Shake with a glassful of broken ice and pour
unstrained. Garnish: slice of orange and
a short straw.

R

Pork Chop on Toast

Cherry flavour   *Alcohol 2.0*

    1 msr Russian vodka
    1 msr cherry vodka
    2 msr tonic water
Shake and strain into glass half filled with
broken ice. Add the tonic and cherry on a stick.

R

Port Side

Blackberry flavour   *Alcohol 2.2*

    1¹/₂ msr cognac
    ¹/₂ msr LBV port
    ¹/₂ msr blackberry brandy
Stir and strain.

B

Porterhouse Blue

Blueberry flavour   *Alcohol 2.0*

1½ msr Canadian whisky
½ msr armagnac
½ msr blueberry syrup

Shake and strain into glass filled with broken ice.
Garnish: slice of lemon and blue cherry.   R

Presidente

Subtle herb flavour   *Alcohol 2.7*

Created around 1920 at the Vista Alegre Bar, Havana, Cuba, for
President General Mario Menocal.

2 msr white rum
1 msr rosso vermouth
⅓ msr dry vermouth
1 teaspoon grenadine

Stir and strain into glass filled with crushed ice.
Originally served straight up. Garnish: slice of
orange and a cherry.   R

Presidente Seco (Dry)

Subtle fruit flavour   *Alcohol 2.5*

Created around 1930 by Eddie Woelke from Paris at the Jockey Club,
Havana, Cuba, for President General Gerardo Machado.

2 msr golden rum
1 msr dry vermouth
1 teaspoon grenadine

Stir and strain into frosted glass, add orange twist.   C
If a teaspoon each of triple sec and lemon juice are added,
this is an El Presidente – a 1940s recipe.

Prohibition Cocktail

Subtle herb flavour   *Alcohol 3.0*

US Prohibition (1919–1933) led to a boom in cocktail invention, mainly
because bootlegged liquor was usually so awful it had to be mixed to
disguise the taste.

2 msr Plymouth gin
2 msr Lillet (dry vermouth)
½ teaspoon apricot brandy
1 teaspoon orange juice

273

Shake and strain. Squeeze twist of
lemon and discard.

C

Purple Cactus
Passion fruit flavour　　　　　　　　　　　*Alcohol 1.7*

    1¹/₂ msr gold tequila
    ¹/₂ msr sweet sherry
    1¹/₂ msr passion fruit juice
    1 teaspoon grenadine

Shake and strain into glass three-quarters
filled with broken ice, add cherry on stick.　　　R

If Greek brandy is used in place of tequila, this is a Purple Lizard.

If Wild Turkey is used in place of tequila, this is a Purple Turkey.

Quilt Lifter
Fruity flavour　　　　　　　　　　　*Alcohol 1.5*

    1 msr white rum
    ¹/₂ msr dry sherry
    ¹/₂ msr creme de banane
    1 msr pineapple juice
    1 msr orange juice
    ¹/₂ msr passion fruit juice

Shake briefly with a glassful of crushed ice.
Garnish: fruit in season.　　　　　　　　　D

If scotch is used in place of dry sherry,　　　*Alcohol 2.0*
this is a Kilt Lifter.

RAC Cocktail
Herb / Fruit flavour　　　　　　　　　　　*Alcohol 2.3*

Created by Fred Faecks in 1914 at the Royal Automobile Club, Pall Mall,
London.

    1¹/₂ msr gin
    ³/₄ msr dry vermouth
    ³/₄ msr rosso vermouth
    1 teaspoon orange bitters (substitute dry orange curacao)
    1 teaspoon grenadine

Stir and strain, add cherry on stick.
Squeeze orange twist and discard.　　　　　C

Randy Andy

Fruity flavour

Alcohol 1.7

   1 1/2 msr white rum
   1/3 msr creme de banane
   1 msr grapefruit juice
   1 msr guava juice
   1/3 msr lime juice
   1/3 msr passion fruit syrup

Shake and strain. Garnish: lime wedge.

C

Rare Beef

Subtle herb flavour

Alcohol 2.0

   1 msr Beefeater gin
   1/2 msr J & B scotch
   1 msr rosso vermouth
   1 msr lemonade

Add to glass half filled with broken ice,
add cherry on stick.

R

Alcohol 2.3

If only 1/2 msr rosso is used and 1/2 msr
Southern Comfort added, this is a
Southern Rare Beef.

Rebel Rouser

Bourbon flavour

Alcohol 2.2

   2 msr Rebel Yell bourbon
   1/3 msr creme de banane
   1 teaspoon Campari

Add to glass filled with broken ice.

R

Red Finnish

Red berries flavour

Alcohol 1.5

   1 msr Finlandia vodka
   1 msr strawberry brandy
   1/2 msr lime juice
   1 msr pomegranate juice
   1 teaspoon caster sugar

Shake and strain into glass three-quarters filled
with broken ice. Garnish: cherry.

R

Red Russian

Cherry flavour   *Alcohol 1.8*

G. Kristjannson, Iceland. This 1969 creation is one of the earliest 'Russians'.

> 1 msr vodka
> ½ msr cherry brandy
> ½ msr apricot brandy

Shake with a glassful of broken ice and pour
unstrained. Originally served straight up.   R

Ridley

Subtle aniseed flavour   *Alcohol 2.1*

Created around 1960 at Duke's Hotel, London.

> 1 msr gold tequila
> 1 msr gin
> 1 teaspoon Galliano

Stir and strain into glass filled with crushed ice,
sprinkle the Galliano on top. Garnish: orange
slice and a cherry.   CS

Rob Roy

Scotch / Herb flavour   *Alcohol 2.5*

> 2 msr scotch
> 1 msr rosso vermouth
> 4 drops Angostura

Stir and strain into glass filled with broken ice.
Garnish: cherry on a stick.   R

If a teaspoon of sugar syrup is added, this becomes a Flying Scot.

If dry vermouth is used in place of rosso, this is
a Dry Rob Roy. Add twist of lemon.

Roman Candle

Fruit wine flavour   *Alcohol 2.3*

> 1 msr dark rum
> 1 msr brandy
> ½ msr LBV port
> 1 msr raspberry syrup
> ¾ msr lemon juice

Shake and strain into glass filled with crushed ice.
Garnish: fruit in season, add straws.   R

Rosalind Russell

Caraway / Herb flavour　　　　　　　　*Alcohol 2.5*

Named after the 1930s film star.

    2 msr Danish akvavit
    1 msr rosso vermouth

Stir and strain, add twist of lemon.　　C

Rose Cocktail

Sour fruit flavour　　　　　　　　*Alcohol 1.5*

"Napoleon I is said to have invented the cocktail. His favourite 'pick-me-up' was called a 'Rose' ". W. M. Thackeray, *The Newcomers*, 1855. This version emerged from the Chatham Bar, Paris, in the 1920s.

    2 msr dry vermouth
    1/2 msr kirsch
    1/2 msr grenadine

Shake and strain.　　C

Round-Up

Sweet brandy flavour　　　　　　　　*Alcohol 2.2*

    1 msr brandy
    3/4 msr creme de banane
    1 msr white creme de cacao
    1/2 msr white creme de menthe
    1 msr 7UP

Shake and strain, add the 7UP.　　C

Royal Passion

Red fruit flavour　　　　　　　　*Alcohol 2.0*

    1 1/2 msr vodka
    1 msr raspberry liqueur
    1 msr passion fruit juice

Shake and strain into glass filled with broken ice.　　R

Rum Ramsay

Lime flavour　　　　　　　　　　　　　*Alcohol 1.9*

Created around 1930 by Albert Martin at the Bon Ton Bar, New
Orleans. He kept the recipe a secret for many years before revealing it to
Trader Vic.

    1 1/2 msr white rum
    1 teaspoon bourbon
    juice of 1/4 of a lime
    1/3 msr sugar syrup
    1 dash Peychaud Bitters (substitute: Angostura)

Squeeze lime juice directly into mixing glass
and add the spent shell. Add remaining ingredients,
stir and strain into serving glass filled with broken
ice. Originally served straight up.　　　　R

Sailing By

Fruity flavour　　　　　　　　　　　　*Alcohol 1.7*

    1 msr blueberry liqueur (creme de myrtille)
    1 msr white rum
    1/2 msr LBV port
    1/4 msr lemon juice
    2 msr dry ginger ale

Shake and strain into glass filled with
broken ice, add the ginger. Garnish: slice of
lemon and blue cherry, add short straw.　　　G

Santiago

Fruity flavour　　　　　　　　　　　　*Alcohol 1.9*

    1 1/2 msr white rum
    1/2 msr triple sec
    3/4 msr lime juice
    1 teaspoon grenadine
    1/2 msr sugar syrup

Shake and strain into glass filled with broken ice,
add cherry on a stick.　　　　R

Saronno Rose

Almond flavour

Alcohol 1.1

   1½ msr Amaretto di Saronno
   ⅓ msr lime juice cordial
   2 msr soda water

Add to glass filled with broken ice.

R

If Southern Comfort is used in place of
Amaretto di Saronno, this is a Snakebiter.

Alcohol 1.5

Satan's Whiskers

Orange flavour

Alcohol 2.6

   1 msr gin
   1 msr rosso vermouth
   1 msr dry vermouth
   ½ msr Grand Marnier
   1 tsp Triple Sec
   1 msr orange juice

Shake and strain, add a slice of orange.
Can be served on the rocks.

C

SAZERAC™

Ready-mixed Sazerac is regarded as being closest to the original recipe,
and comes highly recommended. It is bottled and sold by the Sazerac
Company, Inc. The Sazerac co-starred with James Bond in the film *Live
and Let Die*.

SCAFFAS

Popular in the 1860s until the early 1900s, Scaffas are no longer seen commercially. Scaffa is an old Norse term meaning 'to make something yourself', appropriate as the ingredients were simply added to the glass.

Brandy Scaffa

Brandy flavour

Alcohol 2.3

    1½ msr brandy
    ¾ msr maraschino
    1 dash Angostura
Add to glass.   C

Rum Scaffa

Herb flavour

Alcohol 2.1

    1⅓ msr white rum
    ⅔ msr Benedictine
    1 dash Angostura
Add to glass. Originally occasionally made pousse-café. C
If gin is used in place of the rum, this is a Gin Scaffa.

Scarlett O'Hara

Fruity flavour

Alcohol 2.0

    2 msr Southern Comfort
    1 msr cranberry juice
    ⅓ msr lime juice
Shake and strain into glass filled with crushed ice.
Garnish: cherry on stick.   CS

Scotsmac – *see* Whisky Mac

September Morn

Lime flavour

Alcohol 2.0

Created at the Hotel Inglaterra, Cuba, around 1920.

    2 msr white rum
    ⅔ msr lime juice
    1 teaspoon grenadine
    ½ msr egg white
Rim frosted glass with lime/caster sugar.
Shake well and strain.   CS

Sex on the Beach

Fruity flavour

Alcohol 0.7

²/₃ msr melon liqueur
²/₃ msr raspberry liqueur
²/₃ msr pineapple juice
¹/₂ msr lemon juice

Shake and strain into glass three-quarters filled
with broken ice, or reduce quantities slightly and
serve straight up in a shot glass as a shooter.

R

She's Paying

Sweet orange flavour

Alcohol 2.4

1 msr vodka
1 msr Kahlua
¹/₂ msr Grand Marnier
1 teaspoon amaretto

Shake and strain into glass filled with broken ice,
add cherry on a stick.

R

Shindig

Orange / Peppermint flavour

Alcohol 1.2

1¹/₂ msr peppermint schnapps
2¹/₂ msr orange juice

Shake with a glassful of broken ice and pour
unstrained. Garnish: orange slice and cherry.

R

Ship's Cat

Fruit rum flavour

Alcohol 1.3

1 msr overproof dark rum
1 teaspoon Vimto (substitute: creme de cassis)

Add to glass with one small lump of ice.

S

Sidecar

Citrus flavour   Alcohol 2.0

Created shortly after the First World War at Harry's Bar, Paris. An Army captain was in the habit of arriving in a chauffeur-ridden motorcycle sidecar, and Harry created this for him.

     1 msr cognac
     1 msr Cointreau
     1 msr lemon juice

Shake and strain. Garnish: slice of lemon. A dash of sugar syrup is now often added. The Sidecar is more often served now with broken ice in a rocks glass and with a little less lemon.   CS

If apple brandy is used in place of the cognac, this is an Applecart.

If white rum is used in place of the cognac, this is a Rum Sidecar.

If 1½ msr gin is used in place of the cognac, this is a Chelsea Sidecar.   Alcohol 2.5

If a measure of white rum is added to a Sidecar, this is a Boston Sidecar.   Alcohol 3.0

Slaber

Fruity flavour   Alcohol 1.4

Stanley Caruana, Malta. Courtesy of Bols International B.V.

     1 msr Bols Kiwi Liqueur
     1 msr Bols Blue Curacao
     ⅔ msr Bols Creme de Bananes
     1⅓ msr sparkling water
     ⅓ msr lemon juice
     ⅓ msr orange juice

Add to ice-filled glass.   R

Slippery Dickel

Fruit bourbon flavour   Alcohol 2.3

     1½ msr Geo. A. Dickel whiskey
     ¾ msr Cointreau
     ¾ msr lime juice
     1 teaspoon grenadine

Shake with a glassful of broken ice and pour unstrained.   R

Slow Finnish
Sloe / Cola flavour

Alcohol 1.9

   1 msr sloe gin
   1 msr Finlandia vodka
   1 teaspoon dark rum
   2 msr cold cola

Add to glass three-quarters filled with broken ice.

If the sloe gin is replaced with ⅔ msr Quetsch, this is a Quick Finnish.

Small Nurses, Thank Heaven For
Mandarin flavour

Alcohol 1.8

   1 msr lemon vodka
   ½ msr Drambuie
   ¼ msr Benedictine
   2 msr mandarin juice

Shake and strain into glass half filled with broken ice, add cherry on stick.

SMASHES

The Smash appeared in American literature in 1859, and is believed to take its name from the practice of smashing up ice until it was sufficiently fine for this cocktail.

Smashes are basically scaled-down Juleps. They can be based on any spirit and are usually served in a rocks glass.

Brandy Smash
Mint / Brandy flavour

Alcohol 2.0

   2 msr brandy
   2–3 sprigs mint
   ½ msr sugar syrup

Add to glass and crush mint leaves gently, fill up with crushed ice. Garnish: slice of orange and a cherry, add a fresh mint sprig.

Replace the brandy in the following popular Smashes:

Gin Smash	2 msr gin
Rum Smash	2 msr white rum
Scotch Smash	2 msr scotch

Solitaire

Fruity flavour

Alcohol 1.5

1 msr golden rum
½ msr triple sec
1 teaspoon apricot brandy
½ msr lime juice
2 msr cherryade

Add to glass three-quarters filled with broken ice.
Garnish: slice of orange and a cherry, add straw.

G

Sore Throat

Subtle fruit flavour

Alcohol 2.1

1½ msr gin
⅓ msr Cointreau
⅓ msr rosso vermouth
⅓ msr Rum Tree

Shake with a glassful of broken ice and pour
unstrained, add lemon slice.

R

Southern Delta

Fruit bourbon flavour

Alcohol 2.0

1½ msr bourbon
½ msr Southern Comfort
⅓ msr lime juice
1 teaspoon pineapple syrup

Shake with a glassful of broken ice
and pour unstrained.

R

Space

Hazelnut gin flavour

Alcohol 2.4

1¾ msr gin
1¼ msr hazelnut liqueur
¼ msr lemon juice

Shake and strain into glass three-quarters
filled with broken ice.

R

Spanish Fly

Almond flavour

Alcohol 1.8

1½ msr gold tequila
½ msr sweet sherry

Add to glass filled with broken ice.

R

Spanish Guitar

Red wine flavour

Alcohol 1.5

1½ msr sweet sherry
1 msr dry vermouth
¼ msr cherry vodka

Shake with a glassful of broken ice and
pour unstrained, add cherry on a stick.

R

Stem-winder

Rich port flavour

Alcohol 2.2

1 msr triple sec
1 msr LBV port
1 msr dark creme de cacao
1 teaspoon coffee liqueur
1 teaspoon overproof white rum

Shake briefly with a glassful of crushed ice,
add twist of lemon.

D

Stinger

Mint brandy flavour

Alcohol 2.6

2 msr cognac
1 msr white creme de menthe

Shake and strain into glass filled with crushed ice.
Originally served straight up (pre-Prohibition).

CS

Replace the cognac in the following popular Stingers:

Bee Stinger	1½ msr blackberry brandy	*Alcohol 1.7*
Comfortable Stinger	1½ msr Southern Comfort	*Alcohol 2.1*
Roman Stinger	¾ msr Sambuca	*Alcohol 2.1*
	¾ msr cognac	

Strangelove

Cherry flavour

Alcohol 2.3

    1½ msr vodka
    1 msr cherry vodka
    1 teaspoon kirsch
    2 msr cherryade

Add to glass half filled with broken ice. Garnish: cherry. R

Stratocaster

Fruity flavour

Alcohol 1.7

    1 msr dark rum
    1 msr creme de cassis
    1 teaspoon lemon juice
    1 msr lemonade
    1 msr soda water

Add to glass filled with broken ice.
Garnish: slice of lemon and a cherry, add short straw. G

Strike's On

Fruit gin flavour

Alcohol 2.0

Genever is assumed to have taken its name from the French word *genièvre* meaning juniper.

In the 1680s, the English monarchy greatly encouraged the production of genever and its consumption in preference to imported spirits. Soon the name was shortened to geneva, ginevy and by 1714 to gin.

    2 msr Bols Zeer Oude Genever
    ½ msr lemon juice
    ⅓ msr pineapple syrup
    1½ msr sparkling apple juice

Shake and strain into glass fulled with broken ice,
add the apple and a slice of lemon. R

Superman

Mandarin flavour

Alcohol 1.6

Today London Dry Gin is as popular as ever. Dryness or sweetness in a gin does not refer to sugar content – no sugar is added – but to the proportion of sweet-tasting herbs and spices in relation to bitter-tasting roots and barks used in the infusion.

    1 msr gin
    ¾ msr dry vermouth

¹/₂ msr apricot brandy
1 msr mandarin juice
1 teaspoon grenadine

Shake with a glassful of broken ice and pour
unstrained, add cherry on stick.   R

Supreme

Fruity flavour   *Alcohol 1.9*

R. Reeves, The White House Hotel. Courtesy of Gordon's London Dry Gin.

1¹/₂ msr gin
³/₄ msr peach brandy
³/₄ msr orange juice
1 teaspoon egg white
1 dash Angostura

Shake and strain into glass filled with crushed ice.   CS

Swedish Blue

Blueberry flavour   *Alcohol 2.0*

1¹/₂ msr Absolut vodka
¹/₂ msr armagnac
¹/₂ msr blueberry syrup
1 teaspoon blue curacao
¹/₃ msr lime juice

Shake with a glassful of broken ice and pour unstrained.
Garnish: slice of orange and blue cherry.   R

TNT

Dark mandarin flavour   *Alcohol 2.2*

Aztec Indians traditionally gave *pulque*, the fermented sap of assorted
agave plants, to priests, heroes and sacrificial victims. In 1519, Cortes's
soldiers began to distil pulque, and produced *mezcal*, after the native word
for the agave, *metl*. In the nineteenth century the town of Tequila became
associated with a high quality *mezcal* made from *agave tequilana*. This
became known as Tequila, and today has its own appellation.

1 msr gold tequila
¹/₂ msr Mandarine Napoléon
1 msr Tia Maria

Stir and strain into glass three-quarters filled
with broken ice, add twist of orange.   R

Tailor Made

Fruit gin flavour

Alcohol 2.1

   1 msr gin
   1 msr Pisang Ambon
   3/4 msr dry vermouth
   1 teaspoon watermelon schnapps
Shake and strain into glass filled with broken ice.

R

Tangerine Cocktail

Tangerine flavour

Alcohol 1.9

   1/2 msr vodka
   1/2 msr Cointreau
   1/2 msr Mandarine Napoléon
   1/2 msr amaretto
   1 msr mandarin/tangerine juice
   1 teaspoon grenadine
Shake and strain into glass filled with crushed ice.
Garnish: orange slice and a cherry, add short straw.

CS

Tempo Setter

Sour herb flavour

Alcohol 1.5

   1 msr Canadian whisky
   1/4 msr triple sec
   1/4 msr rosso vermouth
   1/4 msr anisette
   1 teaspoon lemon juice
Shake and strain. Add cherry on stick.

L

Ten Pin Gin

Sharp mandarin flavour

Alcohol 3.0

   1 1/2 msr London Dry Gin
   1 1/4 msr Mandarine Napoléon
   1 msr dry vermouth
   1/2 msr lime juice
   1 teaspoon egg white
   1 msr sugar syrup
Shake and strain, add squeeze of lime twist
and discard. Garnish: slices of orange and lime.

C

Tequila Exotica

Fruity flavour   *Alcohol 1.7*

   1½ msr gold tequila
   ¼ msr white creme de cacao
   1 teaspoon triple sec
   1 msr mango juice
   1 msr white grape juice
   ½ msr lime juice

Shake and strain into glass three-quarters filled
with broken ice. Garnish: fruit in season, add straw.   R

Tequila Shot

Tequila / Lime flavour   *Alcohol 1.0*

Tequila the Mexican way.

   1 msr gold tequila
   1 small pinch salt
   1 wedge of lime

Hold lime between finger and thumb, place salt at
base of thumb of same hand. Quickly lick salt,
down tequila and bite the lime.   S

If the salt is placed on a partner's bare skin, anywhere on their
anatomy, and the lime segment has its juice squeezed on to the
skin next to the salt, when they are licked off in the same order
as above, this is an Idaho Licker.

Tequila Slammer

Tequila flavour   *Alcohol 1.0*

In France – Tequila Rapido, in Germany – Tequila Boom-Boom.

   1 msr gold tequila
   1 msr lemonade, dry ginger ale or sparkling wine

Add to glass. Cover with hand or beer mat,
rap twice on table. Down in one whilst fizzing.   S

If champagne is used in place of lemonade,
this is a Slammer Royale.   *Alcohol 1.3*

Tobago

Guava flavour   ·

Alcohol 2.0

   1 msr white rum
   1 msr gin
   1 msr lime juice
   1/2 msr guava syrup

Blend briefly with a glassful of crushed ice,
add twist of lime.   D

Tonight's the Night

Fruit brandy flavour

Alcohol 1.8

   1 1/2 msr cognac
   1/2 msr rosso vermouth
   1/3 msr passion fruit syrup

Shake with a glassful of broken ice and pour unstrained. R

Torpedo

Brandy / Coffee flavour

Alcohol 2.7

   2 msr brandy
   1 msr coffee liqueur
   1/3 msr egg white

Shake well and strain into glass
three-quarters filled with broken ice.   R

Tour de France

Aniseed flavour

Alcohol 1.8

   1 1/2 msr Pernod
   1/2 msr creme de cassis
   1 teaspoon caster sugar
   1 msr lemonade

Dissolve sugar, add to glass filled with broken ice.   R

Touch of Zam

Fruity / Herb flavour

Alcohol 2.0

   1 msr Glayva
   1/2 msr Benedictine
   1/2 msr sambuca
   1 1/2 msr orange juice
   1/3 msr sugar syrup
   1 teaspoon lemon juice

Shake and strain into glass filled with crushed ice. Add slice of orange.

CS

Tree Shaker

Fruity flavour   *Alcohol 1.0*

   1 msr Rum Tree
   1 msr pear liqueur
   1 msr mandarin juice
   1 msr pineapple juice

Shake and strain into glass filled with crushed ice, add short straws.

D

Tropical Dawn

Sour orange flavour   *Alcohol 2.3*

   2 msr gin
   1/2 msr Campari
   2 msr orange juice

Shake and strain gin and orange into glass filled with crushed ice. Sprinkle the Campari on top, add short straw.

D

Tuna on Rye

Subtle herb flavour   *Alcohol 2.0*

   1 1/2 msr rye/Canadian whisky
   1 msr rosso vermouth
   2 msr ginger ale

Add to glass half filled with broken ice.

R

Turkey Feather

Bourbon flavour   *Alcohol 2.7*

In July 1794, in Western Pennsylvania, USA, 500 armed men, mainly still-owning farmers, staged the infamous Whiskey Rebellion against the new liquor tax.

   2 msr Wild Turkey whiskey
   1/2 msr Drambuie
   1/4 msr Amaretto di Saronno

Stir and strain into glass three-quarters filled with broken ice. Add slice of orange.

R

If only 1 msr bourbon is used and a teaspoon of triple sec added, this is a Barbera.

Alcohol 1.8

Urbinos

Raspberry flavour Alcohol 2.2

> 3 msr pineau des charentes white
> 1 msr cognac
> ½ msr raspberry liqueur

Shake and strain.

C

Vanderbilt

Cherry flavour Alcohol 2.3

Created in 1912 by 'Guido' of Kursaal Bar, Ostende, in Belgium, on the occasion of a visit by Colonel Cornelius Vanderbilt, the American millionaire. The Colonel drowned shortly afterwards in the *Lusitania*, and his cocktail promptly became world famous.

> 1½ msr cognac
> 1 msr cherry brandy
> 1 teaspoon sugar syrup
> 1 dash Angostura

Add to glass filled with broken ice and twist of lemon.

R

Venus Rum

Fruity flavour Alcohol 2.4

> 1½ msr white rum
> 1 msr apricot brandy
> ½ msr triple sec
> ½ msr lime juice
> 1 msr soda water

Shake and strain into glass filled with broken ice, add the soda. Garnish: slice of starfruit, add short straws.

R

Verdi

Peach flavour Alcohol 3.4

Phillippe Galas, France. Courtesy of Bols International B.V.

> 1¾ msr gin
> 1¼ msr Pecher Mignon
> 1 msr dry vermouth
> ½ msr Benedictine
> 1 teaspoon Bols Blue Curacao

Stir and strain. Garnish: slice of peach and sprig of mint. C

Viking Warmer

Blueberry flavour   *Alcohol 2.0*

    1¹/₂ msr vodka
    ¹/₂ msr aquavit
    ¹/₂ msr blueberry syrup
    ¹/₄ msr lime juice
    1 msr lemonade

Add to glass three-quarters filled with broken ice.
Garnish: cherry on stick.   R

Visitor's Treat

Fruity flavour   *Alcohol 2.4*

Written in a nineteenth century hotel visitors' book: 'I came here for a
change and rest. The waiter got the change and the landlord got the rest.'
Anon. *Harpers Gazette*, London 1902.

    1 msr gin
    ³/₄ msr Cointreau
    1 msr creme de banane
    1 msr mandarin juice
    1 teaspoon egg white

Shake well and strain.   C

War Cloud

Coffee flavour   *Alcohol 1.6*

    ¹/₂ msr vodka
    ¹/₂ msr brandy
    ¹/₂ msr Kahlua
    ¹/₂ msr Baileys

Shake and strain.   L

Ward Eight

Lemon bourbon flavour   *Alcohol 2.0*

Created in 1898 at Locke Ober's Winter Place Wine Rooms, Boston,
USA, to celebrate an electoral victory clinched in the city's eighth ward.

    2 msr bourbon
    1 msr lemon juice
    1 msr sugar syrup
    1 teaspoon grenadine

Shake and strain into glass filled with broken ice.
Garnish: slices of citrus fruit and a cherry,
serve with short straws.   G

Waste of Time Cocktail

Fruity flavour　　　　　　　　　　　*Alcohol 1.6*

    1 msr Midori
    1 msr white rum
    1/2 msr amaretto
    2 msr pineapple juice

Prepare two glasses.
Glass 1: rim with grenadine/caster sugar,
add cherry on stick. Garnish: fruit in season.
Glass 2: plain ungarnished. Shake and
strain into glass 2. Serve both.　　Cx2

Western Rose

Sour fruit flavour　　　　　　　　　　*Alcohol 2.1*

    1 1/2 msr gin
    1/2 msr dry vermouth
    1/2 msr apricot brandy
    1 teaspoon lemon juice

Shake and strain.　　　　　　　　　　C

If a teaspoon of grenadine is added, this is an English Rose.

Whisky Mac

Scotch flavour　　　　　　　　　　　*Alcohol 1.3*

Also known as Scotsmac.

    1 msr scotch
    2/3 msr green ginger wine

Add to glass three-quarters filled with broken ice.　　R

White Flag

Hazelnut flavour　　　　　　　　　　*Alcohol 0.7*

    1 msr Frangelico
    1/4 msr Baileys

Gently float Baileys on the Frangelico. Shooter.　　S

White Lady

Lemon flavour   *Alcohol 3.0*

Created by Harry MacElhone in 1919 at Ciro's Club, London. In 1923
he took over a bar in Rue Daunou, Paris, renaming it Harry's New York
Bar. In 1929 he altered the White Lady recipe, using gin in place of white
creme de menthe, and this became a world-wide favourite. He created
many well-known recipes, and the bar flourishes to this day.

> 1½ msr gin
> 1½ msr Cointreau
> 1½ msr lemon juice

Shake and strain into frosted glass.
Often served on the rocks with a little less lemon.   C

White Sands

Fruit rum flavour   *Alcohol 2.2*

Courtesy of Cinco Dias & Co, Havana Club Rum.

> 2 msr Havana Club Old Gold (golden rum)
> 1 teaspoon creme de banane
> ½ teaspoon coffee liqueur
> ⅔ msr lime juice
> ⅔ msr pineapple juice

Shake and strain into frosted glass.
Garnish: pineapple slice and a cherry.   C

Wicked Willy

Fruit wine flavour   *Alcohol 0.7*

> 2 msr full bodied red wine
> ⅓ msr passion fruit syrup
> 2 msr dry ginger ale

Add to frosted glass.   W

Wild Irish Rose

Lemon / Whiskey flavour   *Alcohol 2.0*

> 2 msr Irish whiskey
> ¾ msr lemon juice
> ½ msr grenadine
> 2 msr soda water

Add to glass three-quarters filled with broken ice.   R

Wild Island

Fruit bourbon flavour

Alcohol 2.3

1³/₄ msr Wild Turkey
1 msr tropical fruit schnapps
¹/₂ msr mandarin juice

Shake and strain into glass filled with crushed ice.
Garnish: wedge of orange.

CS

Winter Garden

Peach flavour

Alcohol 1.9

2 msr Canadian whisky
¹/₂ msr peach schnapps
¹/₄ msr sweet sherry

Shake and strain into glass filled with crushed ice.

CS

Witch Hunt

Scotch / Herb flavour

Alcohol 1.5

1 msr scotch
¹/₂ msr dry vermouth
¹/₄ msr Strega
1 msr lemonade

Add to glass three-quarters filled with broken ice.

R

Worried Monk

Lime / Herb flavour

Alcohol 1.8

1 msr white rum
¹/₂ msr coconut rum
¹/₄ msr triple sec
¹/₄ msr Yellow Chartreuse
³/₄ msr lime juice
¹/₄ msr orgeat / almond syrup

Shake and strain into glass three-quarters
filled with broken ice.

R

Yellow Parrot

Herb flavour   *Alcohol 1.1*

Created around 1935 by Albert Coleman at the Stork Club, New York.

¹/₃ msr absinthe (substitute: Pernod)
¹/₂ msr Yellow Chartreuse
¹/₃ msr apricot brandy

Shake and strain.   L

Yeoman's Passion

Passion fruit flavour   *Alcohol 1.8*

A prize-winning recipe, courtesy of its inventor, Brian Page, bars manager at one of London's top casino bars.

1 msr Beefeater gin
1 msr Pisang Ambon
¹/₂ msr dry vermouth
2 msr passion fruit juice
¹/₃ msr egg white

Shake well and strain. Garnish: slices of
lime and lemon.   C

Yum-Yum

Tropical fruit flavour   *Alcohol 1.8*

1¹/₂ msr white rum
¹/₂ msr coconut rum
1 msr mango juice
1 msr peach juice
¹/₃ msr lime juice

Shake and strain into glass filled with crushed ice.
Garnish: lime slice.   D

Cocktails made with less than five measures of fluid before shaking, and with a third of a measure or more of cream, milk or ice-cream.

Absent Friend

Pomegranate flavour   *Alcohol 1.0*

    1 msr gin
    1/3 msr grenadine
    1/3 msr whipping cream
    1/2 msr egg white

Shake well and strain, sprinkle with nutmeg.   L

ALEXANDERS

A group which has grown up around the Brandy Alexander.

Alexander's Sister

Mint flavour   *Alcohol 2.3*

    2 msr gin
    2/3 msr green creme de menthe
    1 1/3 msr double cream

Shake and strain, sprinkle with nutmeg.   CS

Brandy Alexander

Chocolate flavour   *Alcohol 2.5*

The great Brandy Alexander has a sophisticated quality despite its simple construction.

    1⅓ msr brandy
    1⅓ msr dark creme de cacao
    1⅓ msr double cream

Shake and strain. Garnish: grated chocolate or nutmeg.   CS

Replace the brandy in the following popular Alexanders:

| Amaretto Alexander | 1⅓ msr Amaretto di Saronno |
Alcohol 1.8 |
| Rum Alexander | 1 msr white rum
⅓ msr dark rum |
Alcohol 2.5 |

Coffee Alexander

Coffee flavour   *Alcohol 1.7*

    1 msr brandy
    1 msr coffee liqueur
    1 msr cream

Shake and strain, sprinkle with grated chocolate.   CS

Gin Alexander

Chocolate flavour   *Alcohol 2.5*

    2 msr gin
    1 msr white creme de cacao
    1 msr double cream

Rim glass with lemon/caster sugar
Shake and strain, sprinkle with grated nutmeg.   CS

If equal measures of gin, cacao and cream are used,
this is a Princess Mary. Created by Harry MacElhone
at Ciro's Club, London, to celebrate the marriage of
Princess Mary to Lord Lascelles in 1922.

Alexandra

Fruit brandy flavour   *Alcohol 2.6*

    1 msr cognac
    1 msr Cointreau
    1 msr white creme de cacao
    1 msr whipping cream
    1 teaspoon egg yolk

Shake well and strain.   CS

Angel's Kiss

Sweet herb flavour — Alcohol 1.1

½ msr dark creme de cacao
½ msr prunelle liqueur
½ msr sloe gin
½ msr whipping cream
Make pousse-café.

L

Angel's Treat

Chocolate rum flavour — Alcohol 2.2

One for the chocaholics.

1½ msr dark rum
1 msr Amaretto di Saronno
1½ msr whipping cream
½ teaspoon sifted cocoa powder
Shake and strain. Garnish: grated chocolate.

C

Anisette Cocktail

Aniseed flavour — Alcohol 1.2

1 msr anisette
½ msr gin
½ msr whipping cream
½ msr egg white
Shake and strain, sprinkle with nutmeg.

L

Apple à la Mode

Apple flavour — Alcohol 1.0

1 msr dark rum
2 msr apple juice
1 tablespoon vanilla ice-cream
Blend briefly with half a glassful of crushed ice.
Garnish: sprig of mint.

D

Arago

Banana flavour — Alcohol 2.5

1½ msr cognac
1¼ msr creme de banane
1¼ msr whipping cream
Shake and strain.

CS

Banana Bliss

Banana flavour   *Alcohol 1.9*

Expect purrs of delight as they curl around this one.

    1¼ msr creme de banane
    1¼ msr white rum
    ¾ msr filtered orange juice
    1¼ msr double cream
    2 teaspoon grenadine
    2 drops Angostura

Shake all but the grenadine and strain into glass. Carefully pour the grenadine just inside the rim of the glass so it runs down the inside, leaving a red smear as it sinks to the bottom. Garnish: two slices of banana speared either side of a cherry. C

Banana Nutbread

Sweet banana flavour   *Alcohol 1.4*

    1 msr Frangelico
    1 msr creme de banane
    ½ msr dry sherry
    1 tablespoon vanilla ice-cream

Blend briefly with half a glassful of crushed ice. D

Barbary Coast

Sweet scotch flavour   *Alcohol 1.8*

A 1920s recipe, originally without rum.

    ½ msr gin
    ½ msr white rum
    ½ msr scotch
    ½ msr white creme de cacao
    ½ msr double cream

Shake and strain into glass three-quarters filled with broken ice. R

Bazooka

Fruity flavour   *Alcohol 1.3*

    1 msr Southern Comfort
    ½ msr creme de banane
    ⅔ msr whipping cream
    1 teaspoon grenadine

Shake and strain. Garnish: two halves of a cherry. L

Belmont

Raspberry flavour

Alcohol 1.0

    1 msr gin
    1 msr whipping cream
    1/3 msr raspberry syrup
Shake and strain.

L

Black Dublinski

Coffee flavour

Alcohol 2.5

Sold throughout the world, Baileys recently accounted for one per cent of all Irish exports.

    1 msr Baileys
    1 msr Kahlua
    1 msr vodka
    1/2 msr dry sherry
Shake and strain.

CS

Blushin' Russian

Coffee flavour

Alcohol 1.9

    1 msr vodka
    1 msr Kahlua
    1/3 msr amaretto
    1 msr whipping cream
Shake and strain.

F

Brandy Alexander – *see* Alexanders

Brasier d'Ange

Sweet herb flavour

Alcohol 1.4

Courtesy of Marie Brizard Liqueurs, France.

    1/2 msr triple sec
    1/2 msr double cream
    2/3 msr white creme de cacao
    2/3 msr parfait amour
Make pousse-café.

L

Broker's Thought

Lime flavour

Alcohol 1.5

    3/4 msr white rum
    3/4 msr bourbon
    3/4 msr lime juice
    2 msr milk
    1 teaspoon caster sugar
Shake and strain.

C

Butter Pecan

Nutty flavour

Alcohol 0.6

    1 msr Frangelico
    2 tablespoons vanilla ice-cream
    5 pecan nuts – coarsely chopped
Blend briefly.

D

Cadiz

Blackberry wine flavour

Alcohol 1.4

    3/4 msr blackberry brandy
    3/4 msr sweet sherry
    1/2 msr triple sec
    1/2 msr double cream
Shake and strain.

L

Cafe Trinidad

Sweet coffee flavour

Alcohol 2.0

    1 msr dark rum (preferably Trinidad)
    3/4 msr amaretto
    3/4 msr Tia Maria
    1 msr double cream
Shake and strain.

CS

Calvados Cream

Fruit brandy flavour

Alcohol 2.0

    2 msr calvados
    1/2 msr lemon juice
    1/2 msr egg white
    1 msr double cream
    1 teaspoon pineapple syrup
Shake and strain.

C

Candida

Brandy / Mint flavour Alcohol 1.7

    1 msr cognac
    1 msr anisette
    1 msr whipping cream
    1/2 msr egg white

Shake well and strain into glass
filled with crushed ice.   CS

Cape Snow

Orange flavour Alcohol 1.8

    1 msr brandy
    1 msr Van Der Hum (substitute: Mandarine Napoléon)
    2 tablespoons vanilla ice-cream

Blend briefly. Garnish: slice of orange.   CS

Cara Sposa

Coffee flavour Alcohol 2.3

Orange curacao takes its name from the island of Curacao in the
Caribbean, the original source of a variety of orange required for the
production of this liqueur.

    1 1/2 msr dry orange curacao
    1 1/2 msr Kahlua
    1 msr whipping cream

Rim glass with lemon / caster sugar.
Blend briefly with a glassful of crushed ice.
Garnish: slice of orange and a cherry.   D

Caribbean Sunset

Fruity flavour Alcohol 1.8

    1 msr creme de banane
    1 msr gin
    1/2 msr blue curacao
    1 msr whipping cream
    3/4 msr lemon juice
    1/3 msr grenadine

Shake and strain into glass filled with
broken ice. Add grenadine, allow it
to sink to bottom. Garnish: fruit in season.   G

Cavalier

Mandarin / Herb flavour
Alcohol 1.5

1 msr gold tequila
½ msr Galliano
2 msr mandarin juice
1 msr whipping cream
Shake and strain.

C

Cherry Rum Shooter

Cherry flavour
Alcohol 1.5

1 msr white rum
½ msr cherry vodka
½ msr whipping cream
Add to glass. Shooter.

S

Cherry Tree Climber

Sweet cherry flavour
Alcohol 1.7

1 msr cherry brandy
1 msr white creme de cacao
½ msr peppermint schnapps
1 tablespoon vanilla ice-cream
Blend briefly with half a glassful of crushed ice.
If peach schnapps is used in place of cherry brandy,
this is a Peach Tree Climber.

D

Chocolate Gatail

Cherry coffee flavour
Alcohol 2.1

1 msr dark creme de cacao
1 msr Baileys
¾ msr cherry brandy
⅓ msr dark rum
½ msr whipping cream
Shake and strain, sprinkle with grated chocolate.

CS

Climax

Peach coffee flavour
Alcohol 2.1

1½ msr Southern Comfort
1 msr Kahlua
1 msr whipping cream

Shake with a glassful of broken ice
and pour unstrained.

R

Cloudberry
Fruity flavour   Alcohol 1.8

    1 msr vodka
    1 msr Lakka Cloudberry liqueur
    1/2 msr triple sec
    1 msr whipping cream
    1 msr pineapple juice
    1/4 msr lime juice

Rim glass with pineapple/caster sugar
Shake and strain. Garnish: cherry and orange slice.

CS

Coffee Cream
Coffee flavour   Alcohol 1.4

    1 msr coffee liqueur
    1 msr coconut rum
    1 msr milk
    1 msr cold coffee

Shake and strain into glass filled with
broken ice. Sprinkle with sweet grated
coconut, add short straws.

G

Cold Porridge
Scotch flavour   Alcohol 1.5

    1 1/2 msr scotch
    1 1/2 msr double cream
    1/2 msr honey

Shake and strain into glass three-quarters
filled with broken ice.

R

Colditz
Coffee flavour   Alcohol 1.6

    1 1/2 msr Kahlua
    1/2 msr vodka
    1 1/2 msr whipping cream
    1 msr cold cola

Shake and strain into glass half filled
with broken ice, add the cola.

R

Conca de Fuego

Subtle orange flavour

Alcohol 2.7

   1 msr gin
   1 msr cognac
   1 msr triple sec
   1 msr double cream
Shake and strain, add cherry on a stick.

C

Cuban Cherry

Cherry flavour

Alcohol 2.3

   1 msr white rum
   3/4 msr cherry brandy
   1/2 msr bourbon
   1/2 msr dark creme de cacao
   1 msr double cream
Shake and strain. Garnish: cherry,
sprinkle with grated chocolate.

C

Cyndi's Fun

Cherry whisky flavour

Alcohol 1.8

   1 1/2 msr cherry brandy
   3/4 msr scotch whisky
   1 msr orange juice
   1 msr double cream
Shake and strain. Garnish: slice of orange,
a cherry and sprig of mint.

C

Dead Man's Handle

Sweet scotch flavour

Alcohol 1.8

   1 msr scotch
   1/2 msr Mandarine Napoléon
   1/2 msr coffee liqueur
   1 msr double cream
Shake and strain into ice-filled glass.

R

Dizzy Dame

Sweet cherry flavour

Alcohol 1.9

   1 msr brandy
   3/4 msr coffee liqueur
   1/2 msr cherry brandy

³/₄ msr whipping cream
Shake and strain into glass filled with broken ice.
Add a cherry on a stick and short straws.

R

Explorer's Reward

Sweet melon flavour   *Alcohol 1.9*

    1¹/₃ msr coconut rum
    1¹/₃ msr melon liqueur
    ¹/₃ msr dry sherry
    1¹/₃ msr whipping cream
Shake and strain, add cherry.

CS

Failure

Orange brandy flavour   *Alcohol 2.4*

    1 msr Baileys
    1 msr cognac
    ³/₄ msr Mandarine Napoléon
    ¹/₂ msr double cream
Shake and strain. Garnish: mint sprig
and a cherry.

CS

Flapjack Shooter

Sherry flavour   *Alcohol 0.8*

    ¹/₂ msr sweet sherry
    ¹/₂ msr bourbon
    ¹/₂ msr whipping cream
Shake and strain.

L

Fluffy F

Sweet nut flavour   *Alcohol 1.9*

Douglas Brunton, Canada. Courtesy of Bols International B.V.

    1 msr Bols Creme de Bananes
    1 msr Bols White Creme de Cacao
    1 msr Frangelico
    1 msr whipping cream
Shake and strain. Garnish: cherry.

C

French Kiss

Raspberry flavour *Alcohol 2.0*

    1 msr vodka
    1 msr raspberry liqueur
    1/2 msr Grand Marnier
    1 msr whipping cream

Shake and strain. Garnish: cherry or
raspberry on a stick.

F

Gardenia

Pineapple flavour *Alcohol 1.0*

Created by S. Khoury, Savoy Hotel. Courtesy of Gordon's London Dry Gin.

    1 msr gin
    1 msr pineapple juice
    1 msr double cream
    1 teaspoon grenadine

Shake and strain. Garnish: pineapple chunk,
a cherry and sprig of mint.

CS

Girl Scout

Mint flavour *Alcohol 1.2*

    1/2 msr peppermint schnapps
    1/2 msr dark creme de cacao
    1/2 msr Baileys
    1 teaspoon green creme de menthe
    1/2 msr whipping cream

Shake and strain. Garnish: cherry. Shooter.

L

Goat Herder

Cherry brandy flavour *Alcohol 1.9*

    1 msr brandy
    1/2 msr cherry brandy
    1/2 msr kirsch
    1 teaspoon amaretto
    1 msr double cream

Shake and strain into ice-filled glass, add cherry.

R

Golden Dream

Orange / Herb flavour   *Alcohol 1.8*

Created by the Galliano company around 1960.

    1 msr Galliano
    1 msr triple sec
    1 msr whipping cream
    1 msr orange juice

Shake and strain.   C

Golden Sunset

Chocolate / Orange flavour   *Alcohol 2.0*

    1¼ msr white creme de cacao
    1¼ msr Cointreau
    1¼ msr double cream
    ¾ msr orange juice
    1 teaspoon Galliano

Shake and strain. Garnish: half slice of
orange and a cherry.   C

Grasshopper

Sweet mint flavour   *Alcohol 1.4*

    1⅓ msr white creme de cacao
    1 msr green creme de menthe
    1⅓ msr whipping cream

Shake and strain. Sprinkle with grated chocolate.
Add a sprig of mint and short straw.   CS

Hairy Coconut

Sweet fruit flavour   *Alcohol 1.7*

    1 msr vodka
    ½ msr amaretto
    ½ msr Pisang Ambon
    1 teaspoon Green Chartreuse
    ½ msr coconut cream
    1 msr whipping cream

Rim glass with egg white/sweet grated coconut.
Shake and strain. Garnish: slice of lime and
a cherry.   CS

Heart Throb

Coffee rum flavour

Alcohol 1.1

½ msr Kahlua
¾ msr whipping cream
¾ msr dark rum

Make pousse-café. Shooter.

S

Highland Cream

Scotch / Herb flavour

Alcohol 1.8

1 msr scotch
½ msr white creme de cacao
¼ msr peppermint schnapps
¼ msr Galliano
1 teaspoon Glayva
1 msr whipping cream

Shake and strain into ice-filled glass.

R

Irish Cream

Coconut flavour

Alcohol 0.8

1 msr Baileys
⅔ msr coconut cream
⅔ msr whipping cream

Shake and strain, sprinkle with cinnamon.

L

Julia

Strawberry flavour

Alcohol 1.5

Amaretto, 'the lovers liqueur', was created around 1525 by a beautiful young widow for artist Bernardo Luini, a member of the Leonardo da Vinci school. As his model, she was immortalised in his fresco of the Madonna, which can be seen in a Saronno sanctuary to this day.

¾ msr Amaretto di Saronno
1 msr white rum
1 msr double cream
1½ msr strawberry puree
⅓ msr strawberry syrup

Blend briefly with half a glassful of crushed ice.
Garnish: half a caster sugar-dipped strawberry,
add short straw.

D

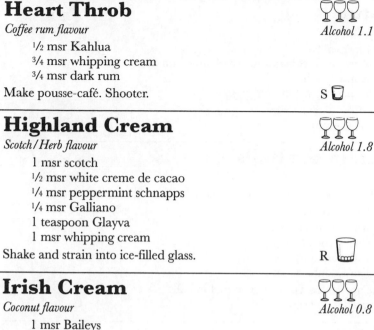

Justine

Almond flavour

Alcohol 1.8

    1 msr vodka
    1/2 msr creme de noyaux (substitute: amaretto)
    1/2 msr kirsch
    1/4 msr orgeat/almond syrup
    1 msr single cream

Shake and strain.

C

Kick in the Balls

Fruity flavour

Alcohol 2.0

A prize-winning recipe, courtesy of A. Beaumont, Australia.

    1 msr dark rum
    1 msr melon liqueur
    1/2 msr coconut cream
    1 msr orange juice
    1 msr double cream

Shake and strain. Garnish: two melon balls
marinated in the rum.

C

Kika

Orange flavour

Alcohol 1.2

    2/3 msr Grand Marnier
    1/3 msr Pisang Ambon
    1/3 msr amaretto
    2/3 msr double cream

Shake and strain, add cherry.

L

Kis-Kesay

Fruity flavour

Alcohol 1.7

    11/3 msr white rum
    2/3 msr white creme de cacao
    1/3 msr lime juice
    1/3 msr blackcurrant juice
    1 msr sweetened whipped cream

Shake and strain, float the cream.
Garnish: orange twist.

CS

Lost Cherry

Cherry flavour   *Alcohol 1.4*

    1 msr cherry vodka
    1/2 msr white creme de cacao
    1/4 msr white creme de menthe
    1 msr filtered orange juice
    1 msr double cream
Shake and strain. Garnish: cherry and slice of orange.   C

Magic Star

Exotic fruit flavour   *Alcohol 1.5*

    1 msr Pisang Ambon
    1 msr white creme de cacao
    2/3 msr kiwi liqueur
    2/3 msr whipping cream
    1 teaspoon grenadine
Shake and strain, sprinkle with grated chocolate.   CS

Mandarin

Herb flavour   *Alcohol 2.1*

Benedictine is believed to be the oldest liqueur in the world. It was first
distilled by an Italian Benedictine monk around 1510 at Frécamp,
Normandy. In 1863 a French merchant discovered the old recipe and
started commercial production.

    1/2 msr Benedictine
    1/3 msr Galliano
    2/3 msr apricot brandy
    2/3 msr triple sec
    1 teaspoon Mandarine Napoléon
    1 msr double cream
    1 msr orange juice
Blend briefly with three-quarters of a glassful of crushed ice.
Garnish: slice of orange speared with a cherry.   D

Maria Mia

Rich banana flavour   *Alcohol 1.8*

Coconut, green banana and almonds. What more could you ask?

    11/2 msr Pisang Ambon
    11/2 msr coconut rum
    11/2 msr double cream
    1 teaspoon amaretto

Shake and strain. Garnish: twist of lemon, slice of banana and a cherry.

CS

Mexican Bliss

Fruit / Herb flavour *Alcohol 2.1*

 1½ msr gold tequila
 ½ msr creme de banane
 ⅓ msr Galliano
 ½ msr mandarin juice
 1 teaspoon lemon juice
 1 msr whipping cream

Shake and strain. Garnish: half slice orange.

CS

Mohican

Sweet bourbon flavour *Alcohol 2.2*

 1½ msr white creme de cacao
 1 msr bourbon
 ½ msr dry vermouth
 1 msr whipping cream

Shake and strain. Sprinkle a straight line of grated chocolate on top.

CS

Moira

Rum / Herb flavour *Alcohol 1.8*

 1 msr dark rum
 ½ msr blue curacao
 ½ msr Galliano
 ½ msr whipping cream

Shake and strain.

L

Motel Wrecker

Orange coffee flavour *Alcohol 1.1*

 ¾ msr Mandarine Napoléon
 ⅓ msr cognac
 1½ msr cold black coffee
 ¾ msr whipping cream
 ⅓ msr sugar syrup

Shake and strain. Garnish: slice of orange.

CS

Mozartus

Chocolate coffee flavour

Alcohol 1.9

1½ msr Mozart
1½ msr Baileys
¾ msr Kahlua

Shake and strain. Garnish: slice of star-fruit.

C

Nut Crusher

Hazelnut flavour

Alcohol 1.0

1½ msr Frangelico
½ msr chocolate syrup
1 tablespoon vanilla ice-cream

Blend briefly with half a glassful of crushed ice.
Sprinkle with chopped hazelnuts.

W

Parisian Blonde

Subtle orange flavour

Alcohol 1.7

1 msr dark rum
1 msr triple sec
1 msr double cream
½ msr sugar syrup

Shake and strain. Garnish: slice of orange.

F

Peppermint Stick

Subtle mint flavour

Alcohol 1.9

A sweet, creamy, mint-flavoured treat for after dinner.

1½ msr white creme de cacao
1½ msr peppermint schnapps
1½ msr whipping cream

Shake and strain. Add a mint-flavoured
candy stick or cherry on a stick.

F

Pink Fingers

Blackberry flavour

Alcohol 2.7

Winning recipe from the Bombay Gin cocktail contest held at the
Waldorf Astoria, New York.

1½ msr blackberry brandy
1½ msr Bombay gin
¾ msr creme de banane
¾ msr double cream

Shake and strain into frosted glass.
Garnish: slice of banana and a cherry.

CS

Pink Forest

Strawberry flavour

Alcohol 2.3

Courtesy of Marie Brizard Liqueurs, France.

    2 msr Fraise des Bois Marie Brizard
    (wild strawberry liqueur)
    1 msr gin
    1/3 msr triple sec
    1 msr double cream

Shake and strain.

CS

Pink Lady

Pomegranate flavour

Alcohol 1.5

Appeared in 1912. Named after a popular stage play.

    1 1/2 msr Plymouth gin
    1 msr egg white
    1/3 msr grenadine
    1/2 msr whipping cream
    1/4 msr lemon juice

Rim glass with grenadine/caster sugar. Shake well
and strain. Garnish: two halves of a cherry.

CS

Pink Squirrel

Sweet nut flavour

Alcohol 1.8

For lovers of sweet almonds and chocolate.

    1 1/2 msr white creme de cacao
    1 1/2 msr creme de noyaux or amaretto
    1 msr double cream
    1/4 msr grenadine

Rim glass with lemon/caster sugar. Shake and strain.
Garnish: cherry, sprinkle almond flakes on top.

CS

Platinum Blonde

Orange rum flavour

Alcohol 2.0

    1 msr golden rum
    1 msr Grand Marnier
    3/4 msr double cream

Shake and strain.

B

Plenty o'Toole

Sweet whiskey flavour   *Alcohol 2.3*

    1 msr Irish whiskey
    1 msr Baileys
    1 msr Frangelico

Shake and strain into glass three-quarters
filled with broken ice.   R

Pompeii

Sweet almond flavour   *Alcohol 1.9*

    1 msr brandy
    3/4 msr white creme de cacao
    1/2 msr amaretto
    1 msr double cream

Shake and strain, sprinkle with almond flakes.   CS

Quick Decision

Coffee flavour   *Alcohol 2.3*

    1 msr bourbon
    3/4 msr Baileys
    1/2 msr dark rum
    1/2 msr coffee liqueur
    3/4 msr whipping cream

Shake and strain into glass filled with broken ice,
sprinkle with grated chocolate.   R

Ready Steady

Coffee flavour   *Alcohol 1.8*

    1 msr vodka
    1 msr Baileys
    1/2 msr sweet sherry
    1 msr double cream

Shake and strain into ice-filled glass.   R

Rêve Satin

Red berry flavour   *Alcohol 1.0*

Courtesy of Marie Brizard Liqueurs, France.

    1 msr Creme de Mure Marie Brizard (blackberry)
    1 msr Fraise des Bois Marie Brizard (wild strawberry)

½ msr double cream
Shake and strain. L

Riviera

Chocolate / Coffee flavour   *Alcohol 2.6*

1¼ msr brandy
1¼ msr dark creme de cacao
½ msr Punt e Mes
¾ msr Kahlua
¾ msr sweetened whipping cream

Shake the alcoholic ingredients and strain into glass.
Float the cream on top and sprinkle with grated chocolate. F

Roadster

Nutty flavour   *Alcohol 1.8*

1 msr Frangelico
1 msr white creme de cacao
½ msr white rum
1 msr whipping cream

Shake and strain into glass filled with broken ice. R

Russian Satellite

Sweet rum flavour   *Alcohol 2.6*

1 msr white rum
¾ msr dark rum
1 msr white creme de cacao
½ msr white creme de menthe
1 msr milk

Shake and strain all but dark rum into glass
filled with broken ice. Float the rum on top
and sprinkle with nutmeg. B

Saronno Peach Fuzz

Almond / Peach flavour   *Alcohol 1.3*

Courtesy of Illva Saronno SpA.

1 msr Amaretto di Saronno
1 msr peach brandy
1 tablespoon vanilla ice-cream

Blend briefly with half a glassful of crushed ice.
Garnish: peach slice and a cherry. W

Seven Dials Cocktail

Fruit brandy flavour — Alcohol 1.7

1 msr cognac
1 msr dark creme de cacao
1 teaspoon Grand Marnier
1 msr double cream
1 egg yolk

Shake well and strain into glass half
filled with broken ice.

R

Silver Jubilee

Banana flavour — Alcohol 2.3

1 3/4 msr gin
1 msr creme de banane
1 msr whipping cream

Shake and strain.

C

Slick Rick

Orange / Herb flavour — Alcohol 1.4

3/4 msr Galliano
1/2 msr Mandarine Napoléon
1/4 msr apricot brandy
3/4 msr whipping cream
1/4 msr lime juice

Shake and strain.

L

Smiler

Almond flavour — Alcohol 1.0

1 1/2 msr amaretto
1 tablespoon vanilla ice-cream

Blend briefly with a tablespoon of crushed ice,
add cherry on stick.

W

Soft Love

Cherry flavour — Alcohol 1.2

3/4 msr creme de banane
3/4 msr cherry vodka
3/4 msr whipping cream
1 teaspoon grenadine

Shake and strain.

L

Southern Belle

Bourbon flavour   *Alcohol 1.9*

    1 msr bourbon
    ¹/₂ msr Southern Comfort
    ¹/₂ msr white creme de cacao
    1 teaspoon green creme de menthe
    1 msr peach juice
    1 msr whipping cream
Shake and strain.   CS

Southern Peach

Peach flavour   *Alcohol 2.3*

In the 1860s Mr M. W. Heron of New Orleans perfected the recipe for
the 'grand old drink of the South'. In 1900 he began bottling his now
famous Southern Comfort.

    1¹/₂ msr Southern Comfort
    1¹/₄ msr peach brandy
    1¹/₂ msr double cream
    1 dash Angostura

Shake and strain. Garnish: slice of peach
speared with a cherry.   C

Stars and Stripes

Fruity flavour   *Alcohol 0.5*

    ²/₃ msr grenadine
    ²/₃ msr double cream
    ²/₃ msr blue curacao
Make pousse-café.   L

Strawberry Dream

Strawberry flavour   *Alcohol 2.4*

A cocktail of strawberries and cream.

    1¹/₄ msr strawberry liqueur
    1 msr white rum
    ³/₄ msr kirsch
    1 msr double cream

Shake and strain into glass three-quarters
filled with broken ice. Garnish: two halves of
a strawberry back to back, serve with short straw.   R

Strawberry Patch

Strawberry flavour   *Alcohol 1.6*

1 msr strawberry brandy
½ msr cherry vodka
½ msr Galliano
1 teaspoon sloe gin
1 msr mandarin juice
1 msr whipping cream

Shake and strain. Garnish: sugar-dipped strawberry.   CS

Strega Sun Witch

Herb flavour   *Alcohol 1.5*

Strega, 'witch' in Italian, comes from Benevento, Italy. Legend has it that a coven of beautiful witches prepared a potion there. If two people drank the magical brew they were for ever united in love.

1 msr Strega
¾ msr white creme de cacao
1 msr whipping cream
¾ msr orange juice

Shake and strain. Garnish: slice of orange.   C

Tête d'Armée

Melon flavour   *Alcohol 2.0*

1 msr Russian vodka
1½ msr Midori
1 msr orange juice
1 msr double cream
1 teaspoon blue curacao

Shake all but the curacao and strain into glass.
Add the curacao, do not stir. Garnish: cherry.   C

Tipperary

Strawberry whiskey flavour   *Alcohol 2.9*

Irish whiskey is traditionally served with water, to be added according to taste.

1¾ msr Irish whiskey
1½ msr Safari (substitute: apricot brandy)
1 msr double cream
½ msr strawberry liqueur
1 teaspoon armagnac

Shake and strain into glass.
Garnish: half a strawberry.   CS

Tornado

Chocolate tequila

Alcohol 2.5

  2 msr silver tequila
  1 msr white creme de cacao
  1 msr double cream

Shake and strain, sprinkle with grated chocolate.   CS

Urban Jungle

Blackberry flavour

Alcohol 1.2

  3/4 msr blackberry brandy
  3/4 msr dry sherry
  1/2 msr triple sec
  1 tablespoon vanilla ice-cream

Blend briefly with a tablespoon of crushed ice.   CS

Velvet Hammer

Sweet coffee flavour

Alcohol 1.8

Of the several versions circulating, this is the most recent and probably the best.

  1 msr triple sec
  1 msr coffee liqueur
  1/2 msr cognac
  1 msr whipping cream

Shake and strain into glass filled with broken ice.
Garnish: cherry.   R

White Christmas

Whisky flavour

Alcohol 2.0

  1 msr creme de banane
  1 msr white creme de cacao
  1 msr scotch whisky
  1 msr double cream

Shake and strain, sprinkle with grated chocolate.   C

White Russian

Coffee flavour

Alcohol 2.2

  1 msr vodka
  1 msr Kahlua
  1 msr whipping cream

Add to glass filled with broken ice,
float the cream on top.

R

Wimbledon Cup

Fruity flavour   *Alcohol 1.6*

    1 msr Pimm's No.1
    1 msr gin
    ¹/₂ msr strawberry syrup
    1 msr mandarin juice
    1 msr double cream

Shake and strain.

CS

Wobbly Knee

Almond coffee flavour   *Alcohol 1.9*

    1 msr Amaretto di Saronno
    1 msr Kahlua
    ¹/₂ msr vodka
    ³/₄ msr coconut cream
    1 msr double cream

Blend briefly with a glassful of crushed ice,
sprinkle with grated chocolate.

D

Wolf's Lair

Peach flavour   *Alcohol 2.1*

    1 msr brandy
    1 msr peach schnapps
    ¹/₂ msr Bärenfang
    1 msr whipping cream

Shake and strain.

F

Xaviera

Sweet fruit flavour   *Alcohol 1.4*

    ³/₄ msr triple sec
    ³/₄ msr Kahlua
    ¹/₂ msr amaretto
    1 msr whipping cream

Shake briefly with a glassful of crushed ice.
Garnish: slice of orange and a cherry,
add short straws.

D

Zipper

Coffee flavour   *Alcohol 2.6*

    1½ msr cachaça (substitute: white rum)
    1½ msr Kahlua
    1 msr double cream
    1 teaspoon Baileys

Shake and strain into glass,
sprinkle with grated chocolate.   C

ZOOMS

Popular in the 1930s, Zooms came and went quite quickly, appropriately enough. They are no longer seen commercially.

Cognac Zoom

Sweet brandy flavour   *Alcohol 2.0*

    2 msr cognac
    ⅔ msr whipping cream
    1 teaspoon honey
    1 msr hot water

Dissolve honey in water and cool.
Shake and strain.   C

Simply replace the cognac to produce a Gin Zoom, Bourbon Zoom or Rum Zoom.

Glossary

(Alcohol by volume)*

Advocaat (17.2%) Netherlands liqueur of spirit and sweetened egg yolks.

Aguardente de Cana (40%) Commonly known as Cachaça, pronounced cachasa. Distilled from fermented and concentrated sugar cane sap. The result is a sugar cane brandy similar to unmatured white rum.

Akvavit or Aquavit (40%) Grain or potato-based spirit usually flavoured with caraway.

Alcohol Ethyl alcohol, with traces of methyl, isobutyl and propyl alcohols.

Amadeus (28%) Austrian almond and orange cognac-based liqueur. A peach-flavoured liqueur of the same name is made in Israel.

Amaretto (28%) Amaretto di Saronno. Almond flavour liqueur from Italy.

Angostura (45%) Angostura bitters. A bitter gentian flavoured tincture with delightful aroma.

Anisette (30%) Sweet aniseed flavour liqueur made with anise and sometimes also aromatic herbs and spices.

Apple Brandy (40%) *See* Calvados and Applejack.

Applejack (40%) American apple brandy, sometimes known as Jersey Lightning after the state where it is produced. Sold straight or blended – with neutral grain spirits.

Armagnac (40%) Grape brandy distilled from wines produced in the Armagnac region in the south-west corner of France and matured in oak casks. The base white wines come from specified vines in a limited area divided into three sectors giving: Haut Armagnac (white), Ténarèze and Bas Armagnac (black). If the spirit is simply described as Armagnac, it is a blend of these types.

Arrack (45%) Batavia Arrack, from Java. Distilled from fermented molasses and cooked rice.

Aurum (40%)   Italian orange flavour liqueur. An infusion of citrus fruits, mainly orange, are distilled three times and blended with specially produced brandy which is left to mature.

Bacardi (37.5%) Brand of white rum originally from Cuba.

Baileys (17%)   Baileys Irish Cream. Sweet coffee-flavoured cream liqueur. May congeal if mixed with citrus juice, tonic water or ginger ale.

Bärenfang (40%) German spirit with strong honey flavour.

Benedictine (40%) Aged distillate of various herbs. *See* Mandarin.

Blueberry Liqueur (15%) Creme de Myrtille. Sweetened extracts of blueberry combined with alcohol and water.

Blue Curacao *See* Curacao.

Bourbon *See* Whisk(e)y.

Branch Water Bottled natural water. The term originally related to water taken from high up in the branch of a river where it was purest. Traditionally added to whisky.

Brandy (40%) Grape brandy. A spirit distilled from wine and made in all wine producing countries. Fruit flavoured varieties include Blackberry (30%), Apricot (20%), Peach (20%) and Cherry (25%). *See also* Armagnac and Cognac.

Cachaça *See* Aguardente de Cana.

Calisay (28%) Spanish sweet herb liqueur similar to Yellow Chartreuse.

Calvados (40%) Apple brandy made in Normandy, France, from fermented apple juice (cider) distilled and aged in Limousin oak casks. The best comes from Pays d'Auge.

Campari (24%) Campari bitters. The red version of an Italian bitter aperitif wine.

Canadian Whisky *See* Whisk(e)y.

Captain Morgan Spiced Rum (40%) Brand of dark rum with spices and natural flavours.

Caster Sugar Superfine sugar.

Chambord (16.5%) Black raspberry liqueur from Burgundy, France.

Champagne (12%) French sparkling wine produced mainly from Chardonnay and Pinot Noir grapes in the Champagne region around Epernay and Reims.

Chartreuse Yellow (40%), Green (55%) An old French liqueur flavoured with many herbs.

Cider (6%) Dry Apple Cider. Fermented apple juice.

Cloudberry Liqueur (21%) Finnish liqueur based on sweet subtle flavour of arctic cloudberry.

Coconut Cream Sweet coconut paste, not coconut milk. *See* Methods.

Coconut Rum (25%) White rum-based sweet coconut liqueur.

Cognac (40%) French brandy distilled from white wine produced around the towns of Cognac and Jarnac. The wines are distilled in traditional pot-stills before maturation in oak casks. VSO – very superior old, VSOP – very superior old pale, VVSOP – very very superior old pale, XO – extremely old.

Cointreau (40%) Orange flavour liqueur made by the Cointreau family since 1849. Orange peel soaked in alcohol is double distilled, diluted and sweetened. (Substitute: Triple Sec.)

Creme de Banane (30%) Sweet clear yellow banana flavour liqueur.

Creme de Cacao Chocolate flavour liqueur. Dark (25%) – distillate of cocoa beans (and sometimes vanilla) macerated in alcohol, diluted and sweetened. White (20%) – more subtle flavour and totally clear, as cocoa remains are absent.

Creme de Cassis (20%) Blackcurrant liqueur usually made by maceration in spirit, filtration, dilution and sweetening.

Creme de Menthe (25%) White or green liqueur distilled from a concentrate of mint leaves. White has a more subtle flavour (substitute: Peppermint Schnapps), green usually contains colourant.

Creme de Noyaux (30%) Persico. Clear almond flavour liqueur made from peach or apricot kernels. (Substitute: Amaretto).

Creme de Y'vette (40%) Liqueur with flavour of Parma violets (substitute: Parfait Amour).

Curacao Sweet orange flavoured liqueur made from infusion of orange peel in spirit, diluted and sweetened. Styles are: Triple Sec (30%) clear/white liqueur, usually the product of redistillation of the base spirit; Dry Orange Curacao (35%) less sweet, clear orange colour curacao. Red, Green, Blue and Yellow Curacao (30%), so coloured mainly for cocktail use.

Double Cream Thick unwhipped cream.

Drambuie (40%) Scotch whisky liqueur with heather honey and herbs.

Dry Vermouth *See* Vermouth.

Dubonnet (18%) Red Dubonnet. An aromatized wine similar to Rosso Vermouth. Extra matured in oak vats. Established 1846 by Joseph Dubonnet.

Framboise (20%) Raspberry liqueur.

Frangelico (24%) Italian wild hazelnut liqueur.

Frigola (25%) Thyme flavoured liqueur from Ibiza.

Galliano (35%) Italian liqueur with over 80 herbs, roots, berries etc., predominantly aniseed.

Genever (40%) Sometimes known as Hollands, it is made from wholly or partly malted grain. It is redistilled with juniper and other botanicals producing a pronounced flavour and aroma. Styles include 'Oude', old genever which is mainly drunk cold and neat; and 'Jong', young genever which is less aromatic and dryer.

GIN

Gin (40%) London Dry Gin. Made from distillate of unmalted grain. The spirit is infused with juniper and other botanicals before and sometimes during redistillation. The result is subtle in flavour and aroma.

Old Tom Gin (40%) A pre-1880s style sweet gin. Occasionally made in London mainly for export. Boord's is the best known brand.

Plymouth Gin (37.5%) A type of dry gin made only in Plymouth, England.

Sloe Gin (26%) A liqueur made from an infusion of sloe berries and gin.

Glayva (40%) Scotch whisky flavoured with honey, herbs and spices.

Gold Tequila *See* Tequila.

Grand Marnier (40%) French Cognac-based Curacao.

Grappa (40%) Italian distillate of the fermented remains of grapes and stalks after pressing for wine production. Maturation is required to smooth this rather fiery spirit. French: Eau-de-Vie de Marc. German: Trester Schnapps.

Grenadine Low or zero alcohol cordial traditionally made from the sweetened juice of the pomegranite 'Punita Grenatum'. Ideal as a sweet red colourant.

Irish Mist (40%) Irish whiskey flavoured with honey and herbs.

Jack Daniels (40%) Brand of American sour mash whiskey from Lynchburg, Tennessee. It is filtered through maple charcoal. Sour mash – after fermentation, some of the solid remains (mash) are added to the following batch to promote flavour continuity.

Kahlua (26.5%) Mexican coffee liqueur.

Kirsch (45%) Clear bitter-tasting eaux de vie (white brandy) distilled from black cherries and their pits.

Kummel (38%) Caraway seed (spearmint) flavoured liqueur.

Lemon Sherbet/Sorbet *See* Methods.

Lemonade Lemon soda. Sparkling sweet soft drink with subtle lemon flavour. (Substitute: 7UP).

Licor 43 (31%) Cuarenta-y-Tres. Spanish sweet vanilla flavour liqueur made with 43 herbs.

Madeira (18%) A fortified dessert wine from Madeira Island off Portugal.

Malibu (24%) Brand of coconut rum.

Mandarine Napoléon (40%) Belgian pure spirit infused with mandarin peel and blended with cognac.

Maraschino (40%) Clear cherry liqueur made from an infusion of crushed marasca cherries macerated in alcohol distilled from the stones. The mixture matures for a few months in larch wood vats. The resulting infusion is purified and matured for several years in ash wood vats. The result is sweetened and filtered to become clear before bottling.

Marc (40%) Pronounced mar. *See* Grappa.

Marsala (15%) A dessert wine from Sicily.

Martini (15%) Brand of vermouth from Piedmont, Italy. Rosso, Bianco and Extra Dry are most popular; there is also a Rosé and a Martini Bitter (20%), similar to Campari.

Melon Liqueur (25%) Sweet green melon flavour liqueur.

Midori (23%) Japanese melon liqueur.

Mozart (20%) Austrian cream liqueur with strong chocolate flavour.

Nutmeg A spice. The pit of the 'nutmeg-apple' – the fruit of the *Myristica fragrans* tree – used grated.

Noilly Prat (17%) High quality brand of dry vermouth.

Okelehao (40%) Spirit distilled in Hawaii from the mashed fermented roots of the Ti plant.

Old Krupnik (40%) Bitter-sweet Polish honey and herb liqueur.

Old Tom Gin *See* Gin.

Orange Bitters (26%) Bitter-sweet liqueur made from Seville orange peel. Substitute: Dry Orange Curacao.

Orangeade Orange soda. Sparkling orange flavour soft drink.

Orange Sherbet/Sorbet *See* Methods.

Orgeat Almond flavour syrup. (Substitute: Falernum or Amaretto).

Ouzo (40%) Spirit distilled with anise seeds. Similar to Pernod.

Overproof Rum (about 62.8%) Rum containing more than 50% alcohol.

Parfait Amour (30%) Fragrant citrus-oil liqueur.

Pastis Generic name for aniseed flavoured liqueurs such as Ricard, Pernod and Ouzo. The name comes from 'pastiche', as these drinks are an imitation of the old absinthe – a health hazard since it contains wormwood, and is no longer widely available.

Peach Brandy (20%) Peach flavoured grape brandy, the sweetened product of the maceration of peaches in brandy.

Peach Liqueur (20%) As above, but containing a lower fruit content and usually made with neutral grain spirits.

Pecher Mignon (18%) Liqueur made from white peaches.

Peppermint Schnapps *See* Schnapps (substitute: White Creme de Menthe).

Pernod (40%) Concentrated aniseed flavour liqueur which turns milky white when water is added. Thus it is sometimes referred to as 'Tiger's Milk' or 'The Green Fairy'.

Pimm's (25%) A bitter fruity summer drink with a spirit base. No.1, gin based, is the popular standard. No.6, vodka based, is hard to obtain. Nos 2,3,4 and 5, based on whisky, brandy, rum and rye whiskey respectively, are collector's items.

Pineau des Charentes (15%) From Charentes, France. The product of grape juice and young cognac blended and matured in cask.

Pisang Ambon (21%) A green banana and herb flavoured liqueur. Ambon is an Indonesian island where 'pisang' means banana.

Pisco (43%) A clear brandy distilled in Peru and Chile from fermented muscat grape remains after pressing for wine production.

Plymouth Gin *See* Gin.

Poire Williams (40%) Delicately flavoured spirit distilled from an infusion of Williams pears.

Port (20%) Fortified wine produced around the town of Oporto, Portugal, on the banks of the River Douro. Fermentation is prematurely arrested by adding grape spirit; this retains sweetness whilst fortifying the wine. Red port becomes lighter and more delicate the longer it is stored in cask whilst white tends to darken. Styles are Late Bottled Vintage (LBV), Vintage, Crusted, Ruby, Tawny, Old Tawny, Vintage Character and White.

LBV port is the product of a single year's harvest, the date of which must be specified on the label. It is ideal for the cocktail bar as it is almost as fully flavoured as vintage port but does not require decanting. (Substitute: Vintage Character).

Prunelle (40%) Clear brandy made from sloes.

Punt e Mes (16%) Dark red bitter Italian aperitif fortified wine.

Quetsch (40%) Clear brandy made from black plums.

Raspberry Puree Smooth raspberry paste. *See* Methods.

Rose's Lime Cordial Non-alcoholic lime cordial.

Rosso Vermouth (17%) *See* Vermouth.

RUM

Spirit distilled from fermented sugar cane sap. The sugar cane is crushed to remove the sap, most of the water is allowed to evaporate and the resulting syrup is centrifuged. The molasses is extracted, and after reduction by boiling, is fermented and distilled. The exceptions are Martinique and Haitian rums which are produced from reduced but otherwise unprocessed sugar cane sap.

Dark Rum (40%) Jamaican style full bodied dark rum. The molasses is fermented usually using yeast from a previous fermentation and this is distilled in a pot-still. Dark rum is usually matured for about five years in barrels previously used for bourbon. The rum is then blended and sometimes caramel (burnt sugar) is added to darken the colour.

Golden Rum (40%) Mostly produced in the same way as white rum but matured for around three years in charred barrels, thus producing a mellow flavour and golden colour.

White Rum (40%) Puerto Rican style clear, dry, light-bodied rum. The molasses is fermented then distilled in a column-still which produces a light clear spirit. It matures for only around one year before bottling.

Rum Tree (24%) White rum-based, sweet, citrus-flavoured liqueur.

Saké (15%) Japanese rice beer. Served warm when neat.

Sambuca (42%) Italian aniseed flavour liqueur made from anise, herbs and roots.

Schnapps (40%) Grain or potato based neutral spirit sometimes redistilled with assorted flavourings such as Apple Schnapps (30%) or Peach Schnapps (23%).

Scotch *See* Whisk(e)y.

Sherbet/Sorbet *See* Methods.

Sherry (17%) Spanish fortified wine. The grapes are gathered and laid out in the sun to increase their sugar content. They are pressed and the must fermented. All the sugar converts to alcohol in dry sherry; for sweet sherry, brandy or dulce is added to arrest fermentation and retain sweetness. They are matured and blended to form various styles. Fino – dry, Amontillado – medium, Oloroso/Cream – sweet.

Slivovitz (40%) Spirit distilled from small plums.

Sloe Gin *See* Gin.

Soda Water Carbonated water.

Southern Comfort (40%) The brand name of a spirit made from a secret recipe believed to contain bourbon flavoured with peaches, oranges and herbs.

Spumante (12%) Italian sparkling wine. There are two types. The superior version is the result of an elaborate process which produces a natural sparkle in the bottled wine from the conversion of sugar during fermentation. The less highly regarded version is made by adding carbon dioxide artificially and is labelled 'vino addizionato in anidride carbonica'.

Strawberry Puree Smooth strawberry paste. *See* Methods.

Strega (40%) Italian liqueur made with 70 herbs.

Sugar Syrup *See* Methods.

Suze (16%) Fortified white wine highly flavoured with gentian.

Tequila A spirit distilled in the Tequila region of Mexico from the cactus-like plant called *agave tequilana*, a member of the lily family. The agave is harvested after 8–10 years' growth, the leaves are removed and the heart is steam cooked and then crushed. The resulting juice is fermented and double distilled.

Gold Tequila (40%) After processing, the Tequila matures in oak vats for three years or more where it mellows and turns golden.

Silver (clear) Tequila (40%) Matured briefly in stainless steel or wax-lined vats, this remains clear and rather coarse.

Thunderbird (17.5%) American fortified and subtly aromatised apple wine.

Tia Maria (27%) Jamaican coffee flavour liqueur.

Tonic Water Carbonated water with traces of bitter quinine.

Triple Sec (30%) *See* Curacao.

Vandermint (30%) Green chocolate and mint-flavoured liqueur. (Substitute: 1/2 Creme de Menthe and 1/2 White Creme de Cacao).

Vermouth (15%) A fortified wine flavoured with herbs, barks, plant extracts etc. They are usually frozen and thawed to encourage the precipitation of impurities, before fine filtering. Dry vermouth is occasionally referred to as 'French', sweet rosso vermouth is sometimes known as 'Italian', both countries make both types.

Styles are: Rosso – based on red wine sweetened and flavoured with caramel. Dry – pale golden white wine based vermouth, the 'French' traditionally matured in oak vats. Bianco – a sweetened dry vermouth. Rosé – based on rosé wine. Individual brands such as the bitter red Punt e Mes do not all fit into these general categories and are referred to by name in the recipes.

Vodka (40%) Almost neutral spirit distilled from a fermented mash of grain distilled and filtered through charcoal. US and UK varieties are odourless and colourless spirits. Russian and Polish possess very subtle flavour and aroma. This is because Polish uses special varieties of grain and traces of aromatic ingredients, and Russian uses filtered but undistilled natural lake and river water.

Other types: Bison Grass Vodka (40%) flavoured with Zubrowka grass. Rowanberry flavour (40%), Cherry Vodka (40%), Lemon Vodka (40%), Pepper Vodka (40%) flavoured with red peppers.

Whipped Cream Whipping cream beaten to form firm peaks.

Whipping Cream A light cream easily beaten into whipped cream. (Substitute: half and half or single cream).

WHISK(E)Y

Whisky in Scotland and Canada, whiskey in USA and Ireland.

Bourbon (40% /US 43%) Used as a generic term for any bourbon-style American whiskey. Bourbon is distilled in a continuous still from a fermented cereal mash containing a minimum of 51% corn. It is aged for 6–8 years in oak casks. These can only be used once under US law and are usually snapped up by distillers of Carribean Rum and Scottish Whisky. (Substitute: American blended whiskey, Tennessee whiskey etc).

Canadian Whisky (40%) Smooth light-bodied whisky made from cereal grains such as barley, corn, rye or wheat in proportions varying with each distiller. The product of the continuous still method, Canadian is usually matured for six years.

Irish Whiskey (40%) Blended Irish whiskey. Similar to Scotch, the main difference being the barley is dried in a kiln rather than over a peat fire.

Rye Whisk(e)y (40%) Produced in Canada and the USA, Rye is distilled from a mixture of cereals but not less than 51% rye.

Scotch (40%) Blended Scottish whisky. Blended Scotch is a mixture of grain spirit, usually made from maize, and malt whisky(s). The malt is made from barley germinated, dried over smoky peat fires, mashed, fermented, distilled and matured in wooden casks for 10–12 years.

Wild Turkey (43%) Brand of straight Kentucky bourbon. There is a 50.5% version (101), and even a Wild Turkey liqueur. Use the lower proof version unless specified.

Yukon Jack (50%) Brand of sweet Canadian herb liqueur.

* The alcohol content of cocktails shown with each recipe is based upon the %/volume figures shown above. Some brands may have a higher or lower alcohol content, often themselves varying in different countries, so check your label if you require accuracy. To calculate the American proof rating, simply multiply the %/vol figure by two.

Index

335

INGREDIENTS INDEX

This index lists cocktails by their main ingredients. To find, for example, Gin and It (which contains gin and vermouth) look under 'Gin-based cocktails' and then under the subheading 'vermouth'. Rare Beef (with gin, vermouth and whisky) is also under 'Gin-based cocktails', subheading 'vermouth-whisky'. To avoid repetition these drinks are not also listed under 'Vermouth-based cocktails' or 'Whisky-based cocktails'. Mixers and non-alcoholic extras are not included.